A NOVEL
OF THE DAMNED

ATTENTION, READER:

This is an uncorrected galley proof. It is not a finished book and is not expected to look like one.

RHEA
RUSS MARTIN

ERMINE PUBLISHERS
Hollywood, California

All rights reserved under International and Pan-American Copyright Conventions. Published in the United States of America by Ermine Publishers, Inc., Los Angeles, California.

Published simultaneously in Canada by Carlton House, Ontario. Distributed in the United States by Whirlwind Book Company, New York.

No reproduction, in whole or in part, in any form, may be made without the written permission of Ermine Publishers, Inc.

SECOND PRINTING

COPYRIGHT © 1978 by Russell W. Martin in the United States of America

Library of Congress Catalog Card No. 78-52800

ISBN 0-89343-048-X

Design by Shawn David

Ermine Publishers, Inc.
6253 Hollywood Blvd.
Suite 312
Hollywood, CA 90028
(213) 461-3256

ERMINE PUBLISHERS
Hollywood, California

1975

Phillip

Phillip Stafford couldn't understand why it was that he followed the woman that Saturday night. He saw her at the party and wondered who she was, at first vaguely, then with mounting intensity. He didn't want to ask because it might cause some raised eyebrows, with Janet and the girls away for the weekend, sunning themselves in Palm Springs. At age thirty-nine, Phillip was known as a bit of a rascal, though he was respected for the fact that none of his escapades had ever caused a scandal. One's extracurricular sexual activities couldn't be kept completely secret, of course, except from one's wife. But to go about asking the names of attractive women at parties would be to forsake discretion altogether. It was there at the party that he began to follow her. He allowed himself some pride in the fact that no one could possibly have guessed that his motions about the Nicholsons' new living room were in any way connected with the tall and slender brunette in the ruthlessly simple black and white dress.

Her features were as stark as her clothing, a study in planes and angles that somehow managed to achieve an impression of softness, possibly through the translucence of her skin and the huge roundness of blue-green eyes. She wore her black hair swept to one side, adding a piquancy to the severity of her features, and for the first time in his life Phillip found himself wishing that a woman were wearing less, perhaps a shorter dress, so that he might see more of her. Her slightest motion, of her hand or her entire body, while smooth and unself-conscious, seemed charged with a subtle vitality that reminded him of something or someone he couldn't place, and that fascinated him. Phillip didn't suppose she would be classified as a beautiful woman in the conventional sense, but there was a quality about her that he could neither discount nor ignore.

Once, when he had lost sight of her for a moment, he twisted his head about to find her looking directly at him, her wide eyes a mixture of innocence and frankness. A young man was whispering something to her, and she smiled in anticipation of the punch line. At the precise moment that Phillip's eyes met hers, she burst into a peal of laughter that made him think of those chimes that summon personnel in department stores; deep, soft, pleasant, yet with an insistent and imperative air not to be denied. He flushed at her laughter and turned away, angry with her and with himself. He had been embarrassed by women very few times in his life. Never before had he been disconcerted by one.

He walked away, determined to ignore the bitch, deciding that he must be developing one of those psychological malaises that men approaching forty were said to be heir to. The thought irritated more than frightened him; it wasn't orderly. So great was his irritation that he managed to make good his resolve to ignore her for ten full minutes. Then he caught sight of her at the door, shrugging into a fur-trimmed cloth coat, long and black, with large red buttons down the front. For just an instant he thought she returned his gaze. Then she was gone.

He was halfway to the door before he realized that he still held a drink. Placing it on a passing waiter's tray, Phillip moved to the closet, plucking his coat off a hanger instead of waiting for the maid, and shrugged into it as he headed for the door. He caught a glimpse of himself in the mirror just before he left the house, a tall, square-jawed, handsome man with fashionably gray temples and a habitual dramatic frown to his brow, dressed in expensively tailored clothes and carrying himself with an air of uncommon assurance, like a man who is accustomed to having his path cleared. Such a man didn't yield to an intense formless panic at the departure of any woman, he told himself, certainly not a girl in her twenties, whom he had never met. Then he deserted the house's warmth for the crisp blackness of the night.

It was hard to see the woman in her black coat, but he caught a glimpse as she moved down the street at a fast pace. Phillip thought about getting his car, driving past her, and then stopping to offer her a ride. A casual offer, he thought, from a gentleman who had seen her at the party and concerned himself with her safety. But the car was in the opposite direction, and he might lose her. He headed down the street rapidly and turned right at the intersection, breathless from the pace she had set. He was hollowly aware that she had vanished, and told himself that she couldn't have gone up in smoke, she must have turned the next corner, and he would find her if only he kept his sense of orderliness about him, moved decisively, and used his eyes with his typical thoroughness.

What he would do once he found her, he had no idea. Finding her was the thing that mattered now, and he felt his lungs beginning to burn, his heart to pump with greater speed and intensity, as he lengthened his strides, almost slipping once in something on the sidewalk. The corner seemed to recede, reducing his progress to a labored slowness. He passed a porticoed house, staying close to the edge of the sidewalk away from the house because he was almost certain that the girl had turned to the right.

"BOO!"

He almost twisted a portion of his spine with fright at the sudden noise. He fought to maintain his equilibrium and his dignity, and did a remarkably good job, but as he turned and saw the girl standing in the portico he was certain that she knew she had given him a turn with her absurd and childish prank. That throaty, exciting laugh erupted from her again just as a car passed, its headlights revealing the impish sparkle of her eyes and glistening on the huge red buttons of her coat. There was a child-woman quality about her, and it excited Phillip even in his momentary anger.

"Gotcha!" she said, making a mock gun of her thumb and forefinger and firing it directly at Phillip's heart. He imagined that he felt something poke through him, as real if not as tangible as an actual bullet.

"I beg your pardon," he said when he had control of his voice. It was a stiff, predictable line, the kind that would have had him roaring with rage if it had come to him from the story department. It brought him the first panicky intimation of defeat at this girl's hands.

"I just said 'gotcha'," she reminded him. "Mr. Stafford."

"How do you know my name?" His voice had lost its tautness. He could tell that she was considering her reply, perhaps making up her mind whether to lie.

"I asked someone at the party," she said finally, stepping out of the portico, standing close in front of him and looking up from under luxurious lashes like a little girl. He had never been so intensely aware of a presence before. He felt an erection stir in his pants, and he had a crazy feeling that she knew it, that she was deliberately putting it there. Suddenly she took his right arm, lacing her left through it and laying her right hand on his wrist. She tucked her fingertips under his cuff in a casual, gentle gesture that seemed intensely intimate to Phillip. Without thinking, he began to walk with her.

"I have the key to an apartment nearby," she said. Phillip thought, *So she's only another actress on the make.* The discovery filled him with an odd mixture of disappointment and relief. He had anticipated some new chapter in his life, something scary and exciting. A new experience.

The apartment house was an old one, probably considered very nice in its day, but now out of place in this neighborhood and doubtless scheduled for early demolition. The halls were carpeted in a faded rose pattern and the new paint on the walls had been spread thinly over the old. Cracks showed through, and Phillip saw some places where it had run. Still, the place was scrubbed, almost antiseptic. The genteel tawdriness of the surroundings added a piquant excitement to their liaison. He hadn't done this kind of thing since long before he had left his twenties behind.

The girl looked at the numbers on the doors as they passed, finally pulling a worn brass key out of her coat pocket, calling to his attention for the first time the fact that she carried no purse. The door squeaked softly as it swung inward. When he hesitated to enter, she subjected him to that conquering laugh again.

"It's all right," she said, and moved past him into the apartment. "You see?" she chuckled, turning to face him and shoving the door all the way open so that it made a clunking sound against the wall. "There's no one here to roll you."

"I admit it crossed my mind," Phillip said. The apartment was one large room, with an alcove of a kitchen to his right and another door, possibly leading to a bathroom, to his left. Opposite the entrance, a huge window let the street peep in between heavy, threadbare drapes. Just beyond the bathroom door was a big double door that undoubtedly opened on a Murphy bed. The walls were a featureless, chalky white, scattered with pictures that had probably come with the place. A gray couch, leaning slightly forward and to the right, stood before the window, and an armless vinyl chair, reupholstered by an amateur, rested near the kitchen.

"These things are a hassle, but they are sexy, aren't they, dear?" the girl said, busying herself with the Murphy bed. It made a tiny squeaking sound as it thumped against the thin carpeting. With one last, furtive glance about the place, Phillip closed the hall door. When he had turned to face her again, the girl had laid her black coat on the couch and kicked off her shoes. She struggled with her zipper, her glance a request. Approaching her, Phillip pulled down the zipper. The nearness of her, the fleeting touch of her body and her emerging nakedness, excited him as he couldn't remember having been excited before. His fingers slipped on the zipper, and his breath grew ragged. He felt like a clumsy schoolboy anticipating his first encounter with an experienced and lovely woman.

"I think I need a shower," she said. "Why don't you go ahead and undress while I see to that, honey?" The dress had slipped from her shoulders, and she held it up unself-consciously, glancing at him over her shoulder. Phillip wanted to call after her, to hold her and tell her that she didn't need a shower, that he didn't want her to leave him even that long. He caught a glimpse of an old-fashioned clawfoot bathtub with a shower curtain and a gooseneck installation, and then she closed the door behind her.

He sat on the edge of the bed and took off his shoes and socks, then stopped and listened to the subtle change in the sound of the shower as she took her place under it. He was actually trembling! It was ludicrous and scary, and he wanted to get up and leave before she came back. Only he didn't know how.

The shower ceased its drumming, and he heard a cabinet open and close, thinking *She's toweling herself now*. He wished he could see her doing that, but if he opened the bathroom door it would be another surrender. By the time she emerged from the bathroom, he was lying atop the bed nude. The erection that had begun on the street was out of control by that time. Phillip didn't know why it should embarrass him. She didn't appear even to notice.

"You're next," she said. "The water's fine." She had let her hair down her back, and he was astonished at the length of it, reaching almost to her fanny. He wasn't certain of whether he would even call her a beautiful woman. What was it about her, he wondered, that reduced him to such a helpless state of excitement?

The last thing he wanted was a shower, but he couldn't think of a way to say so. He rose from the bed and stood for a moment, waiting for his legs to rid themselves of the rubberiness that threatened to drop him in a Mack Sennett pratfall. Then he headed for the bathroom.

When he came back she had turned down the bed, revealing a pink sheet, pale with repeated launderings. The top sheet was white. She lay on the side near him, so he had to walk around the foot of the bed and slip in between it and the wall. His erection was painful, throbbing, and he was actually afraid he might lose control of himself before he got near her. As he lay beside her, she didn't move or even look at him. He thought, in a panic, that she might have been playing with him all along, having a little joke, that she had never intended to let him touch her. But then, as though she had read his thoughts, she laughed and came into his arms.

For the rest of the night he was aware only of skin and hair, blurred with closeness, and the smell of their bodies mingled, and the silky touch of her, and the heat and wetness as he entered her body. It wasn't just the exotic tricks she knew. He had done all of that before. He couldn't decide what it was about her that was so excitingly special. Several times he grew frightened of his own emotions, afraid that his heart or brain might burst with excitement. Even had he known that such would happen, he would have rushed into the mortal pleasure, unable to do anything else. She kept him swollen with pleasure and desire far longer than he had thought possible, and when she finally allowed him his completion, it was the most intense he had ever endured.

Then, as she lay beside him, her thick black hair spilled across his shoulder, just before he fell into an exhausted sleep, he knew the feeling of panic again, panic at the thought that he might not see her after this night. And more frightening yet, he knew that he had felt it even at the height of his ecstasy.

1975

Phillip

Phillip woke with the sun's rays slanting across his feet and a mildly foul taste in his mouth. He lay very still with his eyes closed for a moment and then, remembering where he was, moved his hand, groping for her. There was only an indentation in the sheet where she had lain, and that had cooled. He sat up suddenly, staring about in alarm. There was only an empty room, shabby and, with the unfolded bed, cramped. For a moment he entertained a hope that she was in the bathroom. Then, with the corner of his eye, he saw the note pinned to her pillow. It was scribbled in dull pencil on a scrap torn from a white paper bag.

It was nice. Had to run. Rhea

Beneath the brief message she had drawn two stick figures kissing. One of them wore a Pentunia Pig skirt, and stylized hearts burst all about their kiss. The drawing, like the handwriting, had a subtle elegance about it despite the thick leaded pencil and the wrinkled paper. Phillip tore the note from the safety pin and held it in a slightly palsied hand.

"Bitch!" he muttered, and tossed it aside. Throwing his feet over the edge of the bed he rose, stood for a moment while he collected his faculties, and then padded into the bathroom to rid himself of the previous night's fluid intake. He thought about showering, then realized that he'd have to put on last night's underwear.

Near the front of the building he found a door with a sign on it. MANAGER, it said, and before he thought about it, Phillip knocked. A moment later a trim woman in her late thirites or early forties opened the door. She was dressed in a neat cotton dress, and a brown ribbon held long graying black hair out of her face. She smiled up at Phillip as though she were thinking of inviting him in, so he put on his business expression.

"Do you know where the young lady in Room 10 works?" he asked. "I want to—"

"No one lives in Room 10 anymore," the woman said in a voice that was just a bit more businesslike than his own. She seemed disappointed at his lack of cordiality and determined to do him one better.

She offered no further explanation, and for a moment Phillip was stymied. He couldn't very well insist that he had spent the night with the tenant of Room 10.

"I met her last night at a party," he said. "And brought her here, because she was afraid to walk home. I let her into her apartment myself." The manager looked him up and down, taking in his wrinkled clothes and unshaven face.

"Mister, I don't know where you spent the night, but I can tell you that the tenant moved out of Room 10 three days ago. I haven't been in to clean up yet because the rent's not up 'til tomorrow. But there's nobody there."

"Can you tell me if she left a forwarding address?"

"All she said was she'd had enough of this town and she was going home."

"I see. Well, could you tell me her full name at least?" He was beginning to feel desperate, and was afraid his voice showed it.

"I'm sorry, we don't give out that kind of information on our tenants, past or present. She took such obvious relish in the refusal that Phillip knew he had made a tactical error at the beginning of the conversation. He should have charmed the woman into being on his side. It was too late to mend the error now.

"All right, thank you," he said, and plunged into the sunlit street. On the way back to his car he spotted a coffee shop and decided to ease his morning craving before tackling the freeway. Once he was inside, the food smelled so enticing he decided to have breakfast. As he was paying the check he inadvertantly pulled Rhea's note out of his pocket. The words seemed to mock him, and the stick figure drawing added such an air of gaiety to the message that it galled him.

Nice! Was that the best the little bitch could say about it?

Traffic was light even for a Sunday. Blessedly light, as it

turned out, because ten blocks from his turnoff, he went through a red light. Someone half a block away gave him an indignant blast, or he'd never have known what he had done.

When he activated the garage door opener, the first thing he saw was the ass end of Janet's gunmetal Jaguar sedan. That meant she and the kids had come home a day early, or perhaps even the night before. Phillip pushed the Rolls Royce into its niche on the other side of the station wagon, cut the engine, and hit the remote control again. As the door whirred closed, he opened the glove compartment and removed a motel key he had kept there for over a year and dropped it into his pocket. He felt the note there, and carefully placed it in the glove box, which he locked securely. Janet never used the Rolls Royce.

In the kitchen, Janet heard the muffled rumble of the garage door and stifled a foolish impulse to run and look out the window. It could only be Phillip, since only the two of them had control units for the garage. Unconsciously she straightened the blond hair that hung past her shoulders, glanced at her reflection in the glass table top. Her makeup was sparse enough to be appropriate to the hour and to the blue silk robe she wore. At twenty-nine she still had the smooth, soft skin that had won her a beauty contest ten years earlier, and brought her to Hollywood for a screen test. Through the table she saw her legs, exposed by the robe that had fallen open. They were extremely nice legs and now, crossed one over the other, they looked very inviting. The doorknob turned and, her heart pumping vigorously, Janet fastened her gaze studiously on the copy of *Cosmopolitan* she had been trying to read.

She timed it, raising her coffee and her gaze at the same time and looking at him over the rim of the cup. He was a sight, unshaven and in a wrinkled suit, but just looking at him made her tingle. Feeling a thin sheen of perspiration on her palms, she set her coffee cup down very carefully, with just a normal clinking sound against the saucer. She arched one trim eyebrow at him.

"Well, hello, stranger," she said. He smiled vaguely and moved to where she sat, bending down and kissing her on the lips. She tried to make more of the kiss, but he was already straightening, turning toward the stove, where the coffee sat over the warmer.

"To what do I owe this?" he asked, plucking a cup from an iron tree next to the stove and pouring himself some coffee.

"I just decided to come home a couple of nights early," she explained in a voice that sounded light and effortless. There was something odd about his manner and it worked on her nerves like the wind on a skittish filly. "I met the Crawfords up there, and right away, scheming little wench that I am, I thought 'Aha! A chance to be rid of the monsters for a while. I can get reacquainted with my husband'." Making it look like an unconscious gesture, she turned more fully toward him, moving her legs and causing the silk robe to glide open a bit more. If he noticed it, he gave no sign.

"I wish you'd called me, honey," he reproached her mildly. He moved toward the table in a tired gait. The little slump to his shoulders made Janet want to put her arms around him and mother him. He worked so hard, and all for her and their children, she told herself. "I had a little too much to drink at the party last night, and decided to stay at a motel rather than drive home. Oh, that reminds me." He had started to sit opposite her, but straightened again, fishing a motel key from his coat pocket. It had one of those smudged, worn fobs attached to it. "Would you drop this in a mailbox the next time you're in town? I forgot to leave it."

Janet didn't allow herself to glance at the key, but she felt a painful flood of relief. She knew her husband very well after nine years of marriage, and she was sure he wouldn't be this casual about mentioning the motel if he hadn't gone there alone. She hadn't realized how powerful her fear had been, and she almost laughed aloud with gratitude now that he had put an end to it. He dropped onto the chair with a grunt and took an audible slurp of coffee.

"Well, a late start is better than none," Janet said. He looked down at the cup of coffee, moving it slightly, like a player adjusting a chess piece.

"That's the hell of it, kid," he said. "I have to go back to town and shuffle some papers."

"On Sunday?" She knew she sounded like a disappointed little girl, but she couldn't help it. She had never really had any pride where he was concerned.

"It can't be helped," he said, taking another gingerly sip of the hot coffee. "If you'd called me and let me know you were coming, I could have got it done last night instead of going to that interminable party and earning myself a hangover."

"All right." She spread her hands in a mock placating gesture. "I plead guilty." She moved her legs under the table again, showing him absolutely everything, but he studiously ignored the spectacle. "It's all my fault. Why don't you punish me? Take me upstairs and spank me." He showed her a tight smile.

"Another time, all right?"

Janet shrugged half comically. "Not even a quickie?"

"All I have time for is a shower and change of clothes."

She had to bite off the next thinly veiled plea, looking through the window at the shrubbery and the big elm tree with the bird house, vacant now. When the image blurred, she silently cursed her tear ducts and wished she could turn completely away from Phillip so he wouldn't see her disgraceful reaction. He reached across the table to touch her hand and she avoided contact by picking up the motel key.

"I'll drop this off today," she said. "I may as well drive into town. Maybe go to a movie or something. Or maybe I'll just go on back to Palm Springs. The kids may miss me." She tried to look more defiant than petulant, but her damned lower lip was quivering like crazy. When Phillip answered her, his voice was infinitely tired, infinitely patient.

"Janet, there are two things I don't need right now: a fight or a fuck. I'm too worn out for either." She felt a stab of guilt, and glared at him in defensive outrage.

"Oh, really? Well, you won't get either from me!"

She rose, pushed through the swinging door into the dining room, crossed to the living room and then to the stairs, walking up them in swift but queenly strides until she was almost at the top. Then she broke into a run, almost missing the top stair but one. She went into the master bedroom, threw herself across the bed she had made up with fresh linen twice in the past twelve hours, and shook with sobs. After what seemed like a long time the bed shifted, and she knew he was sitting near her. His hand touched her shoulder, gently lifting. After a moment Janet turned over and looked up at him, knowing her eyes were red and haggard now, the way they always were when she cried even for a few moments. He started to say something, but she cut him off.

"I'm sorry, darling. I know I'm acting like a child. That's why I always get so angry when we argue: I'm always in the wrong. Forgive me?" He shook his head with a wry, avuncular smile and kissed her.

"For what, kid? Flattering the hell out of an old duff after ten years of marriage?" He ran his hand through her hair playfully, then heaved himself wearily up from the bed.

"Have you eaten?" she asked. He nodded, unbuttoning his shirt. He seemed to notice for the first time that he hadn't taken off his coat yet and peeled off both garments at once.

"Damn! I thought I could serve that function at least." His face started to slide into a frown, sending a minor panicky tremor through her. "I'm kidding, darling. Just kidding." She rose. "Now you go in and take your shower and I'll lay out some clothes for you." He slapped her on the fanny as she passed him.

"You know, kid, I could use some more of that coffee."

1796

Elaine

Rhea's story begins on August 6, 1796, when Elaine Carter gave birth to her first and, as it was to turn out, her only child. To the disappointment of Mrs. Carter's parents, the child was a girl. Their disappointment, and her Secret, were the only details of the birth that gave Elaine any pleasure.

She herself had been born Elaine Willoughby some twenty-four years earlier, the daughter of a prosperous merchant of Philadelphia who had soon ceased to be prosperous owing to a penchant for going into businesses, such as shipping, for which he lacked talent. By 1791 the only liquid negotiable asset left to James Stuart Willoughby and his wife was the virginity of their beautiful daughter, and the market for such a commodity was down, so many men of marriageable age having been dispatched in the recent unpleasantness with England. Thus it had come to pass that, at nineteen, Elaine Willoughby had found herself tightly bound in marriage to Lionel Carter, a man of substantial holdings including ships and land, who was fortyish, stooped and balding, with a slightly protruding belly. In time the belly would protrude more than slightly, and the top of his head would show through in lustrous clarity as Nature provided him with a dignified and monkish tonsure.

Unlike the Willoughbys, who had come over from England under William Penn, Lionel Carter was a newcomer to the Americas. He had fought briefly but decently in the Revolution, retired with a dignified shoulder wound that rendered his left arm slightly stiff during inclement weather, and proceeded to capitalize on a fair mechanical talent and a better than fair business acumen by going into the manufacture of musket locks and bayonet studs. Long before the end of hostilities, he had graduated to the production of the whole musket and even some artillery pieces, and in the process had made the intimate acquaintance of men who had the intimate acquaintance of such luminaries as White Horse Harry Lee and John Adams. Almost as important, Carter muskets had a reputation for durability and dependability far better than the general run of weapons, though they also tended to be a bit thick and clublike.

Using his connections with restraint and decorum, Lionel Carter had amassed a modest fortune by the age of thirty-five, when he had decided it was time to look about for a wife to share his gains, and to provide him with an heir who might enlarge them after his retirement and even his demise. In his characteristically methodical manner, Lionel took five years to consider the possible choices. In the beginning he had briefly considered an older cousin of Elaine Willoughby, but before he could make up his mind she had married a third cousin from New England. When he had first cast an appraising eye on Elaine herself, she was only sixteen, already an exquisite young lady but hardly of a proper age. She had the reputation of a stubborn child, given to alternate fits of sulking and rage, but once Lionel had seen her in a low-cut gown, the burden of his chaste life grew odious to him, and no other female would suffice to relieve him of it.

One of his finest assets in the siege he laid against the young lady was her family's straitened financial condition. One afternoon, over James Willoughby's last good port, the two gentlemen discussed the closely related subjects of the Willoughby estate and Lionel Carter's chafing bachelorhood. Since they were alone in the Willoughby parlor the whole time, and since neither man ever discussed their conversation later, no one knew exactly the arrangements that were made. Still, the following day all the Willoughby debts were consolidated under a loan from Lionel Carter. Further loans were quietly negotiated during the next three years; and on the day when Elaine Willoughby was tugged sulking to the altar, all debts were cancelled and a further gift of five thousand dollars was bequeathed to James Willoughby and his wife. In the days when a young woman was expected to bring with her a dowery, the parents considered themselves incredibly well blessed, and were puzzled that their daughter was less than elated at her near escape from a penurious spinsterhood.

Lionel Carter's expectations of sanctified joy, together with his yearning for an heir to the Carter fortune, were frustrated. His lovely bride didn't like him, and made no pretense otherwise. The long awaited wedding night was filled with very little pleasure and a great deal of unpleasantness. After that, overtures were seldom made and usually parried. Elaine had been brought up to believe that a wife's duties were sacred, but her own personality militated against the acceptance of the earthier of these obligations.

She discharged the others, those relating to the house and servants, and the acceptance of guests, with a perfunctory but acceptable efficiency. Lionel's ordinarily easygoing nature was exacerbated by frustration; he felt a potent and erotic affection for his young wife, and infrequently in the ensuing five years his chafing continence drove him to the point of threatening her with divorce, and with a vaguely defined law suit against her father. On these occasions, scarcely more than a dozen in number, did Elaine, in the gloom of her bedchamber, open her thighs to her lord and master, every muscle in her elegant body taut with revulsion as she prayed that this sweating, grunting animal would finish his depredations and leave her alone, and that there would be no issue from their joining. Both prayers were always answered.

"Perhaps, dear, you should consult a physician," her mother suggested timidly when Elaine had been married four years and had still not presented her parents with a grandchild.

"Mother, I'm certain that if God wishes Mr. Carter and me to have a child, He will see to it in His good time." Like most Philadelphians of long standing, Elaine was not above the dropping of great names when it seemed expedient. Nevertheless, her mother's entreaties were becoming bothersome, and she had the feeling that others were beginning to speculate about the Carter marriage. With great reluctance Elaine finally concluded that a child would be necessary in order to still her mother's suggestions, forestall the cryptic looks she had been receiving from time to time from her father, and maintain her own precarious status among their old friends, most of whom considered the family debased by the marriage as it was. While Elaine concurred in this belief, she didn't want to aggravate matters by failing at the marriage, or by giving rise to speculative titters. Still, the thought of carrying this tinker's brat in her belly for nine months was too great to bear. And so it was that Elaine embarked on the plan that would culminate in her Secret.

For a month she considered candidates, inspecting and appraising young men from behind her casually friendly gaze at parties and teas and dinners. This contemplation was a source of mild amusement. Only one candidate was seriously considered.

Richard Phillip Dawson, at the age of twenty-four, was perfect for the role in which Elaine had decided to cast him. He was handsome, with a bit of a rascally reputation; he was married to the daughter of a wealthy and influential family, and therefore certain to be discreet about matters; and, as Elaine's second cousin, he was certainly worthy of her favors, something she would have been loath to admit about very many other men.

Having made a conscious decision, Elaine set about implementing it with efficiency and directness that would have astounded, if not delighted, her businesslike husband. Richard Dawson's home was with his in-laws, who owned a large estate just outside of Samuelsburgh, a small town twenty-five miles from Philadelphia. However, since it was his function to look out for his father-in-law's interests in the city, he lived there much of the time, abiding at one of the better hotels. He had never brought his wife with him on these long sojourns, a fact that encouraged Elaine to believe the rumors about her cousin's roguish behavior. The mechanics of their relationship, then — seeing to their privacy and secrecy — she could safely leave to him.

He normally left his hotel at seven in the morning and walked to his office, three blocks away. It wasn't difficult to find out such things about one's cousin without arousing unwelcome curiosity. Thus, on a Wednesday in early December, bundled in her lovliest winter coat, Elaine Willoughby Carter had a servant drive her to within a block of her cousin's hotel. Then, instructing him to wait, she strolled down the street, her hands thrust into a light gray muff which matched the fur collar of her coat, and with her usual precision arrived at the front door of the hotel just as Dawson emerged, resplendent in tight breeches and light brown boots polished to a soft luster, his wig expertly powdered under a light blue three-cornered hat. The hat came off with a flourish and his face showed courteous pleasure as he bowed.

"Odds, cousin, but it's a pleasant surprise," he said with proper enthusiasm. "But surely you haven't walked here from your house?" He looked about in wonderment. The sky was only tinted with grayness. A man in worn breeches and soiled white stockings walked along the cobbled street snuffing the lamps.

"My coach is just up the street Richard," she replied. "May I walk with you?" The fact that she had not offered him a ride, at which her servant might be within earshot, was not lost on Richard. He bowed again, replaced his hat with deceptive casualness — it was perfectly squared on his head — and took his place next to the curb, offering his cousin an arm. She leaned into his body slightly, which also was not lost on him.

"Why is it that you never visit me while you are in town, Dick?" she asked. "I have always had the feeling that we were more than cousins. As a child I often fancied that we might one day marry." She looked up at his eyes, which revealed mild astonishment at the boldness of her conversation, and went on. "In time, of course, my father's reverses rendered all such fancies vain." Her demeanor and his instincts told Richard that this was a time for frankness.

"Alas, sweet cousin, there are times when our preferences, even our passionate desires, must bow to practicality."

"Oh, well put, cousin, and I certainly agree. Still, will you concur that there is a place for passion, provided one remains practical about it, and keeps it in its proper place?" They were nearing his offices, and might soon be within earshot of others who shared them. He stopped and faced her. Elaine withdrew her arm from his and began to thrust her numbing hand back into her muff, but Richard took it between his for a moment. The roughness of his leather gloves, the massiveness of his hands compared to her own, excited her in a way she had never known before.

"How could one dispute such a statement, Elaine?" he asked, meeting her honest gaze. "Even if one wished to. I shall be in Philadelphia for a fortnight more, and then I simply must return to my father-in-law's estate. I pass this way each morning."

"I know."

"Above all else one must, of course, be discreet."

"May discretion be left to one who is more practiced in it?" He nodded slightly, as pleased with her wording as he was with the agreeable prospect which this morning had brought.

Elaine Carter had never been a dutiful wife; on the following afternoon, in a room provided for Richard by a friend and business acquaintance who could be trusted to harness his curiosity, she in fact ceased to be a faithful one. She found the experience far more palatable than she had thought possible. Richard was much more attractive than her husband; far more adept and experienced at the art of arousing a woman, as well. These differences were paltry, however, compared to the very important psychological advantages he held, being of Elaine's class, and thus nearly worthy of her favors. While she still couldn't give herself entirely to the sensations of erotic love, a total surrender being beneath her ladylike station, she was far more open and relaxed with her cousin Dick than she could ever be with the lout her parents had forced her to marry.

Additionally, the fact that their assignations were forbidden, and that a certain amount of danger attached itself to them, made the matter all the more exciting, though Elaine felt no sense of wickedness about their relationship. To her it was a more proper match than her lawful marriage.

For the first time in her twenty-three years, Elaine had a glimmering of what sex could be, and in the few afternoons she shared with her cousin she learned to take sensuous delight in his touch and a womanly pleasure in the excitement he displayed at the sight of her naked body — a sight she had never allowed her husband. By the time Dick Dawson returned to Samuelsburgh and his wife, she was reasonably certain that her purpose had been accomplished, and that her parents' grandchild would not be her husband's offspring.

1975

Phillip

A job well done. Phillip allowed himself a touch of smugness over the way he had handled Janet. Apologizing brought her a kind of catharsis, and once he had allowed her that, she was always grateful enough so that there were no problems between them for weeks. And she wanted to believe in his rectitude and his superiority because it made her feel secure, so there was never any difficulty in maneuvering her into position to tender the apology.

He was still congratulating himself as he pulled into the driveway of the studio. He showed his pass to a sleepy Sunday guard and drove onto the grounds. They were deserted, providing a startling contrast to the activity of weekdays now, with a plethora of TV shows in progress.

His office was stunningly quiet, almost tomblike. The secretary's swivel chair, nestled neatly under her desk, the vacuumed red carpet, the Picasso and Van Gogh prints on the walls, the tall plants in the corners, seemed different in this silence. It gave him the feeling that he had wandered onto a set that had been put together for a picture that would take place in his office. Phillip walked with silent purposefulness across the plush carpet and let himself through the door marked PHILLIP STAFFORD — PRIVATE.

His private office seemed less bizarre in the silence of a Sunday. He had spent a lot of time alone here. He walked to the vast walnut desk, checked the answering machine hooked to his private telephone and saw that there had been no calls since his departure on Friday. Walking to the couch he sat down, pulled off his shoes, and stretched out. The instant he had done so, the telphone rang.

"Shit!" He rose and plodded to the desk. "Hello." Deliberately, he made his voice brusque and uninviting.

"Hello yourself, lover."

Phillip wiped the palm of his free hand on his pants and waited for his breathing to come under control. She didn't prompt him, and though there was no audible sound from the other end of the wire, he detected an almost palpable amusement there.

"Hello," he said. Then, in a vague, defeated voice, "How did you get this number?" It was his personal direct line. Only a dozen people in the world knew it, including Janet, who had been instructed to use it only in the direst of emergencies, and not including his private secretary, who didn't need to know it. If Rhea heard the question, she didn't consider it important enough for an answer.

"Do you know where the White Cockatoo is?"

"I don't even know what it is."

"It's a cocktail lounge, about four miles north of you. I'm calling from there." She took a long pause, during which he said nothing. "Yes, I thought that would interest you," she said. "I'll be here for exactly fifteen minutes after I hang up. Then I'm leaving."

"But listen — !" He was talking to a dial tone. He stood looking at the receiver for a moment, then, recalling her confident, patronizing tone, slammed it onto the cradle and crossed the office in long strides. He had put on his shoes and was heading for the outer office before he realized what he was doing. Cursing his heart for pounding that way, feeling the sting of sweat in his armpits at the thought of her, he could feel the beginning of an erection. This was insane, and he wouldn't yield to it. Fifteen minutes. As though he were some tardy delivery boy. What did he need her for, anyway? He had a lovely wife, and the choice of a hundred beautiful young actresses.

"Fuck you, Rhea whatever-your-name-is," he mumbled, and walked with deliberate slowness to his bar, where he poured a straight whiskey and downed it.

Stop looking at your watch, asshole.

He went to his desk to find something to do, but there he saw his clock, so he went back to the bar and poured another whiskey. And that was how he wasted eight of his fifteen minutes.

When he finally gave up and started toward his car, he found the impulse to break into a run irresistible. He didn't bother to fasten his shoulder harness, which was a rule he never broke, and when he went through the gate he almost hit the guard's kiosk. Turning north on a squeal of expensive rubber, Phillip broke the speed limit all the way. Then he nearly missed the place, catching sight of the sign just before it would have been too late. He parked blocking a driveway, left the keys in the car, and ran huffing into the White Cockatoo.

He was blind for a moment. Then he headed for a front booth, where a woman with black hair sat, her back to him. Even before the woman turned her head to glance at the clock on the wall he saw that it wasn't Rhea. In a panic, he looked about the lounge. She wasn't there.

"But that's not fair," he said almost sobbing. The Patek Phillipe watch on his wrist told him that he had nearly two minutes left. She had said fifteen minutes, and he had got there in thirteen, and she wasn't there.

"Gotcha again!" Her voice was right at his shoulder, and he felt a slender finger jab him in the flank. He spun about like a startled child and almost laughed with relief. She was dressed in a red pantsuit with ornate brass buttons, and she had tied her hair into an elaborate bun at the back of her head. The severity of the hairdo made her face like something engraved on an ancient coin. The trimness of her figure, the sumptuous bulge of her breasts, the graceful line of her neck, all invited a man's touch. He kept his hands at his side through a conscious effort. Rhea gave him one of those maddening little smiles that said she could read his mind, and brushed past him, giving him a whiff of subtle perfume. Following obediently, Phillip waited until she was seated in a back booth, then slid in across from her. Under the table her foot brushed his ankle once, lightly, and then no more.

"You cut it close," she said. Her smug assumption that getting here before she left was important to him angered Phillip, but he maintained an impassive expression. "That was nice last night, wasn't it?" she said with that mocking lilt to her voice. The waitress appeared at his elbow. Rhea ordered a margarita and Phillip a Beam and water. "I'm sure you liked it even better than I did," Rhea said when they were in privacy again. "Would you like an encore?"

"I guess I wouldn't be here otherwise."

"Well, I only give one free sample, dear. This time it's going to cost you something." Phillip felt a flood of relief. So she was a bargainer after all, just a common hooker, even if she had been the most incredible fuck of his life.

"How much?"

"It isn't money, Phil, dear. I don't want your money."

"A screen test then." When she smiled, he hurried on. "Or a part in a picture. If you're after a contract, I can't swing it."

"Of course you can. You're a very big man at that studio. You can swing just about anything."

"No, really. The way things are—"

"Philly, dear. If you lie to me once more, I'm going to walk

27

away from you for good." He felt the smoothness of the table under his fingertips, saw and smelled and thought with the acuity of a man who knows he may be dead in a moment. He thought about making a contest of it, but something almost unconscious told him that he would lose any contest with her. He pushed the knowledge down, out of sight, and told himself that he could always handle her later. It would be very satisfying to bring her to heel and make her pay for all this patronizing, for the smugness and elaborate self-confidence with which she badgered and tormented him.

"All right," he said, feeling a sinking sensation in the bottom of his stomach. He thought that for the first time in his life he knew what a general must feel like before ordering a retreat. "All right, maybe I can swing it." His mind was flicking over the factors of this decision: the valuable favors he had done that he would have to call in, the favors he would have to ask of people who would be only to happy to obligate him, the deterioration that would accrue to his prestige, formerly unassailable. It would amuse and relieve a lot of his professional colleagues to discover that Phillip Stafford was capable of lowering himself to such an extent. But she was laughing at him again, with such full throated mirth this time, it startled and puzzled him more than it made him angry.

"Don't worry, Philly. You don't have to endanger your supremacy at the studio. I don't want to be an actress."

So this is what it's like to hate someone, Phillip thought.

"All right," he said in a very quiet, tightly controlled voice. "Will you tell me what you do want? Or are you having too much fun?"

"Oh, now I've made you cross with me." She reached across the width of the table to touch his cheek with a light, parental gesture that made him want to grab her hand and twist it until she screamed. At the same time it made his member so stiff he was glad they were sitting in a booth. He sipped his drink, which tasted bitter to him. "All right," Rhea said, leaning back and taking a sip of her margarita. "I'll get down to business. Your wife has a pin in the form of a peacock, understand she's very fond of it."

"It was left to her by her mother," Phil said blankly. Twist upon bizzare twist. This was the most mystifying girl he had ever encountered.

"That's the one. I want it." He stared at her for a moment before he could find words.

"But it's only a gold-plated pin with some rhinestones. It's worthless. I'll buy —"

"I don't want you to buy me anything, Philly. I want that particular pin, and I assure you I'll recognize it."

"But why?" There was something chilling about this, something that frightened him almost to the point of flight.

"You're not to ask me that," she said, and her gaze was as uncompromising as a pawn broker's. Phillip looked away first.

"Would you mind telling me how I'm supposed to get it from her?"

"That's your affair. Tell her you want it. After all, the poor girl worships you to the point of absurdity. Or just take it, if that would be easier."

"I suppose you want it in advance?" The woman was obviously insane, which was scary, but Phillip felt a strong tinge of relief that what she wanted was so easily provided, that it wouldn't cost him anything he couldn't afford to give up.

"Not at all. I trust you, Philly. Because if you don't give me the pin, you'll never see me again." He was astonished at the desolate, physical sickness that thought gave him. And he hated himself for the weakness that forced him to ask the next question.

"And if I do?"

"Oh, well." She took another sip of her drink and smiled at him with apparent enjoyment. "In that case — maybe."

1975

Phillip

He took the pin the next morning. It was in the top drawer of Janet's bureau, with the rest of her costume jewelry, mostly stuff she had brought from Washington State when she had come to California for the screen test, ten years before. Her real jewelry, the things Phillip had bought her, were locked in a strong box. His heart pounded absurdly when he took the pin out of the drawer, and afterward, crazily, he wiped his sleeve across the drawer to eradicate his fingerprints. Janet was in the shower at the time. He dropped the piece of thin metal into his coat pocket and walked out of the bedroom without looking back. All through breakfast he had difficulty looking at her, and hid behind his newspaper. Things had been strained between them since the previous day, and so it seemed natural enough. The words he read were nonsense to him. He kept wondering how long it would be before Janet noticed the absence of the pin, and just how hard she would take the loss.

On the way into town he thought about the previous day, and his second sexual encounter with Rhea. He had hoped that the magic of her had been the product of novelty, and that this time would prove a disappointment. He hadn't for an instant entertained the possibility that it could be more intense the second time.

Possibly a part of the power she held to excite him lay in her casualness to all of it. Even in the throes of multiple orgasms she seemed in control of herself, aware of her every action and its effect on him, amused at her own emotions and far more amused at her ability to reduce him to a helplessness of desire and unendurable pleasure.

When she was finished with him, he lay staring at the ceiling of the hotel room, listening to the percussive sound of her shower. She dressed without self-consciousness, as though he weren't there.

"I'll be in touch with you about the pin tomorrow," she said from the door. "Or the next day." There was no repetition of her threat not to see him again. None was required.

Phillip skipped his usual turnoff and drove into Los Angeles, only vaguely aware of his reason. He parked at a lot and walked half a block to Slavick's. The salesman looked at his clothing and smiled respectfully.

"I'm looking for something for my wife," Phillip said.

"And the occasion, sir?"

"No occasion," Phillip said a bit snappishly. Then he smiled, with effort. "I haven't been very nice to her lately." The clerk gave him an understanding, almost conspiratorial smile, leading the way to one of the showcases.

"I think this is rather smart." He withdrew a pin in the form of a starburst. It was white gold with a diamond in the center and chips all about. The price tag read six hundred fifty dollars.

"No, no," Phillip said with a touch of impatience. "I want something nicer than this."

"Of course, sir." The clerk's icy good breeding gave way just a bit, revealing his excitement, as he moved toward the back of the store, and the vault.

Phillip finally settled for a thirty-five-hundred-dollar diamond and ruby pin. He had narrowly avoided selecting one in the form of a bird of paradise before he realized that that would have been too obvious. The one he bought was in the form of a pentagram. It should make up for the cheap thing he had in his coat pocket, he told himself. It should make up for whatever anguish Janet would feel at the loss of her mother's one bequest to her. And it should make up a bit for the fact that he felt not the least touch of redeeming remorse for his act.

1955

Phillip

When Phillip Stafford arrived in Hollywood in 1955, he was twenty years old, not yet legally entitled to vote or order a glass of beer. He was the holder of a freshly granted B.A. from a university in the state of Washington, having skipped a grade in grammer school and attended summer sessions during his college career. His degree was in business administration with a minor in theater arts, and now, having produced two student films, he had arrived at the Mecca for the hopeful.

On the day he arrived, before unpacking, he went straight to one of the large studios and sought an interview with an executive who had held out some hope for him during a visit to his university, only to find that the gentleman had been ousted in a recent internecine struggle, and that the personage who had replaced him was supremely uninterested in college boys, believing that the only way to become a film-maker was to have been born to the business, or to have been fortunate enough to have attracted the attention of someone firmly established, and thus to have wormed one's way in. That was the way he had made it. Phillip sat in the outer office, enduring the pitying and rather supercilious glances of the secretary, for some three hours before he gave up and went looking for his new home, an apartment in Hollywood which he was to share with a former college chum, a diplomate in theater arts who had been working at becoming a director for the past twelve months.

"Well, you've already been initiated, then," said Charlie Moulton when Phillip had described his day at the studio. "This is the one industy in America that's designed as a fort, to keep new talent out."

"Christ, Chuck, they're always shouting about how they need new, talented people," Phillip said.

"Sure. But number one, there are a hundred more or less talented people out on the streets for each job, and two, there are at least twenty untalented schmucks for each one who could amount to something, and, three, nobody in this business really cares about the future of the industry. The person he hires today may take his job, so it's best not to hire him in the first place, unless he's an accountant or a janitor or something. How much money do you have?"

"Three hundred dollars and a few cents."

"Well, you'd better find yourself some gainful employment. This apartment costs seventy-two-fifty a month, half of which is your responsibility starting the first of next month, and you're going to have to pay for your own food. Your wardrobe all right?"

"This suit, two more about as good, and a couple of sport coats."

"You're in good shape there. Getting a job is the most important thing."

"I thought I'd get a job at the studio."

"Jesus, was I as naive as you just a year ago?" Chuck asked the mottled ceiling. The apartment had turned out to be a small living room, a smaller bedroom and a kitchenette, plus a cramped bathroom with a stall shower, a basin, and a Sears Roebuck medicine cabinet. There was a fairly good-size closet in the bedroom, which Chuck had consented to share.

"Well, what kind of job do you have?" Phillip asked.

"I work in an all-night ice cream place on Hollywood Boulevard."

"A soda jerk?"

"Listen, don't knock it. I eat there, two meals a night, and manage to spirit out some goodies once in a while. Night jobs are at a premium in this town. Every would-be actor and actress wants to work at night. You sleep in the afternoon. That leaves you eight hours every morning to pound the pavement. The best thing is a job that allows you to work weekends. That means a couple of days during the business week, you're fresh and rested. Can you cook?"

"Anything that's canned or frozen."

"Well, you'd better get a girl friend who can do it for you, then. I'm no better, and we probably won't be seeing much of each other once you get your job, anyway." Chuck rose from the worn and lopsided chair in which he had been sitting and walked into the kitchenette. Opening the tiny refrigerator, he took out a can of beer. "You want another?" Phillip nodded somewhat disconsolately. "We're celebrating your arrival," Chuck informed him. "After today, you buy your own beer if you want any." He rummaged through a drawer, found the opener.

"Hell, I'll go get a six-pack later," Phillip said a bit defensively. "Why won't we be seeing much of each other?"

"I work an afternoon and early evening shift at the ice cream place and I'm in a play at night. It's a semi-pro thing, with a few professionals and the rest of us working to get the exposure. Listen, another thing, no borrowing clothes, all right? Roomies have to maintain some rules, or things get unpleasant."

"Your clothes won't fit me, and I never cared for your taste anyway. I thought you came here to be a director, not an actor."

"An in is an in. If you don't like my clothes, that's George with me. That couch opens out into a torture device, and that's where you sleep. I get the bedroom because I was here first."

"Okay. Any suggestions about finding work?"

"Try the city and the county. They have some jobs that require nothing but a college background."

"Where do I go?"

"Ask a bus driver. When you get up, fold the couch back up and stuff the bedding out of sight. You can wash the sheets at the laundromat on the corner."

"Is there an ironing board in the place?"

"What the hell would I do with an ironing board? Sally does my ironing."

"How nice for you. Who the hell is Sally, or dare I ask?"

"Sally is my girl, Sally Platz."

"Platz? Platz?" Phillip laughed, then took a sip of his fresh beer.

"You think her name is funny? Fine. You can't fuck a name. And you keep your hands off her, Buddy. I remember how you always were with the broads back at school."

"Did I ever try to take any of your girls away?"

"I never had a girl like Sally before."

"Okay, okay, I'm not out to plunder your treasure. Word of honor." Phillip meant it. Girls weren't that hard to find, and he had always had a healthy respect for Chuck Moulton, who was half a head taller than he, and had been on the varsity football team at school.

The next day he started to hunt for a job. Following Chuck's advice, he went to the Los Angeles City Hall and put in for any promising positions. Then he did the same thing at the county. It took most of the day, and he was told that his applications would be reviewed for qualifications and his name put on the proper lists, but not to expect to hear anything for the time being. Then he had his first stroke of luck. A large downtown hotel, where he stopped for lunch, turned out to need someone for a job described as "assistant night auditor." He overheard two employees discussing it, and went up to the personnel department. He hadn't the slightest idea of what an assistant night auditor did, but he managed to convince the man who interviewed him that he was thoroughly conversant with the operation of the NCR 2000, whatever that was. The job paid twelve dollars a day and the shift was from eleven p.m. to seven a.m., though he was told that if the night auditors managed to balance the accounts in less time they were allowed to go home. He was asked if he could start that night.

One thing that restored a bit of the Hollywood luster was Sally Platz. Sally was precisely the kind of girl one associates with the film industry. She was tall, about five-nine Phillip judged, and there wasn't one ounce of surplus weight on her. She had a perfect face, with high cheekbones, a classic nose and finely chiseled features from which smoldered a pair of green eyes that seemed to see everything inside a man at the first glance. She had the quality of seeming to find every man attractive, as though something in her chemistry responded instantly to maleness in any form. Everything about her was sensuous: her long-fingered hands, the copper colored hair that always appeared to billow about her face as though fanned out on a pillow, every slightest move she made. Even the negative action of standing or sitting still seemed to become incredibly suggestive in her, as though she were holding herself in check, barely mastering the intense vitality of her sleek body. Her voice was almost masculinely deep, yet very luxurious, like the purr of an expensive and finely tuned engine at the idle. Phillip had to remind himself that at least while he was rooming with Chuck he had better keep his promise. Charles Moulton had earned something of a reputation for an unpredictable temper while at the university. It had only surfaced twice during his four terms there, but on each occasion it had become something of an event, an entry into the school's annals.

One of the incidents had involved a term paper which matched that of another student almost word for word. Though the two papers had been turned in to two different professors, somehow they had come to be compared. The other student, a member of the track and football teams, had insisted that his was the original and that Chuck had got hold of it somehow and copied it. To be accused of such a subterfuge could mean expulsion, or at the very least some strong disciplinary action, but more than that it had constituted an impugning of Chuck's integrity, and he had met the accuser on the green that evening. As a result, the football team had had to do without the other man's services for some time while his nose knitted itself back together.

The other occasion had concerned a girl, one of the cheerleaders, who had been going more or less steady with Chuck for two semesters. Another man, this time a member of the boxing and wrestling teams, had offered her a ride one evening, had taken her against her will to a secluded spot, and had tried to make out. When she put up a struggle, he had reportedly become more forceful than prudence permitted, and the girl had barely escaped with her virtue (though not her skirt) intact. In a state of near hysteria, she had been picked up by the Highway Patrol, and her parents and the school notified. She had refused to press charges, but as soon as Chuck heard about the incident he had taken out after the culprit, who by this time had been convinced of the wisdom of his voluntary withdrawal from school. Chuck had caught him loading his car with luggage, and without notice had begun to bombard the man with blows. Phillip had happened to be present at this confrontation, had seen the kind of ferocity of which his roomie was capable. The other man, though certainly an able fighter, was like a fighting dog up against a Bengal tiger. Nothing he could do seemed to have an effect on his adversary. Chuck's hands and feet seemed to become, alternately, bludgeons and claws. Long before he was finished, his victim's shirt was soaked in blood and his face was unrecognizable. Some of the other students, who had stopped to observe the fight, finally dragged Chuck away from the man, who had long since ceased even trying to defend himself. All the while Chuck had been screaming obscenities, which had finally dissolved into meaningless but frightening sounds.

Though Chuck's temper had never again erupted while he was at the university, or since Phillip had undertaken to share his apartment, Phillip had never been completely comfortable in his presence. It was rather like sharing living space with a tame and lethargic jungle cat. While he was fairly certain that sooner or later he would have his try with Sally Platz, he wanted to be certain that Chuck wasn't around when that happened.

In the meantime, he had decided to take Chuck's advice and procure a girl friend for himself. The perfect candidate seemed to be Sally's roommate. Not only was Claudia a pretty girl, and adept at the domestic arts, but her address was a convenience since it would give him greater access to Sally.

"Go ahead and take her out," Chuck urged him after his first meeting with Claudia. "She's already half sweet on you. I can tell. Just don't push her. She's a smalltown girl, and scared to death of losing her high standards now that she's moved to Babylon."

In those innocent days there were two kinds of girls: those who kissed on the first date and those who didn't. From what Chuck had said, and from his own observation, Phillip decided that Claudia was a nonkisser. Nevertheless, at the end of their first date, she stood in front of her door expectantly, obviously waiting for him to make the try. Probably, he thought, so that she could prove she was a lady by fending him off. But when he took her in his arms, she neglected to do any fending. Rising on tiptoe, she allowed herself to be kissed. It was obvious that his judgement had been sound. She knew nothing about the process, yet her lips were supple and he tasted just the fleeting suggestion of a sweet, retreating tongue before she twisted from his grasp and fled, clearly flustered and embarrassed, into the sanctuary of her apartment. When the door had closed Phillip started to turn away, then hesitated. The hallway was deserted. With the excitement of an inexperienced burglar, he leaned forward, pressing his ear to the door. From inside he could hear an excited babble. He couldn't make out any words, but the tone was enough. Sally's deeper, calmer voice, soothing and perhaps a bit patronizing, replied.

With a smirk on his face, Phillip turned and moved toward the street, whistling softly. From this point he knew he could coast, right into Claudia's pants.

1796

Rhea

When, on that sixth of August, 1796, Elaine Willoughby Carter's daughter was dragged into awareness of her own existence, already showing signs of that physical beauty which had run like a vein of gold through her mother's family, George Washington was making ready to retire from public life, soon to be replaced in the Presidency by John Adams. The young nation was beginning to spread westward. Treaties were enacted with the Indian tribes, and swiftly abrogated as more and more whites pressed into Indian land. Far to the west Spanish colonies slumbered, oblivious of the day, sooner than seemed possible, when it would prove more than expedient for the United States to engulf them. American political thought was being written down and published, and read and criticized, and was already beginning to make its slowly deepening print on the rest of the western world; for in those days giants lived.

Besides these historical events, it seems almost wantonly trivial to mention that Elaine Carter, to spite the parents whom she had never forgiven for pressing her into an unsuitable marriage five years earlier, insisted on naming her daughter after a Greek goddess instead of a saint, or one of the Christian virtues, as would have seemed proper in those days.

Rhea Carter weighed six pounds, three ounces at birth. She had the appetite of a dray horse and the voice of a sergeant of fusilliers. She was, by the accounts of those who saw her, an unusually beautiful baby. Elaine was less than mildly interested in the fruit of her illicit relationship with her cousin, except insofar as the child helped her to maintain her status in society, and to quell the urgings of her parents.

Of course it had been necessary to yield to the importunities of her husband a few times when she had first become certain of her condition. Her greatest fear had been that he might fail to make his usual pathetic advances, and that she might have to invent occasions to invite him into her bed.

Lionel, however, with his accustomed cooperativeness, had chosen the right time to plead and cajole and finally resort to his usual threat. Simulating intimidation, and concealing her relief, Elaine had suffered her husband's touch a full half dozen times. By the sixth of August, pride had left no room in Lionel Carter's heart for so base an emotion as suspicion.

Cared for by servants, Rhea grew rapidly. Her putative father quite forgot that he had had his heart set on a male heir. He doted on the daughter God had finally given him. Taking a new interest in his business, he increased the fortune which had ceased to hold his attention of late and still, with the stamina of joy, found time to stroll the streets of Philadelphia with his baby. For a while his wife accompanied him on these promenades, having decided that to do so would enhance her flagging image among her peers. After a few months, however, Elaine decided that enough was enough, and left her foolish husband to dote alone. The child had served her purpose, and no longer concerned Elaine.

Some things, however, are most difficult to ignore, and a growing child is among them. Before long Rhea's presence began to impinge on Elaine's consciousness, as it would on other people's for a long time to come. Even if she shut herself in her room, as she was loath to do, Elaine was constantly aware of the babble of child sounds, the rumble of toys pulled through the house, the arrival of guests, including her pesky parents, to visit, not her, but the brat she had whelped. She put up with it for three years. By that time Rhea's incredible mental precosity, which at times frightened Elaine, as though it might have been visited on her by Divine Will, had manifested itself. That intelligence, however, was what gave Elaine her opportunity to be rid of the child for most of the time, and she seized the chance with eagerness, hesitating only long enough to lay her plans with the exquisite care that was one of her strongest traits.

She found her husband sitting in his den, surrounded by the personal accumulations of his life: pipes, solid furniture, a few books, and the single painting over the fireplace that had been left by the previous owners of the house. His Continental musket, which he had carried into battle and fired at a British officer once (and missed) was suspended beneath the painting. It looked slightly at odds with the subject of the portrait, a middle-aged woman who seemed to be trying to look half her age for the benefit of the artist. Lionel was clearly delighted at being visited here by his wife, whom he seldom saw at all apart from mealtimes. Elaine seated herself opposite him and smiled most becomingly.

"I have been giving some thought to the matter of our child's education," she said by way of preamble.

"Of course. Well, we can't start thinking about such things too soon, I suppose. She will have to be trained in the domestic arts."

"Of course, Mr. Carter," Elaine agreed. "But a mind like our daughter's shouldn't be wasted. I have been giving some thought to sending her to school right away, if you will consent. There is a school right here in Philadelphia where she can board. She would be able to come home on weekends, of course."

"What, send my daughter to a boarding school when she's only three years old?" He seemed shocked out of his usual composure by the thought.

"This school is very —" She struggled for the word. "—progressive in its approach. They feel that a child should be sent to school not according to his or her chronological age, but with concern for the child's readiness to learn. In the case of an exceptionally gifted child, such as Rhea, they will consider an admission at the age of three, or even earlier. Particularly if the child is from a background of proper substance, of course." Lionel Carter shifted in his seat, nearly writhing under this unaccustomed flattery from his wife.

"Well, I shall think about it, dear," he promised.

"I hope you will give it your earnest consideration. It is nearly time for school to begin." She looked at the clock on his desk, a clock which he had bought at the beginning of his prosperity, and which had never ceased to keep perfect time since. "Our dinner tonight will be roast lamb," she told him, apparently dropping the subject of the school. Roast lamb was his favorite dish, though he seldom enjoyed it because Elaine couldn't stand it. "And now, so that I shall be fit company, I think I'll go up to my bed and lie down for a while." As she spoke these apparently innocent words, Elaine looked directly into her husband's eyes with an expression of invitation that he couldn't possibly misunderstand. Then she rose and curtsied briefly and left him to finish his pipe. Minutes later, fairly trembling with anticipation, he left the pipe half smoked and stone cold, and followed her to her chamber.

The following month Rhea was admitted to Mr. and Mrs. Cameron's School. It was located, conveniently from Elaine's point of view, directly across town, too far for casual visiting. Now she had her child out of her hair and no longer had to listen to her idiot of a husband making mewing sounds and laughing like a buffon in a stage play. More important, she had demonstrated to her own satisfaction that she could control her lord and master, provided she wanted something badly enough to resort to extreme measures.

As for Lionel Carter, he retired earlier than had been his wont, and spent the early evening hours in his den, seeing to business concerns, which meant that Elaine had him out of her way, too, for the most part. It never occurred to him to inquire into the kind of things which the very "progressive" school to which he had entrusted his daughter would be teaching her. He naturally assumed that they would limit their pedagogical efforts to the conventional pursuits of a female's life: sewing, spinning, and what have you. He would have been scandalized quite beyond even his wife's control had he known that Mr. and Mrs. Cameron could be so depraved as to teach a girl to read and write.

1955

Phillip

Like her roommate, Claudia had come to Hollywood to break into the movie business. Not for a moment did Phillip believe she would make it. That was just one of the differences between the two girls. Sally, with her incredible loveliness and the animal vitality that radiated from her, had every chance. In all likelihood, she would win a career and then chuck it for the kind of marriage that it would open up for her. From the way things looked, Phillip guessed that her marriage would be to Chuck Moulton, if Chuck had anything to say about it.

That Chuck was in love was unquestionable. Phillip could see it in every glance the man gave to Sally. Even the fact that he worked so hard to find his break in the film industry spoke of his feeling for Sally, since she was obviously the kind of prize that went to the successful and the ambitious. For her part, Phillip decided that Sally was fond enough of her boy friend, but that she could just as easily gravitate to any man who promised her the kind of life she sought. Her kind of sensuousness seemed to accompany, in many cases, a shallowness of outlook and a mediocre or less than mediocre mind. In Sally's case, these negative qualities weren't immediately noticeable because her deep green eyes suggested an intelligence that wasn't there and because she had learned to speak seldom and with authority. Like many stupid but ambitious people, she had developed a kind of craftiness which, coupled with a jungle tenacity, could go a long way as a substitute for genuine mentality.

All of this information could be of use when Phillip got ready to make his move, but he still had his own roommate's temper and emotional involvement to consider. Since he had no desire to have some intern at the county hospital sew his ear back on, Phillip limited his immediate progress to reconnaissance.

Meanwhile there was Claudia. Phillip had scored with her on the second date, to his mild surprise and her complete astonishment, he thought. She had accompanied him to the apartment, possibly thinking that Chuck would be there, or perhaps she had consciously or semi-consciously abetted the deception. At any rate, Phillip hadn't mentioned the matter of his roomie's whereabouts.

Once she was there, it was almost ludicrously easy. She came into his arms willingly, and only began her fitful protests when matters had proceeded to the point where she would be unlikely to prevent their consummation.

"No, Phil, you—you musn't," she whispered, pressing her hot little body against him as he began to knead her buttocks through the thin summer skirt she wore. Through her blouse he could feel the quickening of her breathing, and he fancied that he could sense the hardening of her nipples. In a tango-like embrace, she allowed herself to be backed to the couch, where she fell back across the cushions. Phillip's body pressed her into the softness of the cushions.

"Phil, no. I mean it, now —" Her words glided into a breathy quiet while Phillip slipped a hand beneath her skirt, stroking the abrasive surface of her nylon stocking. Suddenly her body pitched, her legs pressed together for an instant, fluttered apart and pinched closed again as his fingertips crossed the border of her stocking, slid over the wire jaw of one garter and stroked bare skin. Thus did she refuse and entice, resist and yield in the timeless and instinctive manner of a nice girl whose time has come. Minutes later, bathed in sweat and gasping with beloved pain, she surrendered her virginity. In the weeks to come, she would learn, and he would teach her, to be voracious where she had been apprehensive, eager where she had been fearful.

"I love you, Phil." That came on their third time in bed. Phillip had heard it from enough girls so that the novelty had worn smooth. Still, something told him that this time it was a genuine sentiment, not the kind of expression that sprang solely from the heated loins and guilty conscience of a girl who has just discovered what it's all about.

To Phillip it was an encouraging bit of intelligence, since it granted him a degree of comfort in their relationship. It assured him of his ability to take without giving. In her innocence Claudia had no idea of what she had given away. To Phillip her confession of love amounted to a surrender, possibly unconditional.

"Shee-it, man, goddamn!"

It was a Friday afternoon when Chuck bolted through the door. Claudia stood in the far corner, ironing a shirt for Phillip. He had purchased a new ironing board out of his first paycheck, storing it under the couch on which he spent his nights. Now starched white shirts lined the wall behind her, the hangers suspended from a cornice three-quarters of the way up from the floor. She stood and stared at Chuck, too surprised to be embarrassed, for the moment, at having been caught in the apartment while Phillip was still abed. Claudia still imagined that their sexual relationship was a secret. Phillip played along with her by discussing it with Chuck only when she wasn't around.

"What's up, buddy?" Phillip asked. His eyes were still gritty from too recent and too little sleep, but he pushed himself to a sitting position, leaning back against the upright portion of the couch.

"I got a job!"

"Oh. What about your job at the ice cream joint?"

"Christ, man, I'm not talking about that kind of thing. I mean a job!"

"A movie job?" Suddenly Phillip was completely awake. "Doing what?"

"Nothing much. Just assistant to the second-unit director on a big-budget motion picture, that's all." He seemed ready to explode with delight and self-approval.

"Where? Here in town?"

"Arizona. Right outside of Phoenix." He moved to the bedroom door, paused. "Of course the studio will fly me there and back." Then he entered the bedroom, moving with jubilant purpose. Phillip looked across the room at Claudia, then threw back his covers and rose. Claudia came around the ironing board with astonishing speed as he moved toward the bedroom door.

"Put something on!" she breathed. Ordinarily he slept in his shorts, but Claudia had arrived before he had fallen asleep that morning, and they had done some screwing. He picked up his pants and stepped into them, walking into the bedroom as he zipped them. His belt hung loose. Chuck was throwing things into a suitcase. "They going to shoot over the weekend?"

"No, but the second-unit man wants me there to scout the locations with him." He could scarcely contain himself. "You know what this means?"

"I just came over to do a little ironing for your roommate," Claudia said, walking into the room with the shirts as though offering proof of her innocence. Chuck stopped in the middle of putting his

45

undershirts into the suitcase.

"Huh? Oh, sure."

"Now that you're making it, don't forget your friends," Phillip said. He felt more than a tinge of envious resentment.

"You think you're kidding? Listen, just as soon as I make a name with this guy, I'm going to tell him about you."

"I usually take the shirts home and do them," Claudia said from the vicinity of the closet, where she was hanging the shirts with considerable care. "But our iron went on the blink today."

"You realize I get screen credit for this? My first goddamn job and I get screen credit."

"I'll have to buy a new one," Claudia said.

"What?" Chuck paused, looking at her with mild annoyance.

"A new iron," she said.

"Oh. Sure." He scooped some white shirts out of a drawer and carried them to his suitcase. "Listen, buddy, you can use the bedroom for the next couple of weeks." He looked straight at Phillip as he spoke. His face was diverted from Claudia's gaze and he winked. "It ought to be more comfortable."

"And convenient," Phillip said. "Have you told Sally about this?"

"I went straight over to the paratment, but she was out."

"She had an early call for some television thing," Claudia volunteered. "She woke me up getting ready. I couldn't get back to sleep, so I decided to come over here and do the ironing for Phil."

"I sure appreciate it, too, honey," Phillip said, hooking an arm about Claudia's waist as she came within range. "There's nothing like having a woman take care of your ironing early in the morning." He kissed her on the temple, and she blushed with pleasure. Chuck bit his lip and turned away.

"Listen, will you get in touch with Sally and tell her where I've gone?" he requested, busily stuffing clothes into his bag. Phillip tightened his arm about Claudia's waist.

"Guaranteed," he said. "Consider it done."

That night Phillip called in sick. He knew that Sally had a habit of coming over to "visit" Chuck late at night. He didn't bother to tell Claudia that he wasn't going in to work. Going to bed early, he left the door to the apartment unlocked, as Chuck had mentioned doing on such occasions. At eleven-thirty he heard the knob rattle, and he turned over in bed, pulling the covers up until only a thatch of his hair showed against the pillow.

"Chuck?" It was a whisper, incredibly sultry. Phillip pretended unconsiousness, but the erection he had attained at the first rattle of the knob grew painfully hard. He was suddenly struck by the childishness of this gag, the astronomical odds against its success, but at the same time it was an erotic situation that he wanted to prolong.

"Chucky-boo?"

He buried his face more deeply into the pillow to stifle irrepressible laughter. Chucky-boo? It would be hard to keep from mentioning that one to Chuck. His own silent laughter was answered by a throaty chuckle from Sally. He heard the rustle of cloth and had to exert considerable discipline to keep from looking. Moments later the bed swayed, creaking a mild protest, as Sally slid under the covers. Her animal heat seared his skin. The musk of her body, unencumbered by perfume, caressed his nostrils as a hand, astonishingly soft and long-fingered, rested on his hip for a moment, then slipped to his waist. In the instant he turned over, she withdrew slightly, apparently more baffled than shocked.

"Hi, Sally." He smiled at her in the dimness. The only light came through the window. Their thighs brushed under the covers.

"Phillip?" she asked stupidly.

"Chuck's out of town. He asked me to tell you." As casually as though he had done it a thousand times, Phillip laid a bare hand on one naked, luxurious breast. It quivered like an awakened bird.

"Well, this is a hell of a way to tell me." But he could see that she was fighting laughter. "Why didn't you – ?"

"I just now woke up." She seemed not to have noticed the presence of his hand, except that her nipple was prodding his palm almost angrily. She looked at him for a moment, studying the bland expression on his face, as though wondering whether to believe him.

"Oh, she said finally. "Well, I guess I'd better go home then."

"Had you really?" His hand slipped down the flat plane of her belly, then skirted around her hip and rested on her thigh.

"You know it." She stared at him for a moment longer. Her voice had grown more breathless than usual, and she had done nothing to avoid his hand's attentions. "What do you think would happen if Chuck found out about this?"

"He'd never understand."

"Well, then?"

Phillip shrugged, stroking the inside of one superb thigh.

"Well, then, let's not tell him."

"Phillip, you shouldn't do that."

Phillip rolled onto his side and slipped his hand up to the moist heat of her crotch, smiling with a confidence that grew more authentic every moment.

"Really," she said. "I mean, what about Claudia? She's in love with you." Her eyes and the tone of her voice seemed to plead with him to come up with an answer to that one that she could accept.

"Claudia's a nice girl," he said. "I took her cherry. She has to be in love with me for a little while to make it all right."

"You really think that's all?"

"One of these days she'll find an excuse to go home and marry the guy who owns the gas station." He leaned down and kissed the juncture of her neck and shoulder. A violent shiver ran across her body, from the middle both ways. The thickness of her hair caressed his face. Phillip nibbled at her earlobe and then spoke soothingly into her ear. "I've only been going with Claudia because it gave me an excuse to be around you. If I can't make it with you, I won't have any reason to hang around anymore. You're doing her a favor."

"You shouldn't say that." She tried to make her tone reproachful. "She works her fanny off for you." Phillip slid his hand over her hip and down underneath.

"It's not as nice a fanny as yours. No contest."

"You're determined to have your way, aren't you?" She asked as though it constituted an excuse for yielding. Phillip kissed her full on the mouth, barely touching her tongue and bringing it thrusting into his mouth. "She told me she was coming over here today to iron all your shirts."

"That makes her feel like a wife. I do her a favor by letting her do those things for me."

"Jesus, you're fast with the answers."

"But I'm very slow with something else," he said. And suddenly she was all over him.

1799

Rhea

As Rhea Carter's personality developed, it became plain that she was a mixture of Lionel's practicality — learned no doubt, since it couldn't have been inherited — and Elaine's will. The latter caused her to chafe under the rigid discipline enforced by Mr. and Mrs. Cameron. The former occasioned an acceptance of that discipline, there being no other course open to her. One other trait which came to the fore once she was in school was an astounding intellect.

"Simply astounding, mum!" Mr. Cameron averred to Elaine on one occasion. "Never, in twenty-three years of teaching, have I seen the like of it." At the age of three and one half years, Rhea was reading better than many educated adults. Her manual dexterity proved exceptional, too, and before long she was writing as well as she could read. Once she had been told something — the meaning of a word, the way to make a letter, the name of a foreign capital, or the sum of two numbers — she remembered it permanently, and was able to apply it in practical ways far beyond the ability of students who had been at the school for several years. By the time she had been at the Camerons' institution for a year, Mr. Cameron was alight with the fervor of a discoverer.

"I should like your permission, mum, and the permission of your husband as well, to move Mistress Rhea on to more advanced studies."

"What sort of studies, Mr. Cameron?" Elaine asked, displaying something of the interest expected of a mother. The previous twelve months had been very pleasant, and she really didn't care if the man taught her child devil worship and cannibalism, provided he kept her away from the house five days and nights a week.

"This may seem startling, Mrs. Carter, but I think your daughter is ready to start learning French. And perhaps even Latin?" His inflection rose at the end of the unprecedented suggestion. He expected some objections here. Had the child only been a boy, he would have anticipated unalloyed joy on the part of its parents. But few people were daring enough to risk over-educating their daughters. The search for suitable husbands was harrowing enough without finding oneself with a young woman who was too intelligent and too erudite for the prospective bridegrooms.

"Well, if you think she is ready for such training, I shall leave the matter in your capable professional hands," Elaine said, eager to end the conversation. Mr. Cameron was one of the few things she found more boring than the subject of her daughter. "It is highly gratifying, of course, that you feel Rhea is worth this extra consideration."

"Excellent," Mr. Cameron said with the apparent relief of a man who has achieved far more than he had expected, and at a lower cost in terms of effort and time. "And the child's father?"

"Her —? Oh." Elaine caught herself just in time to thwart a cryptic smile. "You needn't concern yourself with Mr. Carter's reaction. I shall broach the subject to him. Unless you hear otherwise by tomorrow, you may proceed as you please. I give you and your wife carte blanche in the matter of my child's education, sir." Having received his permission to proceed and his dismissal from his client's presence in one voice, Mr. Cameron posted back to his school, content. He was a man dedicated to the craft of teaching the young, and he had never before been given the opportunity to work with such fine material as the mind of Rhea Carter. Had he known in advance the result of the course he had plotted, it is quite likely that he would have gone ahead anyway. Certainly there was no way to foresee what would follow. It was not his fault or even, logically, the fault of Rhea's mother. It was pure chance that led to the first dramatic turn in the child's life. Chance, or perhaps some force that rules and directs chance.

On her fifth birthday Rhea was allowed, against the better judgment of her teachers, to spend the day at home. It was not that the Camerons were opposed to birthday celebrations on principle. They simply considered it a heinous offense to interrupt the progress of a child's education for such frivolities. Nevertheless, Lionel Carter was not to be denied.

Recognizing the determination that surfaced so seldom in her husband, Elaine threw herself into the preparations with admirable enthusiasm. She instructed the servants in the preparation of the meal, including a small cake, saw to the decorations, and went so far as to shop personally for a gift. She selected a tiny purse with a matching pair of gloves. And then, as was customary, she inserted a coin into the purse. This custom almost went unobserved when Elaine discovered that she couldn't find a penny in her own purse. So determined was she, however, to join in the spirit of the moment that she dropped in a silver coin, a ten-cent piece. She regretted her unwonted lavishness at once, but had a serving girl wrap the gift and put it away before she could change her mind.

The birthday dinner went perfectly. Rhea, dressed in stiff crinoline, her blond hair hanging in ringlets past her tiny shoulders, was a sight to melt the heart of any father, and even her mother felt a tug at her heart. Rhea went through her meal with enthusiasm, partly because the presents would be opened afterward; but she never misplaced her manners. They had been too well ingrained in her as they were in all children of well-to-do parents in those days.

The family sat at a small table instead of the long one usually used for the evening meal, with mother and father bracketing their child, who occupied the head of the table for this special festivity. In the soft glow of the candles Elaine allowed herself to mellow for the moment, looking on her child with what she fancied was love while even her paunchy and balding husband began to look less offensive than usual. Part of this felicity came from a crystal decanter on the table, but some of it was the ordinary maturation of a woman now in her late twenties, seeing the sum total of her life gathered about her and unwilling to admit that it meant nothing to her.

Lionel had bought Rhea a large handmade doll imported from Paris, and a carousel that turned and played a tune when it was wound. She was delighted with these gifts as would be any child; but her most intense joy was reserved for the gloves and purse from her mother, partly because she had never received more than the most casual of notice from that lady before, and partly because these were such items as a grown-up woman might use. They seemed to beckon her toward, if not yet into, the status of young womanhood. And the ten-cent piece, gleaming brightly in the candlelight (because the serving girl had had the wit to polish it), capped the present. Unable to contain herself, Rhea dismounted her chair and ran around the corner of the table to hug her mother with all the strength of her chubby, five-year-old arms.

"Oh, Mommy, thank you! Thank you!"

"You're welcome, dear. Now stop this nonsense before you get yourself all wrinkled, and me as well." But her husband, looking across the narrow table at her, saw the flush of her cheek and a glow in her eye that was like nothing he had ever seen there before; and he reached across to squeeze her hand.

The next morning Rhea wore her new gloves and carried her purse with proper ladylike self-importance. The ten-cent piece rested in its depths. It was a moment of great importance in Rhea's life, though as yet she didn't know it, and wouldn't until, years later, she would smile, examining that morning in retrospect.

Her mother stood near the front door as Rhea came down the stairs, waiting with scarcely concealed impatience. Candlelight had nurtured the tender feelings of the previous night, and wine had fertilized them; in the cold light of day these feelings evanesced like a mist.

"Will you hurry, Rhea!" she hissed. Rhea came down the stairs at a speed that was not quite safe, but managed to negotiate them without mishap.

"I'm sorry, Mommy," she said, looking up at her mother with an expression of contrition calculated to soften even Elaine Carter's heart. "I was trying on my new gloves, and seeing which coat—"

"Yes, yes, all right. You're going to be late returning to the school, and Mr. Cameron will be upset. We must learn to consider other people's inconvenience," Elaine said on the way out the door with the age-old hypocrisy of parents: she didn't give a fig for Mr. Cameron's inconvenience.

Furthermore, contrary to her prediction, they arrived at the school with more than a quarter of an hour to spare. As woman and girl alighted from the coach, an ancient wagon pulled by an equally venerable horse came rattling over the cobbled street. The driver saw Elaine and her daughter and reined the weary horse to a stop.

"Pots and pans, ma'am?" he offered. Elaine ignored him. She considered it an affront that he thought she would concern herself with such sordid matters as pots and pans, which were properly left to servants. But the man, a scrawny and vulpine sexagenarian in filthy trousers and a shirt of indeterminate color, was not to be ignored. "A bit of cloth, then. I have some real good cloth, ma'am."

"No, thank you," Elaine said frostily, moving toward the wood frame building that was her daughter's school. Rhea, however, had noticed something, and glided toward the cart, standing on tiptoe to study the object of her attention. The old man saw the direction of her gaze and winked.

"You like the book, miss? It's a fine old volume for sure."

"Rhea, come away this instant," Elaine commanded. Rhea pretended not to have heard.

"How much is it?" she inquired.

"Oh, well, such a fine volume is worth a good deal of hard

United States currency, miss," the man said, his eyes narrowing a bit as he studied the girl's clothing, and the look of her mother, and the coach from which they had just alighted.

"I only have ten cents," Rhea said, extending her purse slightly, as though she thought the man might see into its interior.

"Ten cents! Well, now, that don't seem like very much for such a fine old volume as this," he said.

"Rhea! This instant!" Elaine said, and her coachman made ready to take a hand if he should be needed.

"Mommy, the book," Rhea said, pointing. Her mother walked swiftly to the girl's side and reached for her hand, which eluded capture. "But, Mommy, it's in Latin!" The keen eyes of childhood had seen the title carved in the leather binding. Even had her mother observed the letters clearly, she wouldn't have known Latin from English, having had a proper and ladylike education.

"I don't care if it's in Greek, it's filthy."

"I'd be happy to wrap it up for you, ma'am," the peddler said quickly. "A bit of cleaning and it would grace any bookshelf."

"Please, Mommy, please!" Rhea looked up at her mother with the importunate gaze of a child who has found a treasure. It wasn't tenderness for her daughter that softened Elaine's resolve, but a desire to be done with the matter.

"Oh, all right," she said, "if you want to waste your money on trash, then go ahead. Give the ten cents to the man and come along!"

The peddler, almost as delighted with the transaction as his youthful customer, wrapped the ancient tome in a piece of cloth that was almost clean as Rhea fished through her purse for the ten-cent piece, which she relinquished to him. The coachman accepted the book for the little girl, since it was of folio size and stuffed with hundreds of thick pages. Having made a sale, the peddler hastened to make himself scarce. The transaction was pure profit to him, since he had discovered the book among the ruins of a house that had burned long before. Like Elaine Carter he couldn't read, but had merely hoped that someone would be foolish enough to part with some coin of the realm for the volume. That there were men who would trade hard cash for such trivia as books was a fact he had ceased trying to fathom; that he might clear ten cents on the sale was astonishing to him, and that he would sell the book to a little girl in a gray coat was even more amazing.

1955

Phillip

There was a brief time when Phillip was sorry he had put the make on Sally Platz. His assessment of her qualities had been borne out by subsequent observation. She was a stupid and vacuous girl, who substituted slyness for intelligence and stubbornness for character. She was a good actress, which reinforced a theory Phillip had held for some time, that intelligence and acting talent were irrelevant to one another. Phillip had no compunctions about sleeping with his roommate's girl friend. Quite the contrary, there was a spice to the relationship that would have been absent had she been fair game. It was just that he kept remembering what Chuck Moulton was capable of when he felt threatened, or when his sense of outrage was activated. Sally's awesome stupidity, taken in that context, became scary, because it seemed all too likely that some night in bed with Chuck she might let something slip, bring up a subject she had discussed previously, under similar circumstance, with Phillip, or in some other way arouse her boy friend's suspicions.

It soon became obvious that his fears were groundless. Sally showed no change in her attitude toward Chuck. She was as casually affectionate around him as before, and her relationship with Phillip showed no outward change, either. There was no sign of strain or formality that might have given them away. Her natural acting ability proved a decisive advantage, but it also put Phillip on his mettle. If Sally was this much a natural at dissimulation, then he would have to be careful about trusting her motives too, and weigh the things she said to him for hidden meanings.

"We'll have to cut this out when Chuck and I are married," she said one night after a particularly furious and satisfying coupling. The silence that followed the pronouncement was barely perceptible.

"Well, that's up to you," Phillip allowed. "If you're positive you're going to marry him."

"Why not?" She disentangled herself from his arm and rose to support herself on her elbows, looking down into his face in the dimness. They were in Chuck's bed while Chuck was at work. "He's ambitious, and he treats me well. Someday he's going to be a fairly big man in this town, I think. He'll be able to help me in my career. I think that's the best offer I'm likely to get. Don't you?"

It was obvious what she was trying to pull, and Phillip felt a prickly sheen of sweat on his palms and forehead. To insult her now, to make the rejection too obvious, might bring disaster. To lead her on could, in the long haul, prove just as calamitous. Also, he didn't want things between him and Sally to end before they had to. She had proved the best lay in his already long string of conquests. A natural fuck, she didn't know how to do anything wrong, and her passion was so colossal that even now, when she was keeping Phillip satisfied, Chuck apparently had noticed nothing different in her response. Keeping Claudia around was handy, but she had already become the side issue, the appetizer in his sexual diet.

"Chuck loves you," he said. "The kind of love a guy like me doesn't know anything about." He injected a note of wistfulness into his tone, making it seem that he envied Chuck his ludicrous dependence on Sally. "I guess marrying him will be the best thing for you. But I don't want to think about it until I have to."

"Chuck is a very talented man," Sally said as though she hadn't heard him, as though she still thought it necessary to justify her intentions. "Have you seen that script he's been working on?"

"Chuck? Working on a script?" Despite himself, he asked it in an incredulous tone. He was sure, after two years, that he knew Chuck's abilities pretty well, and he had never heard the man speak of a desire to write.

"Sure. Why not? Don't you think he can handle a script?" She sounded as though he had challenged her veracity. Responding to instinct, Phillip sustained the note of incredulity in his voice.

"Oh, sure, I guess so. I just never thought of Chuck as a writer, that's all."

"You don't believe me, do you?" Sally's anger, already incited by his evasion of her bait, grabbed at this pretext. Before he could deny the charge, she rose from the bed and headed for Chuck's dresser. "I'll show you, smart-ass," she said, padding across the carpeted floor. Sinking to her haunches, she opened the bottom drawer of the dresser and delved under some clothes to produce a large manila envelope, which she carried back to the bed to drop heavily on Phillip's belly. He grunted from the impact, then looked down at the envelope with mild and polite interest.

"Look at it," she ordered. "Go on." Phillip stared up at her for a moment, undecided whether to greet her imperative attitude with anger or indifference. Then he looked at her breasts, juggling slightly with each short, intense breath, and decided that the best course would be tractability. Scooting up against the headboard, he picked up the envelope and emptied it out. The sheaf of papers was heavy and loose, spilling across his stomach. Sally switched on the lamp next to the bed, making him blink. He picked up the manuscript and glanced through it. It was a screenplay, right enough.

"Okay," he said. "You've proved it, honey. But I believed you anyway. Now how about coming to bed?" She looked at him, still petulant if not angry, probably stung because her blatant ploy hadn't worked as she had obviously hoped. Finally, she picked up the manuscript, rearranged it carefully, and placed it in the envelope.

"I'd better put this away first," she said in a voice that sounded as though she had recently been crying. Since she hadn't shed a tear in the past several hours, Phillip decided she must be acting for his benefit. Tucking the flap of the envelope inside, as it had been when she took it out of the drawer, she padded back and put it away under the clothes, then covered it over, carefully rearranging things exactly as they had been. When she turned and approached the bed again, her walk had that sensuous little swing-bounce that appeared when she wanted to put it on. Not having made it with hints, Phillip thought, she probably intended to fuck him into proposing. Well, she had every right to try.

He didn't think about the manuscript for a week. Then one night when he was alone in the apartment with nothing to do, he went to the dresser and dug it out. His motive at that point was curiosity reinforced by boredom. It was his night off. Chuck was working late at the ice cream parlor, the picture on which he had been working having run its course. Sally was working for some rich bitch from San Francisco, and was spending more and more of her evenings at her employer's temporary residence. Roles had been scarce for her of late, and she had taken this job to supplement her income until the TV season opened up several months hence. From what she had told Philip, the job was a glorified stenographer's position, but paid remarkably well. And the woman for whom she was working seemed to have taken an inordinate liking to her new employee.

He had made an excuse to keep Claudia from coming over. She had become an irritation, her sexual expectancies burdensome. It wasn't that he couldn't cope with the servicing of two women. It was just that going from Sally to Claudia was like rising from a dinner of duck a l'orange to munch on a green apple. The excitement he had garnered from the girl's innocence had worn through to the primer like a cheap paint job, and the lovemaking was perfunctory, at least on his part.

He took the manuscript into the living room, got a beer from the kitchen and opened it, then sat down on the couch, under a single shaded lamp, and began to read the screenplay.

He grew excited before he had scanned the first page. It reminded him of the Hitchcock thing, *I Confess*, but with a twist: instead of the priest's life being threatened, it was the life of an innocent third party. The priest, who had heard the confession of the killer, knew that only by breaking the seal of the confessional could he save the life of the accused person. The trouble was that Chuck, having come up with a basically sound, even stirring, idea, was botching it badly.

In the first place, the personality of the priest was all wrong. He was presented as a bloodless Christ figure, with no negative traits at all. Secondly, the accused party was intensely likable, a friend of the priest's who had once saved his life when the two of them were skiing, prior to the priest's taking Holy Orders. The character of the murderer was pure deep-dyed-villain of the East Lynne school. He was presented as crude, insufferably overbearing, deliberately insulting, even sadistic. There was no ambiguity to the story, and no tension. Phillip found himself pulling his ball pen out of his shirt pocket, and caught himself just in time to avoid marking the script. He scrounged a tablet and took notes as he went through the screenplay, then placed the sheets of notes securely in his coat pocket, hanging in the closet.

As he lay in his unfolded bed that night, he found it impossible to fall asleep because the story, and all that was wrong with it, kept flitting through his mind like a gaggle of moths. He woke the next morning, after finally dozing off at dawn still thinking about it. The sleep must have released something in his unconscious, because the ideas, simple and effective, flooded through his brain almost too quickly for him to pin them down. He entered the bedroom and moved silently to the closet. Chuck was a thick, twisted lump under the bedding. Phillip found his coat, took out the notepaper on which he had written the notes the previous night, and moved toward the living room.

"What's up?"

Phillip almost twisted his sacroiliac.

"Jesus, buddy, don't do that," he said with genuine asperity. "I thought you were asleep."

"Sorry. What have you got there?" His glance indicated the notes in Phillip's fist. They had become crumpled.

"Just some notes. An idea I've been working on in my spare time. And don't ask me anything about it, because I'm not sure I can trust you."

"A script idea?" Chuck asked, a cryptic, dreamy smile playing at his lips.

"Right."

"Okay. I won't ask you anything about it." There was a faint note of fatuous superiority to Chuck's tone, so slight that Phillip wouldn't have noted it had he not expected it. Chuck rolled over and placed his nose in the pillow, and Phillip knew he was already drifting back to sleep.

He went into the living room and made up his bed, then dressed and left the apartment with his notes and the remainder of the tablet. Walking to a coffee shop on the nearest corner, he ordered some breakfast and sat doodling with the ideas he had written the previous night.

His notes consisted entirely of negative comments on the script as written. Now he rewrote these objections, forming them into a column down the left half of a fresh sheet. Drawing a wavy line down the middle, he proceeded to write his amendments on the right side of the line.

To begin with, he altered the priest's personality and outlook. Instead of the plaster saint of Chuck's version, he came out as a man with problems, doubts as to the genuineness of his vocation. There would be a strong hint that he had entered the priesthood on a kind of rebound after serving as a Ranger in World War II. He would have an eye for the girls, though, of course, it would have to be suggested very subtly to get past the Johnson Office.

Phillip simply reversed the characters of the murderer and the accused innocent man. It was the innocent man who was now the crude, unlikable person, while the murderer was a man who had redeeming qualities, and who had killed in a fit of rage. There would be a suggestion that the victim had brought his fate on himself.

Written that way, Phillip thought as he dug into his ham and eggs, the story would have tension born of ambiguity. If the priest maintained his vows, could he ever be certain of his motives? Or could the viewer be certain, for that matter? It would be tempting to allow an unattractive curmudgeon to go to the gas chamber, especially when he would be taking the place of a generous, lovable victim of circumstance. For a while Phillip toyed with the idea of introducing a hint of love interest between the priest and the accused man's wife, this providing more doubt as to the former's motivation. In the end, though, he decided it was too pat and, anyway, the censors would shit a ring around themselves.

On the other hand, should the priest elect to break the sacred seal, he would be damned in the eyes of the Church, but that would provide him with a kind of release, which might be tempting in itself.

By the time he had written this much down, he was excited, but not satisfied. The story needed something more, some gimmick to resolve matters. He felt that he was on the verge of figuring it out, but his mind, after its furious activity, was a blank.

It will come, he told himself with a wistful hopefulness. It has to come.

1799

Rhea

One of the Camerons' progressive policies was that which allowed the boarding children to stay up later than would have been allowed, provided they used the time for scholarly pursuits. There was a library available to them, of modest size but excellent range of subject matter. It pleased Mr. Cameron so mightily that his prize student had spent her birthday money on an old Latin book that he quite forgot his earlier outrage regarding the child's absence from the dormitory for an entire night.

He didn't even bother to inspect the book, assuming that Rhea's mother had supervised the selection. He did note, from a distance, that despite its worn and tattered condition, and the layer of smut that covered it, the book had an exceptionally fine leather binding. This should have been no surprise, since human skin always makes soft and pliable leather; but Mr. Cameron didn't know that the book was bound in that material, any more than he knew its title. Had he taken the time from his teaching to inspect the book, Rhea's life would have been drastically altered. Even so liberal and progressive an eighteenth-century pedagogue as Mr. Cameron would never have allowed a five-year-old of genius and sensitivity to leaf at will through a book entitled *Liber de Malo*, The Book of Evil.

Rhea took advantage of the extra time allowed the students

that first night. The book made little sense to her at first. She had to stop and look up many of the words, since her Latin was not yet as solid as it would soon be. Even when she had translated the words, Rhea could make little of them. Whole sentences baffled her with their lack of logic. The chapters seemed to contain instructions for calling up various people with funny names, interspersed with repetitive warnings to follow the procedures to the letter, since one departed from them even slightly at one's peril. It was rather scary, but since Rhea didn't comprehend it perfectly, not as scary as it should have been.

The next morning when Mrs. Cameron entered the dormitory to wake the children, she found Rhea already awake, propped up in her bed, a book almost as big as she laid across her lap. Mr. Cameron, upon hearing of this laudable application on Rhea's part, hit upon his brilliant plan. He would allow the child to read her book only during the scanty free time allowed the children at the Cameron school. Since she would be engaged in the curriculum he had outlined for her during school hours, and since she was so fascinated by her own book, she would spend that much more time on her Latin, which was all to the better.

If the Camerons had been astonished by Rhea's intelligence in the past, now they were almost stupefied by her progress. She spent almost all of her time in reading, and Latin had become her favorite subject. It became troublesome even trying to get her to interrupt her studies to take nourishment. At an age when most children are readying themselves for the first shock of combat with studies, and looking forward with glee or dread to the task of learning to stumble through an elementary reader, Rhea spent her mornings reading Pliny and the orations of Cicero, and her afternoons and evenings pouring over an esoteric work which she was slowly and excitedly beginning to understand.

She had come to dread weekends. The relationship between her mother and the man she thought to be her father had deteriorated in the days since her birthday, when all had seemed briefly rosy. It was still a delight to spend time with her daddy, but even her love for him had begun to take a second place to her fascination with *Liber de Malo*. Her studies had opened new vistas for Rhea, and she had begun to see her daddy as a lovable but rather dull man who had never read anything more stimulating than a business report, and who seemed defeated and baffled by his inability to get along better with Mommy.

There came a time when reading the book would no longer suffice. It was a set of instructions, and Rhea's brilliant mentality was still harnessed to a sensitivity that was sufficiently childlike to need to discover the utility of those instructions.

She chose one of the simpler incantations in the first part of the book. The ingredients were easy to assemble for such a ceremony; all of them were available in the house itself, though such things as chicken blood had to be obtained clandestinely. A candle was no problem, since she had them in her own bedroom, and a piece of chalk was simply brought home from school on Friday afternoon.

On Friday night Rhea repaired to the basement of her parents' house and drew the proper figure on the stone floor. It had been a difficult evening, with her mother and father not speaking to each other. For a five-year-old even of Rhea's mentality, it was impossible to understand the cause of her parents' disharmony. Sex was a word she had never heard; the emotions it excites in adults would have been beyond her experience. She only knew that they seldom spoke, and were barely civil when they did, and that her daddy spent increasing amounts of time away, and that when he returned he smelled of liquor. Once he had been sharp with her when she had burst in on him in his room in the morning. He had made it up to her later, with a gift and a kiss, but the experience had frightened Rhea. Her daddy had never spoken to her in such a manner before, and she found it very hard not to blame her mother for this first, terrifying fissure in her security.

"*Show no fear; for if the demon senses weakness in you, he will rend your limbs from your body—*"

Rhea had read the graphic warning many times, and had learned it by heart. It didn't frighten her because, first of all, she wasn't certain of what a demon was, and secondly, so long as she wasn't afraid of one, it obviously couldn't hurt her. Otherwise, why would anyone want to summon one in the first place. To an exceptionally intelligent child, it all made sense.

She drew the proper figure on the basement floor with her chalk, studying its shape and reading its description over and over again, and then drawing it once more, to be certain there was no break in the line.

"*The form is a triangle superimposed on a five-pointed star, but no line must cross another: the points of the triangle must grow as by nature from the flat sides of the star. All lines must be sharp and clear, and with no break in the marking. The star must be thirteen units in size, whether feet or some other unit of measurement, or some number divisible by thirteen, for this number is pleasing to Him Who Must Be Obeyed; and no point of the star or triangle must point precisely north, or south, or east or west, for if a line runs in a precise direction, the demon will gain his bearings and will find his path from the figure and devour you.*"

Rhea made the lines thirty-nine inches in length, because that was a practical size in the basement, necessitating no shifting of cartons or stored furniture which inhabited the place. She was sweating when she had finished, and rechecked everything to ascertain that all directions had been followed to the letter. She sprinkled the chicken blood about the periphery of the design after placing the candle inside and lighting it. Then she stood back and spoke the words, reading aloud from the book. They were words she didn't fully understand even yet, but according to the book they would call forth a demon with a funny name she couldn't pronounce. She read the words three times, translating them from Latin to English in her mind, as one will do who is still new to a foreign tongue.

"*Amite, Male Spiritu, mihi tuum, servum—*"

"Spirit of Evil, send forth your minion to me. I bind him to do my will before he may return to the great domain of wickedness."

When she had read the words three times, nothing happened.

She stood looking at the crudely chalked form, at the old half-consumed candle in the middle and the mildly disgusting splotches of chicken blood that surrounded it all, and she felt stupid and embarrassed. She had come down here in her nightie and robe, lugging this huge useless book and those equally useless implements, and for what? It was all as silly as the prayers she said every morning and every night to please the Camerons.

The candle began to smoke.

It was an expensive candle, guaranteed never to smoke, but now the smoke rose from the tip of the flame in a thin black plume.

A chill passed through Rhea's tiny body.

At first she thought it was caused by a breeze, but no breeze could possibly find its way into her father's basement. No, the chill, whatever its source, was inside her. And it wasn't going away. She hugged the book to her as though for warmth.

A prickly sensation covered her skin.

The chill wouldn't go away, but this burning was just as real and just as insistent. The smoke from the candle had begun to billow outward, as though it were backing up against the ceiling. She couldn't see the ceiling. It was well cloaked in gloom. The candle's light, too, had begun to bow outward, as though something heavy rested upon it. Rhea could see only the candle now, and the pathetic scribble she had made around it. But she knew there was something in the basement. She was no longer alone.

Then she heard a sound, something between a sigh and a chuckle. The candle's halo flattened even more. And a voice spoke in her head, without coming through her ears.

"A child?" the voice said. It was like a magnified whisper, except that there was no sibilance to it. The chill that invaded Rhea's body seemed to fluctuate with the words and syllables. *"Have I been summoned by a little girl?"*

"I —" For the first time since she had started to talk at the age of five months, Rhea was without words. Except for the fancies of infancy, through which she had passed quickly and emotionally unscathed, she had never known what it was like to be afraid. The Presence hung over her in the dimness, almost invisible but somehow darker than the dark itself. Her heart beat frantically in her tiny chest, and she avoided speaking for the moment because she knew her words would come out all crooked and shaky. "I wanted to see if — whether it would —" She stopped, gulping for air. The Presence seemed to grow denser, mashing down the candlelight a bit more.

"Yes, little one," the whisper said inside her skull, *"the incantation is genuine. Perhaps you wish now that it were not?"*

"I'm — I'm not afraid of you," Rhea said, forcing a tone of defiance into her voice to keep it from failing her. That sound came back, half chuckle and half sigh.

"Of course you are afraid. You would be a fool if you were not. But you have courage, little one. Let me come to you, and show you that there is nothing to fear. I shall come out of the figure that you have drawn, and you will see that I am your friend, ready to do you great favors." She could feel the Presence gathering itself, moving toward the border of the form she had chalked on the basement floor. Rhea sensed a warmth from it, a feeling of friendliness, and she lowered the great book slightly from where she had held it before her. She smiled. The light from the candle became a fuzzy-edged bar, horizontal, its topmost line only a foot above the wick.

"No!" She said it more loudly than she had intended and then winced because one of the servants, who slept on the ground floor, might hear her and come to investigate. "No," she commanded once again, more quietly but with equal authority. "You shall not!" The sigh and chuckle wafted through her once again. The burning sensation on her skin was more intense than before.

"Very well, little one," the Presence acceded. *"You are brighter and stronger than I had understood."*

"And don't call me little one! My name is Rhea."

"As you wish, Mistress Rhea. What is your will?"

"My will?" The question left Rhea baffled. It had never occurred to her to wonder why one would want to summon a demon. The possibility of doing so had seemed fascinating enough in itself.

"Why have you summoned me?" The voice took on a vague note of impatience. Then, more slyly, *"Or if you have no task for me, then give me my leave, and I shall return to my own realm."* Rheas felt a rush of relief. She opened her mouth to tell the demon he was free to depart, but some tiny apprehension stopped her.

"If I give you permission to go back without commanding you to do something for me, what will happen?" she asked in her crispest voice, copied after her mother's. "Tell me the truth." When the Presence answered there was a subtle but distinct note of disappointment in the words forming in Rhea's skull.

"If you summon me without reason, the form you have drawn will cease to be a charm, and will no longer protect you. I shall depart from it, little Rhea, and crush your body into a spot of grease on this floor, and your soul will be my property through all eternity." Rhea overcame a momentary impulse to step back. The book was full of warnings that the demon would do all it could to trick whoever summoned it, and to destroy any person who tried to command it. Like most of the instructions and admonitions, these warnings had been no more than an exercise in translation to her. Now their meaning was brought home to her with the force of immediate and palpable danger. Unbridled, unprincipled hatred was a new concept to Rhea, and she fairly gagged on her first taste of it. Her fright numbed her mind for a while, so that she couldn't think of a command to give to the demon. The lack of a command was the thing to fear, and so she nearly fell into a funk of panic born of the viscious circle. She thought flittingly about being the property of the demon, and what unspeakable things he might do to her. And she thought about Daddy, who would be alone except for Mama, who didn't care about him.

And suddenly it seemed very simple.

"Your task is this," she said in a clear, forceful voice. "Make my mommy love my daddy."

The Presence chuckled and sighed again.

"By your daddy, you mean that fat gentleman who is sleeping in an alcoholic stupor uptairs at this moment?" Rhea bristled.

"I mean my daddy, yes! I mean my father, who owns this house and a lot of other things, and is a very smart man."

"I suppose that is clear enough," the demon replied with a note of cryptic amusement in his voice. *"Are you certain that this is your will? A wish granted is a relentless thing, Mistress Rhea."*

"It's what I want you to do if you can," Rhea said. Her voice quavered a bit as she thought of how much there might be to this matter of summoning up demons that she hadn't fully understood.

"It will be a simple matter," the demon sighed, *"to give you that which you think you want. I was required to warn you. As you will, so mote it be."* Something went through Rhea at these words, passing through her flesh and permeating the house. *"I leave you now, little mistress. Summon me again at your peril."* The voice dwindled at the final two syllables, and suddenly the light from the candle leapt upward as though relieved of a great weight. At the same time the cold feeling, of which Rhea had nearly ceased to be aware,

vanished, as did the burning sensation on her skin. It all happened at once, with such uncanny speed that Rhea was unsure that any of it had been there at all. The candle stood there, in the middle of the intricate design she had made, flickering but not smoking, an ordinary candle once more. The blobs of chicken blood had dried, blending into the dark stone so that they were scarcely visible. It looked silly to her once more, like the games played by the other children at Mr. and Mrs. Cameron's school.

She put down the book and retrieved the candle, using it to relight the lamp she had brought with her to work by, and had snuffed earlier, in compliance with the book's rules. In the stronger light the scene was even more foolish, and she began to feel ashamed of herself for having imagined so much. It couldn't have been real, she thought almost hopefully as she blew out the candle. But real or not, she knew her parents would disapprove of her nocturnal ramblings if they discovered them. Possessed of a drawn weariness that was unfamiliar to her, Rhea went searching for a damp cloth to wipe away the chalk and the melted wax from the candle. And to do her best to eradicate the dried splotches of blood.

Make my mommy love my daddy, she thought. If only it were real. . . .

A coldness seemed to pass through her slender frame, and for just an instant Rhea thought she heard in the distance a soft laugh that was like a sigh.

1975

Janet

To Janet Stafford it was like living through an interminable, frustrating dream. She had given up trying to get through to her husband by herself. Like many beautiful women, Janet lived with an innate sense of inadequacy. She knew that her husband was handsome, and that he possessed that rare charismatic attractiveness that defied description and transcended looks. Throughout their decade of marriage she had dreaded exactly the thing that had apparently happened: his loss of interest in her. She had never deluded herself about the depth of her husband's feelings. She loved him far more than he had ever loved her. Nor had she even tried to convince herself that he was faithful. Instead, she had managed to generate in herself a feeling of gratitude for his discretion, and the manner in which he covered whatever sexual escapades he might have indulged in. She didn't even take any credit for her own fidelity, knowing as she did that it was based on a total indifference to all other men. But now....

Now he hadn't touched her in — how long? Since she had gone to Palm Springs with the children.

When frustration turned to desperation, Janet decided that she would have to share her plight with someone who could offer her professional help.

Since her marriage, Janet's church attendance had been sporadic, a fact which had raised some feeling of guilt in her, though she had tried to make up for it with frequent and generous donations to the nearest Quaker church. Her family had all belonged to the Society of Friends for generations, and she knew that at home her father and siblings all prayed regularly for her return to the fold. One day, when the gloom of her present predicament had seemed overwhelming, she had dressed in one of her more sedate outfits and driven to the church. The pastor, whom she found in his office poring over his next Sunday's sermon, had had little solace to offer her.

"Mrs. Stafford, I can't promise you that there is any way to make your marriage stronger," he had said. "Christ didn't promise anyone an easy time on this planet. Personally, I think that a good deal of your present trouble flows from the fact that you have deserted Him, but don't think that He is going to bribe you back into His service by guaranteeing to restore your husband's love. All I can tell you for certain is that if you truly accept Jesus into your heart, He will bring you a peace and joy that will allow you to surmount any earthly troubles. The Lord Himself has told us not to pray for things, for our Father in heaven knows what we need and will provide it. Pray, rather, that you may be pleasing to God. And that is something that may only be accomplished through the blood of Christ, shed for our sins."

Janet had thanked the man and gone home. For the next few weeks she had prayed, as the pastor had suggested, for the strength to accept her lot, but the prayers seemed empty to her, as though they went nowhere beyond her own skull, and finally she concluded that it was because she didn't want to surmount her problems, or at least not this problem; she wanted to get rid of it.

To tell a friend of her situation was a grave risk. Even to be seen entering the office of a psychiatrist or a marriage counselor, for one in her position, could result in snide paragraphs in the gossip columns, which were bound to come to Phillip's attention and make matters worse or at least overtly hostile rather than silently estranged as they were at the moment. Still, the pressure of her fear and frustration built daily, even hourly, and she knew that she would have to confide in someone very soon. The smart thing to do, she reasoned, was to choose the right friend, someone who could be trusted, rather than waiting for the words to blurt themselves at the worst time.

"I feel the need of some outside help sometimes," she said to Nancy Wood, a woman whose background was similar to hers. Nancy had come to Hollywood two years before Janet, had married a middle-grade director who did a lot of TV work, and had gradually drifted out of her fairly promising acting career in order to become a full time wife and mother. Since then Nancy had seemed happy enough, animated and outgoing. She had taken up many outside activities to fill her time, and still seemed to have plenty of leisure left over. They were having lunch at the Brown Derby when Janet made her tentative and cryptic opening remarks.

"Well, I don't know what kind of trouble you're having, honey," Nancy said in that amalgam of California straightforwardness and southern accent that her voice had become in a dozen years. She looked at Janet across the crisp white tablecloth and two huge green salads, her expression expectant.

"It's nothing in particular," Janet said. "I just feel a bit depressed lately, Nancy. I thought that, since you're my best friend, you might —"

"In other words, it's none of my damn business. Quite right, too. Still, that does make it hard, hon. I know a good marriage counselor, if it's that sort of thing, and a good agent if you want to go back to work. I also could give you the names and addresses of some medics who might prescribe vitamins or tranquilizers." She munched on some lettuce and looked expectant again. Janet forked some of her own salad into her mouth and waited. "Look." Nancy's voice took on a tinge or irritation. "How about me telling you some of my juiciest troubles? Then you'd have something to hold over me if I should suddenly turn gossip?"

And suddenly Janet was crying. She wasn't even aware of when the tears had started. She scraped half her lipstick off with her eyeteeth and put down her fork, plucking her napkin from her lap and pressing it to her face. She couldn't seem to stop, and she was embarrassed, and horribly afraid she would embarrass her friend, but the tears wouldn't stop boiling up from her eyes, and now she was beginning to sob, too. She felt a surprisingly strong grip on her wrist.

"All right, honey. I'm sorry. That was pretty callous of me, but then I've never claimed to be the soul of tact. Just calm down. You don't have to tell me a damned thing if you don't want to."

Somehow Janet got herself in hand and looked across forlornly at Nancy, feeling that diminished state that always came over her when she knew she had been weak and that her makeup was destroyed.

"I'm sorry."

"Nothing to be sorry about, hon. You know, it just occurred to me that you apologize a whole lot. Maybe that has something to do with your troubles."

"Maybe." Janet picked up her fork and took another mouthful of salad. She chewed on the crisp lettuce until she thought she would choke. It seemed inexhaustible. Nancy was looking across at her with a speculative glance. Abruptly, as though arriving at a decision, she picked up her purse, which had rested on the floor beside her chair, and pulled out a white pocketbook.

"Well, here's where I maybe lose some respectability in your eyes, hon, but I'll take that chance." Janet looked at her in a mixture of confusion and hope as Nancy opened the pocketbook, fished around the pockets and compartments, and finally came up with a creased and a dog-eared business card. It was off-white, with a speckle finish, and the lettering on it was in a red and white fancy script. Nancy held onto it, as though having second thoughts, then thrust it across the table with the air of someone plunging into cold water. "I don't know if you believe in this stuff, but you don't have a thing to lose." She laid the card next to Janet's salad bowl. Janet read it without picking it up.

MRS. BAKER — PSYCHIC READER

In the bottom corners were a telephone number and an address, together with an admonition against arriving without a prior appointment. Janet looked at the card for a moment and finally managed to swallow the mouthful of salad. Then she looked across the table at her friend.

"The way this woman works is unusual," Nancy said, talking fast. "You send her a letter asking for an appointment, and you enclose something of your own in the letter. Something you've worn, though it doesn't have to be an intimate item. I mean, you don't have to send her a pair of your panites," she explained in a strained attempt at wit.

"Nancy, really—" Nancy threw up her left hand, palm forward, thrusting another mouthful of salad into her mouth with her right.

"It's up to you, hon. But give it some thought. This woman has told me things about myself that no one could have known, and she's predicted things that have come true right down the wire. She's no con woman, Janet. I mean she won't keep you coming back just to make money off of you. She doesn't have to. She's done readings for some very big people in this town and from all over the country. Pick up the card, hon. Just in case you decide." Janet placed a fingernail under the card, hesitated.

"Maybe that's the problem. Maybe I'm afraid she will know all about me. I'm not certain —"

"Well, that's a point. If you're embarrassed about your problems, perhaps you'd better not go to Mrs. Baker, because she'll take one look at you and know all about you. But she's like a priest. She'll never divulge anything she knows, even with your permission. She believes it's bad luck or something, and that she'll lose her power if she tattles."

Janet picked up the card and tucked it into her purse.

"Just out of curiosity, will she return what I send her?"

She had been taught by her Christian parents that such things were of the devil, but she had gained in sophistication since then. Now she wasn't sure whether she still believed that. But if Jesus wouldn't help her she thought, then maybe this woman — or the devil — could. Three days after her luncheon with Nancy Wood, Janet decided that she had wrestled with her conscience long enough to prove her essential virtue, and wrote a letter to Mrs. Baker. She had placed the letter in one of her personally imprinted envelopes and sealed it when she remembered that she was supposed to enclose something personal.

A handkerchief seemed sensible, but she had no old ones, and she recalled, after looking for one, that Nancy had said it should be something she had worn. Concerning herself with such niceties made her feel ridiculous, but she had decided to go through with it, and so she might as well obey all the rules. Finally, she decided that an old piece of costume jewelry might be sensible.

It was a comment on her state of mind that she had rummaged through her costume jewelry box for five minutes, rejecting this piece and considering that, before she noticed that the peacock was missing. Then she spent an additional five minutes going through all the pieces assiduously to be certain that she was right. Finally she got down on her hands and knees and looked under the dresser. She went and found a flashlight and looked again; and finally moved the dresser, raising a sheen of sweat on her forehead and upper lip from the effort.

But the peacock was gone.

She sat on the foot of the bed and cried. It was silly, she told herself, to get this sentimental over a worthless piece of glass and metal, something she hadn't worn in years and would doubtless never have worn again. She would have felt less despondent had she lost one of her really valuable pieces of jewelry, even the expensive star Phil had bought her a few weeks before. This was just a capper, she thought, after all the anguish she had suffered the past month or so.

Finally, to occupy her mind, she took out the box of fake jewelry and went through it again, eventually selecting a rhinestone bracelet which her younger sister had given her as a high school graduation present, and which she had worn almost constantly during her first year in Hollywood as a kind of talisman. She went downstairs and thrust letter and bracelet into a small flap-end manila envelope, sealing it with its own glue and some Scotch Magic Tape.

She decided to take the envelope to the post office right then, buy the stamps, and mail it. Afterward she went shopping, buying some new lounging pajamas that were black and would go with the slippers she had bought three days previously. Then she went home and lay down. She was asleep when Phillip arrived. It was dark outside, and the clock next to the bed told her it was after eight o'clock.

She looked a sight, but she only took time to run a comb through her hair and put on some lipstick before running downstairs. He was in the kitchen, rummaging through the refrigerator.

"Hi," he said, straightening up with a quart of low-fat milk in his hand. He lifted the cap on the carton and went to the cupboard.

"Phillip, have you seen my pin?" she asked. It sounded like an outlandish greeting for a wife to give her husband, but it had jumped out of her mouth and there was no calling it back. He seemed to stiffen for a moment, but she wasn't certain, and his back was to her. He took a tall glass out of the cupboard and began to pour milk into it carefully.

"Which pin is that, kid? The new one?"

"No, I suppose that's in the wall safe, with the rest of our valuables. I'm talking about that old pin my mother gave me just before she died."

"I don't recall it." He turned and faced her, his face gnarled into a frown of contemplation. "Oh, yeah, that swan, or chicken or whatever it was?"

"It was a peacock, and it's missing."

"Well, I sure didn't wear it last." He smiled, and as good as the smile was, she thought she detected a bit of tightness around his mouth. "Have you asked the kids about it?"

"I don't think either of them would go into my things without permission."

"No, I suppose not. Well, it's just misplaced. It'll turn up."

"How could it have been misplaced? It was always kept right in the box with the rest of my costume jewelry?"

"Goddamn it, I don't know, Janet. Shit, I come home after a bitch of a day, and you ask me to worry about some pin your father bought at Woolworth's for your mother in 1937."

Now, don't cry! Janet told herself silently. You're just going to make things worse. But the tears welled up in her eyes, threatening to run over. Phil sighed and put down his glass of milk. He walked to her and placed his hands on her shoulders.

"Honey, I'm sorry," he said. "That was a cruddy thing for me to say."

"No. You're right. Now you go take your shower, and I'll throw something together for you to eat."

"I'm really not hungry. I just want to go straight to sleep."

Well, you've made that point right off, Janet thought. But she produced a smile.

"Did you stop to eat on the way home?"

"No, but —"

"Then don't be silly; of course you're hungry. I defrosted some pork chops. They'll go just fine with eggs and coffee. Now you go and get cleaned up."

Moments later, as she scrambled three eggs for him, she told herself that he really had been right. He had much more important things to concern himself with than the loss of an old pin that the insurance company wouldn't even value at a dollar. Still, she couldn't help wishing he had shown just a little more sensitivity to her feelings. And there was the tightness around his mouth, the way he had stiffened when she had brought up the subject in the first place. For the first time in her married life, she was unable to dismiss or erase those little clues from her memory.

1955

Phillip

He wrote the script at the hotel, after hours. The hotel job proved ideal for his purposes because, once the figures had been balanced, Phillip was free to go or stay. There was an IBM typewriter in the office, and he was able to put in at least two hours a night with it before the morning crew came on. He kept the manuscript in one of the hotel's safes out of fear that if he took it home Chuck might come across it.

His gimmick, the resolution he had sought, didn't come to him until he had been writing almost blindly for three nights. Then it finally occurred to him that the only out for his priest character was to go out and plant evidence that would incriminate him. By laying his life on the line, he would be able to maintain the sanctity of the confessional and rescue the accused man at once. He would simply refuse to answer any question or to take the stand in his own defense.

Once the idea had solidified, he wrote at white heat, resenting the inexorable advance of the clock that would force him to fold his manuscript and go home. For a while he considered letting the priest go to his death, but he knew that such an ending wouldn't be commercial even if it could be got past the censors. Reluctantly, he also yielded to the necessity of having the priest joyously reconciled to his calling at the end of the film. Yet, through careful writing he managed to leave in some ambivalence about that, and just a touch of foreboding that the character was in for an arid future.

Up to this point he had kept his activities secret. He had briefly considered going to his roomie with the finished script and explaining that he had come across the original quite by accident and decided to redo it as he felt it should have been done. But the idea seemed fraught with danger and, besides, he didn't want to share his screenplay now that it was finished.

That he might share the secret with Sally was a notion that had briefly occurred to him, too. He had even begun to think of marrying Sally. For a young man on the rise, she wouldn't be a bad choice, particularly in the movie industry. He had decided against letting her in on things, first because he was afraid that she might yield to an attack of conscience and blab the whole matter to Chuck, and later because of an increasingly obvious change in the girl's personality.

To begin with, he was seeing much less of her. And so was her ostensible boy friend. To Phillip this constituted an annoyance, but he knew that it was tragic to Chuck. A man in love is always insecure, and that insecurity was being aggravated by his loved one's increasing spells of absence. She always had the best of excuses: she had to work. Her employer, the older woman from San Francisco whose name Phillip had never heard her mention, was making increasing demands on her time. The worst part of it was that Phillip seemed to detect a kind of complacency in the girl. On the increasingly rare occasions when he and Sally managed an assignation, he had the weird feeling that she was there, not because she preferred to be, but because it would constitute an infraction were she not to show up: failure to repair, perhaps. She gave him the impression of having been assigned to him for the night by some unanswerable authority. And although she was still the most glorious fuck he had ever enjoyed, he had the feeling that she was no longer yielding to her own insistent desires, but was putting on a show for his benefit, performing like a trouper. There was a detached air about her, as though she would have preferred to be somewhere else; and at the same time an almost palpable nervousness that he couldn't interpret. Despite the sensual pleasures she could still bring him, he found himself relieved when she departed, and for a while he revived his affair with Claudia because he found her wholehearted devotion reassuring, and her propensity for losing herself in the act of sexual intercourse refreshingly normal.

To take Claudia into his confidence with regard to the script was unthinkable. She had a smalltown, Midwestern conscience that couldn't be trusted. He thought he could probably keep her in check for so long as he continued to screw her, but he could never be sure. And when the time came to make the clean break, he didn't want a vengeful female around who was armed with that kind of information.

So it had proved wisest to keep things to himself. But he knew the time was coming when he would have to abandon secrecy. He had a good script, perhaps a great script, and the time had come to do something with it. Getting it to the right people would be hard, but Chuck was a connection, if he could manage to manipulate him without giving away the fact that he had expropriated Chuck's story.

As it turned out, the connection worked for him without his having to take any overt action. It was one of those weird, almost creepy experiences that seem inevitable when middle-aged, successful men look back on them, but that are really miracles when they occur.

It happened on a Monday. Chuck had stepped out of the apartment for a moment to pick up his dry cleaning. During the quarter hour that he was absent, the phone rang, bringing Phillip up out of a light, intermittent sleep. He padded to the table on which the instrument rested and picked it up, concentrating on making his voice coherent and authoritative.

"Mr. Moulton?" a woman inquired from the other end of the wire. She had a voice like a busy signal, rough-cut and imperious.

"He's out right now," Phillip replied, making his own voice flat and without a trace of deprecation.

"Can you tell me when he'll be back?" the woman asked in a tone that implied he shouldn't have made her inquire. Something about her tone put Phillip on his mettle.

"No, I can't," he told her. "He left this morning on urgent business and I have no idea what time he'll return." That was true enough. Having clean pants to wear was urgent, and there was no telling what Chuck might stop to do on the way over.

"I see. And you can't tell me where I might get in touch with him?"

"I'm afraid not. May I ask who is calling?" Phillip asked in a tone that implied she shouldn't have made him inquire.

"This is Anthony Hatfield's office," the woman said in the same portentous tone she might have used to inform him that the call originated from the White House. For a moment Phillip couldn't imagine who Anthony Hatfield might be, and he almost said so. Then the name rolled over in his mind, and he remembered Chuck's using it in a casual, name-dropping way around people who were working in studios. His heart began to pound, and he spoke before he realized what he had decided to do.

"Oh, well, why didn't you say so?" he asked. "I'm Chuck Moulton. I'm trying to shake someone, ma'am. That's why I didn't identify myself right away. What can I do for Mr. Hatfield?"

"I see." The woman sounded as though he had stolen thirty precious, irreplaceable seconds from her life. "Mr. Hatfield would like to see you today about a possible assignment, Mr. Moulton. Would two o'clock be convenient?"

"Let me see." Phillip put down the phone with just a touch more clatter than was necessary and stood looking out the window for ten seconds. "Two-fifteen would be better," he said.

"Very well. Two-fifteen, then," the secretary replied in an I-see-through-you voice. "Mr. Hatfield will be expecting you at two-fifteen sharp." She gave the last syllable just a fillip of emphasis.

"Sharp is the word," Phillip said, and hung up. He walked back and sat on the edge of the hide-a-bed. There was just a touch of raggedness to his breathing. What the fuck did you do that for? he asked himself.

It was still possible to abort the plan that had formed in his mind. All he had to do was tell Chuck that he had an appointment with Anthony Hatfield at two-fifteen. But he knew he wasn't going to do that.

"Who the hell are you?"

Anthony Hatfield turned out to be a fiftyish, ucler-ridden man with gray complexion and watery blue eyes. He looked like an actor playing his own part in a B movie. Phillip walked across the immaculate but boorishly decorated office toward the cluttered desk.

"I'm Phillip Stafford, Mr. Hatfield," he replied.

"My secretary told me Chuck Moulton was outside."

"It's not her fault, sir. I gave her that name. You see, I'm Chuck's roommate, and this seemed like a good way to gain entry."

"Is that right? Well, listen, horse's ass, you go home and tell Moulton that if he ever gets another chance in this town, he'd better have a smarter roommate."

"Aren't you even interested in why I took a chance like this?"

"I'm not blind, Stafford. I can see that sheaf of paper under your arm. It's a script, right? The best thing since *The Birth of a Nation*. And you're giving me first crack at it."

"Only because I'd never have got in to see Sam Goldwyn." Phillip was astonished at the easy smoothness of his voice. He had played a lot of poker at college, and the skills he had developed stood him in favor now. Only he had never played for table stakes before. Apparently the right amount of sassiness was a good tactic here, as he had hoped and surmised, because Mr. Hatfield's lips curved into the faintest and briefest of smiles before he spoke again.

"Is that a fact? Well, listen, mister. I may not be Samuel Jesus Christ Goldwyn, but if I read every piece of shit some huckster snuck in here I'd be in the fuckin' poorhouse now. Why don't you take that stationery home and wipe your ass on it? That's prob'ly all it's good for anyhow."

"Once you've read it, you're going to apologize for that remark." The statement proved to be a prophetic one. Twenty years later, at a banquet in Phillip's honor, the apology was publicly and charmingly tendered. For the moment, however, the predicition had its intended effect. Mr. Hatfield looked as though he had been struck in the belly. But he smiled again, not quite as briefly as before. Phillip walked to his desk and set the manuscript in the middle of the green blotter. Hatfield looked at it as though it were oozing pus. "I know you're a busy man, Mr. Hatfield, so I won't take up any more of your time. I'll just leave this here. If you're as smart a man as I think, you'll read it."

"Get this fuckin' piece of shit off my desk," Hatfield commanded as Phillip walked to the door. When he had it opened, Phillip turned and smiled in a conspiratorial manner. Hatfield depressed a key on his intercom. "Mrs. Wanamaker, after this, if some schmuck wanders in off the street, you check his I.D. before you admit him." Phillip laughed good-naturedly and fought an impulse to wipe his palms on his trousers. "Hey, tell me something, Dudley Nichols. How come you haven't got an agent to pull this kind of schtick for you?"

"I'm new in town," Phillip replied. "Agents' offices are just as hard to enter as this one, so why not go right to the top?" This time Hatfield smiled openly, and Phillip could almost hear him thinking, At last! Some respect from this pup! Phillip waited precisely the right interval before throwing out his joker. "Now I'd like to ask you a question, sir. How come, with a name like Anthony Hatfield, you talk like a Jew in a black and white movie?" He walked out, leaving Hatfield swallowing something between laughter and outrage.

1801

Rhea

To a child every wait is a long one. Though Rhea's mind was sharper than that of most adults, it lacked the perspective that only time can bring. Thus it was that Rhea was reinforced in her belief that the episode with the demon had been a phantom experience. It takes time for a human being to realize that she is in love, and the results of Rhea's wish weren't apparent that weekend. But when she came back the following Friday night, everything had changed.

For one thing, her mother's clothes had been moved into the master bedroom. The room she had kept for her own was just another guest room now. But this was only an outward and obvious manifestation of something that made itself evident to anyone who had been in the house before, and who entered it again.

The air of tension was gone. The servants seemed more relaxed, though they were no less conscientious in their duties. Lionel Carter had had no more than a moderate amount to drink in the past five days, and the diminution of his alcohol intake had worked wonders in his personality.

The most obvious change, however, was in Elaine Willoughby Carter. She was too intelligent and practical a woman not to have recognized that something in her had been altered, and that her husband was the focus of it. She had devoted some fleeting moments of introspection to the matter, but had not bothered to pursue it even in her own good mind. A sudden and inexplicable wretchedness of the soul gives one pause to consider; but happiness does not invite questioning. And for the first time in her twenty-nine years Elaine was happy. She woke happy and retired happy. She found delight in fulfilling her functions as mistress of Lionel's house. A smile played at her lips and often, as she walked about, supervising the house-cleaning, whatever tune she was humming would give way to a chuckle, or even a hearty laugh. Many times the laughter would know no direct cause: Elaine hadn't thought of something funny; she had merely felt the urge to express her joy. She was like a woman who, poverty-stricken all her life, had just discovered a fortune.

The ironic thing was, and it was a good joke on her, she averred, that the fortune had been hers all along. This fine man, whom she had been fortunate enough to take to husband, was her fortune, and she was determined not to squander a second's worth of it ever again.

Everything he did was beautiful to her. When he left for his offices in the morning she would gaze out the window until he was gone from sight; and when he came home at night, she would be there to greet him at the door with a wifely kiss. The servants no longer even attempted to approach the door when the master came home.

To dine with him, to enjoy a glass of wine while he sipped at his whiskey, just to sit and share a room with him was an intense joy to Elaine. How was it that she had never noticed the noble slope to his brow, the majestic look of his nose, the way his face seemed to light up all about him when he smiled, and made the world a more solemn and dignified place when a frown creased his forehead? How could she have escaped marking the way his glance made her feel so alive, and his touch turned her body all weak and watery?

It had come over her gradually. At first she was only aware that she found his presence less objectionable than she had in the past. Then she had found herself seeking him out in the evenings, deliberately spending with him the time she had previously expended in solitude, or with those rare friends who visited. Then, just two nights before Rhea's return from Mr. and Mrs. Cameron's school, they were sitting across the narrow table, sharing their dinner, and he was making her laugh with a wit she had never heeded in the past. The use of the more intimate table had been Elaine's idea. Without examining her own motives, she had so instructed the servants, simply because it seemed a pleasant notion to follow. Then, when he had pleased her with an especially subtle witticism, Elaine, quite unconsciously, had reached across the table and covered his hand with her own.

Lionel had looked down at her hand and then had shifted his gaze to her eyes. Elaine felt herself flush hotly, filled with the idea that he, with that wonderfully perceptive mind, had read her thoughts. Or not her thoughts exactly, because she had had none at that moment, but something more subtle: her emotions, and before she was fully aware of them herself.

Suddenly her heart fluttered wildly against her breast, she was a bit dizzy, and her hand trembled. Her breathing was shallow, her skin all prickly; and she was pleasantly conscious of a glow of perspiration on her forehead.

With elaborate slowness she withdrew her hand from his, never looking away from his eyes because she feared that to do so might shatter this fragile moment. She rose with great care, pushing back her chair with her knees. Lionel sat looking up at her, making no move to rise himself, as though, wonderful and considerate man that he was, he feared to assume intentions on her part which might prove mere fancies on his own. Elaine felt a keen pang at the thought that she had given him ample reason in the past to entertain just such doubts. Now it was her place, even at the risk of boldness, to allay his doubts emphatically. She leaned forward slightly at the waist, raising the skirt of her long dress slightly with her right hand preparatory to moving away from the table, and took his hand in her left. Still he sat there. She knew a moment of self-comprehension when it occurred to her that this would have seemed like denseness on his part, just a short while ago. Now she found his reluctance, his apprehension at offending her through presumption, to be charming. She tugged lightly at his wrist, and smiled softly.

"Come, husband. Please."

He rose finally, nearly upsetting his wine glass in the process, and followed her. Fortunately the servants were nowhere about, having retired to their own quarters for the night. Elaine could feel herself blushing furiously, and she was certain that the chance presence of another party would have filled her with an anguish of discomfort, for the things she was feeling were too intensely personal to be shared with outsiders.

She led her husband to his own room because the thought of being there with him, of being possessed by him while surrounded by his furniture and his belongings, seemed both exquisitely exciting and appropriate.

The room flickered with light from the oil lamps, lit with efficiency by the servants before they had retired. The bed had been turned down, and looked crisp and inviting.

In the opening years of the nineteenth century, undressing for bed was something of a chore, taking a goodly amount of a woman's time and threatening to wear down the passion of the most heartily erotic person by the sheer, arduous delay. It is a tribute to the human libido that the race survived the era of layered underdress and tight lacings. To Elaine it had never seemed other than natural that undressing required as much time as dusting a good-sized room or unhitching and bedding down a team of horses. Now, for the first time in her life, clothes were an irritating encumbrance, something that would not yield quickly enough to her demands to be out of the way. Never before in the ten years of their marriage had she disrobed before her husband's rapt and grateful eyes. He sat fascinated as her loveliness emerged with tortuous slowness from the yards of expensive linen that encased it. Elaine was vaguely surprised that she felt no embarrassment. No man had seen her naked, except for Dick Dawson, since she had been a child. Lionel might have glimpsed her a time or two as they prepared to make furtive love beneath the covers of the bed, but to expose herself so brazenly before him should have had her in a fit of humiliation. Instead, she blushed with a pleasant physical excitement and a joy at the pleasure she was bringing to him.

Lionel stared at her body with open admiration, sitting on the edge of the bed, as still as a painting, as though afraid that any movement on his part might break this instant. Elaine felt an overwhelming tenderness for him, and she moved to the bed quickly, taking his head in her arms and pressing it to her naked bosom. Now even the pleasant embarrassment was extirpated from her; there was no room for any emotion in her being except for the overwhelming love that she felt for this man. Timidly his arms encircled her hips, his hands shyly clasping her buttocks. Her entire body covered itself in gooseflesh as she trembled with a kind of desire she had known with Dick Dawson, which she had taken for the fullness of sexual passion, was as nothing compared with this feeling, in either intensity or complexity. The reticence of his caress seemed dear to her, but she was determined that the time would come soon when his hands would travel over her flesh with casual boldness.

That night was a revelation to Elaine and to her husband. He had lived a life of probity, with a wife who cared nothing for him. He was as ignorant of the full joy of erotic congress as he was clumsy in its execution. His wife had had little more opportunity to learn, and so they were bride and goom that night, lost in the wonder of discovering each other's bodies. Four times they fell into exhausted sleep, pressed together in an embrace that had lost none of its passion for their momentary inability to satisfy that desire. Twice during the night they woke together, as though their bodies and nerves responded to a single impulse, and resumed that which exhaustion had interrupted. And in the morning, before rising, they locked their bodies together in one last erotic embrace before ringing for the servants, putting on some clothes, and ordering breakfast to be brought to them. They spent most of that day in the bed chamber, like children who had just discovered the use of it.

Into this whirl of connubial rapture stepped Rhea Carter, five years old but with the intelligence of an extraordinary adult, and with the secret knowledge of how it had been brought about. It wasn't exactly as she had expected. When she had ordered the demon to make her mother love her father, she had envisioned the casual affection she had noted among the parents of other children, not this fervid and fanatical passion. In its own way this ardor was more disturbing than the animosity it had replaced. She had sought a more pleasant atmosphere in the presence of her parents. Instead, she found that she was deprived of that presence for the most part. Her parents seemed virtually unaware of her existence, and for hours at a time, in the middle of the day, they would vanish into their bedroom. Rhea didn't know what they did there all that time. It was possible, she supposed, that simply loving each other so much made them terribly tired, and they had to sleep more than people did otherwise. She wished now that the demon had made her mother love her father only a little bit. She had learned her first two lessons with regard to wishing: be certain you want what you wish for, and be precise in your instructions.

What was worse, the new ambience of love in the Carter household didn't include Rhea. In her child's way she had assumed that when her mother loved her father, she, Rhea, would be loved as well. Her father already loved and cherished her, and when her mother loved him she would feel the same way. At five years of age Rhea had only a child's understanding of what fathers and mothers were; that paternity could be dubious was a fact she had no way of understanding. For that reason, her mother's fresh resentment of her was a puzzle. To Elaine, the exquisite little girl who came to the house on weekends was worse than a stranger: she was an abomination, a diabolical reminder of the sin she had committed against the only man who meant anything in her life. The child was repellent to her as a reptile, and it was only through a supreme exertion of will that she was able to conceal this aversion and display nothing more than a cool indifference in her daughter.

At first Rhea retreated into her books. She had proved the golden expectations of Mr. Cameron to be paltry and unambitious. After only a few months she was reading Latin like an ancient Roman, and had begun to write in that language. *Liber de Malo* now yielded more readily to her study, and she was disturbed to note the errors she had made earlier, and slightly puzzled that the creature she had summoned, an immensely powerful being by human standards, had not squashed her for her impertinence. Many of the necessary rites had been observed by her through instinct, or by sheerest accident. Her belated terror at the possible consequences of her rashness brought about a determination never again to use the book's powers.

The thing that changed her mind was an event that was as unexpected and as inexplicable to Rhea as it would have been obvious to any adult cognizant of the Carters' new relationship. The disturbing insularity of their love seemed all at once to take on a greater intensity three weeks after Rhea's wish was granted. She hardly had an opportunity to speak to either of them because suddenly, even when they were at dinner or luncheon with Rhea, they were caught up in one another, lost in their own mutual existence, and apparently sharing some tender secret. The whole thing made Rhea sick, and once she had an opportunity, having caught her father alone on his way out to attend some weekend emergency at his offices, she broached the matter with the directness of a child coupled with the adult's obvious intention of being answered. Her father stood before her for a moment, a large portfolio under his arm, and cleared his throat loudly and repeatedly before he thought of a way to reply.

"Well, you see, my dear, that is, your mother is —" He broke off suddenly, red-faced, and Rhea knew it was one of those matters about which adults were so cloyingly and frustratingly cryptic. "What I mean to say, my dear, is that you're soon to have a little sister. Or perhaps —" and here his face and voice grew wondering, "—perhaps a little brother." Rhea actually drew back in shocked surprise. This was a development she couldn't have anticipated.

"How do you know?" she asked.

"We—well, we just know, Rhea. You'll have to take your father's word on the matter. And now —" He fished his watch out of a vest pocket like a talisman intended to make her vanish, but Rhea was determined.

"Where is my little brother or sister now?" she asked with narrowed eyes.

"Why, in heaven, of course, waiting to be born." Rhea clenched her tiny fists in frustration. Heaven! Probably the one place where she couldn't get at the little brat.

"Then how do you know about him, Daddy?" she asked with the insistence of an attorney determined to find a flaw in the witness' testimony. "Or her?"

"Because God has a way of revealing these things to grown-ups, Rhea," her father answered with a desperate sternness. "And now I must go." He was down the walk and into the waiting coach before Rhea could insist on more answers.

She stood looking after him resentfully. The spring in his step, the disgustingly childish joy in his voice as he called to the coachman, were all the more difficult to bear because she recalled when only she had made him feel that way. And now he obviously cared not so much as a rusty nail for her. In her confused and instinctual way, Rhea knew that her wish, her mother's new love, had something to do with this new and totally repulsive development. Well, she had brought about that love. And what had been done could easily be undone.

1976

Phillip

By this time, Phillip Stafford thought, he should have been drawing unemployment insurance. He had lost track of the mistakes he had made in the past weeks. Once he had sent a whole unit off to a location a week before the time agreed upon by the man who owned the land on which the shooting was to take place. It should have cost the studio hundreds of thousands of dollars in salaries and other costs. When the unit had arrived the owner of the land had expressed bewilderment, but he had smiled at the assistant director and said that another project of his had fallen through unless he could put it off for a week. He had given up on the other project because he had agreed that Phillip's studio could have his land during that time. Now, he said, if they could finish up their shooting and get off the place within a week, he would be willing to rebate twenty-five percent of the rental he had agreed upon. The result was that the studio had saved several thousand dollars in rent and had also managed to accelerate the schedule of the film by a week.

"How did you know to send those people out there seven days early?" one of the company vice presidents had asked Phillip in a voice filled with wonder. Phillip had shrugged, playing his famous poker face.

"You don't expect a man to give up all his secret sources, do you?"

In another instance he had allowed an actor's contract to

lapse without picking up the studio's option. The actor had signed with another studio for a big increase in salary. Phillip's prestige at the studio had suffered for a while. Then it had become known that the actor was suffering from cancer of the larynx, something he hadn't known about himself when he had pulled his tricky exit from the studio. The subsequent operation had deprived him of his voice, which had been one of his chief assets, and had left the other studio holding a very expensive dead asset.

"Did you really know about that?" the same vice president had asked Phillip with a note of comical dubiety in his voice. Once again Phillip had shrugged.

"Have you ever known me to slip up on an option before?"

As a result Phillip was being considered for a vice presidency himself. He had always known that he was destined to head the studio someday, but he had never believed that he would make it on a series of mistakes. And how long could he expect the mistakes to remain lucky?

He knew what was wrong with him: Rhea. He had tried to rid himself of her, but his need for her grew daily. He had made a play for another woman and found himself incapable. After that humiliating and possibly pernicious experience, he had resolved not to attempt again. The woman involved, a young actress, had done well from the incident, getting a juicy part that was actually beyond her in terms of popularity and talent. Phillip knew that he couldn't afford to shut up many sluts in such an expensive manner.

He had tried to go cold turkey once, changing the number of his private line at work and instructing his secretary to intercept any calls from a woman named Rhea, and from anyone who didn't identify himself. He had felt proud of himself afterward, but three days later, when Rhea had called him over his new unlisted number, he hadn't even asked her how she knew it. He had been too relieved, and too excited, to hear her voice.

"I'll be at the usual place a half hour or so from now," she said.

"Rhea—"

"If you're not there to meet me, I'll leave, Philly."

"Damn it, Rhea —" But he was talking to a dead line. This time he didn't go through the charade of trying to stay away. He tossed off his drink and told his secretary to cancel all his appointments for the afternoon. Driving like a crazy man, he had arrived at the lounge ten minutes early, had taken their rear booth and ordered a drink. An hour and a half later he was on his fifth drink when Rhea walked in, resplendent in a lime-colored pant suit and clog shoes, with her black hair flowing freely down her back. With just a touch of lipstick and eye makeup she looked startlingly lovely to him. He reached across the table, half rising, to touch her hand, but she avoided him, sliding into the booth and looking across at him with that maddening twinkle.

"Je-sus it's hot," she said. "I'll have something cool. A gin and tonic, I think. Order it for me will you, Philly?" The waitress was already on her way over. Phillip ordered the gin and tonic and another whiskey and water for himself. He was angry by then, freshly aware that he had cancelled appointments in order to be here at the time she had specified.

"Know what time it is?" he inquired, fingering his watch.

"I never carry a watch. They annoy me," she said. Her gaze asked him if he wanted to make something of it. Phillip shrugged and picked up his drink.

"I only thought that if you had come earlier, we could have spent more time together."

"Philly, dear, you shouldn't assume that I want to spend more time with you. Anyway, you didn't have to wait, you know. You probably shouldn't be here now, considering your recent performance at work."

"How do you know—?" He stopped himself too late, wanting to cry because she found it so easy to rob him of his usual composure. Someday, he thought, he was going to choke the life out of her, if he went to prison for the rest of his life. She threw her head back and laughed and then, just as the waitress brought their drinks, leaned forward and patted his hand in a gesture of mock comfort. Her touch, the way she bestowed it upon him, was an exciting humiliation.

Phillip busied himself paying the waitress. He was too drained even to be angry with Rhea, or with himself. Anger was something he still occasionally knew when she wasn't around, but aside from a brief and occasional flash, he couldn't sustain it in her presence. He could only feel the most demeaning emotions: anxiety, fear that she would leave him or never let him touch her again and, lately, a sense of hopelessness.

"It's pay-up time again, Philly." He stared at her, hating her for her self-assured, patronizing tone, and himself for yielding to her even while he hated her. He had a stick in his pants, just because she had tacitly suggested that they were going to do some screwing. There had been a few times these past weeks when she had met him at this bar, patted his cheek and played footsie with him under the table while drinking a few drinks, and then left him there with his pants afire.

"What do you want?" he asked, staring at his drink, staring at anything but that taunting expression in her deep blue-green eyes. She had made few demands of him, but those had been freakish, bizarre to the point of frightfulness. After the pin he had taken from Janet's dresser, there had been trinkets that belonged to his daughters, things that could be of no possible value to anyone but their owners. The purpose of her exactions had to be to force him to hurt the few people he cared about, and so he had dutifully pretended that it pained him to see his younger daughter cry for four hours over the loss of a stuffed doll she had had since her birth. He had even gone through the motions of buying the child a half dozen new dolls to make up for the loss, knowing that Rhea would know about it, as she seemed to know about everything he did. Actually, the only thing that had bothered him about Rhea's demands was their irrationality.

His home had absorbed an air of hysteria of late, as Janet suspected the servants of stealing the hodge-podge of objects, and the servants suspected each other. The only two people who were above suspicion were Janet and himself.

Another time Rhea had made the queer demand that he give his older daughter nothing for her birthday. The child was devoted to him, and he had known that it would crush her to be forgotten. He had taken a detached interest in his own reaction to his little girl's disappointment. He had been bored by it, slightly annoyed that such trivia insinuated itself into his life. Once again, only the meaninglessness of Rhea's demand had disturbed him. He knew she must be insane to make such demands of him. There was no other explanation. And now he knew he would yield again. Before answering his question, she took a long sip of her gin and tonic, apparently to savor and extend a delicious moment.

"There's an old man working for your studio," she said. "His name is Gustav Schnertzlinger."

"Gus? That's right. He's a custodian."

"He's been out sick for the past two months because of an extended illness."

"He needed a gall bladder operation," Phillip said stupidly: Obviously she knew as much about it as he did, and probably more.

"Gus has used up all of the sick leave he's entitled to. Now he has asked for a leave of absence, because the doctors have found some complications and want to open him up again."

"Well, that's no problem." Phillip felt a cautious sensation of relief. What could Gus prossibly be to Rhea? Father? Uncle? He'd have got his leave of absence without her, but if she wanted to make it a condition of their continued relationship, it was a good joke on Rhea for a change.

"Of course it isn't," she said, and took another sip of her drink, holding the straws in the long, slender fingers of her left hand. "He's not going to get it." Phillip stared at her, trying to swallow something in his throat that wouldn't go down. Rhea met his gaze serenely, an expression of impish amusement in her eyes, the corners of her mouth curled up slightly.

"Gus has been with the studio longer than I have," he said.

"Much longer."

"He's over sixty years old. He can't possibly get another job." She said nothing. "He's due to retire soon."

"Then think of the money you can save the studio by firing him now."

"Maybe he won't quit. Maybe he'll come back to work without the second operation."

"Yes, that's quite possible," Rhea said, stirring her drink with her straws.

"And that could shorten his life."

She dropped the straws into the drink and stretched her slender body, seemingly bored at his recitation of obvious and irrelevant facts. "What's the answer? Yes or no?"

Phillip answered between clenched teeth. "I'm not in the business of hiring and firing janitors. This won't even reach my desk."

"But if you say the words, in the properly imperative tone, Mr. Schnertzlinger loses out." Her tone told him to stop trying to con her, or stall her. "Yes or no?"

"You know it's yes."

"Well, shall we go?" She slid gracefully from the booth and stood looking at him with an air of indifference. Phillip wanted to cry. He also wanted to pick up the remainder of his drink and throw it at her, but instead he slid out of the booth and walked beside her toward the door. "We ought to find another place to meet," she said in a langorous, mildly distracted voice. "This one is beginning to bore me."

Outside the traffic was sparse. The sun was barely clear of the tops of the buildings. Phillip led her to the parking lot. A taxi was disgorging three men, who looked at Rhea with interest. Phillip unlocked and opened the car door for her, and she smiled at him, giving his cheek a little pat.

"I can't do it." The words were a total surprise to him, but Rhea didn't seem at all taken aback by them. She looked at him a bit quizzically, still smiling that smile of vague amusement.

"Are you certain that is what you want?" she asked. Phillip felt a bitter galling frustration in his chest.

"What I did before was between myself and my family," he told her. "But this has to do with business. I won't give you charge of my job." Her look only showed more amusement, and a more cryptic amusement. "What are you?" he hissed, leaning close to her.

"You'll find out, Philly," she chuckled. "And when you do, it won't matter." Then she turned and walked to the empty taxi. Phillip clutched the jamb of the car door for support, and to keep himself from running after her. Halfway to the cab, she turned. "If you change your mind in time, I'll know."

1801

Rhea

This time Rhea was very careful. She understood the book better than before, and she took all precautions. The figure she drew on the basement floor was only slightly like the first one, because she took it from a middle chapter, which promised to raise a more powerful demon. Each chapter instructed the reader in the summoning and control of a mightier spirit than the previous one.

"*The design is two triangles, crossing each other, their axes at right angles, with no line crossing another, and with no breaks in the lines at any point. A circle rests in the center, touching no line of the triangles, or any point where lines would exist if they crossed one another....*"

It was past midnight when she lit the three candles at the three prime points of the design, the bases of the triangles and the center of the circle. Then she snuffed the extraneous light and recited the words in a loud and steady voice.

"*Mitte, Imperator Erebu....*"

"I implore thee, Emperor of Hell...."

"*... orate tumme servum and me....*"

"... dispatch your servant to me, in keeping with the pact you have made with mankind, and bind him to my wishes. Despise not my supplication because I am a mortal and unworthy, but consign your minion to the hottest depths of the fiery sea should he fail to carry out my decree."

There was no steady gathering as there had been the first time. This demon made himself known instantly. A rush of air inward occurred from all sides, as though to fill a sudden vacuum, and he was there. She could only see him in vague outline, and just at the bottom, above the yellow candlelight, which flickered but somehow managed to avoid extinguishment in the stiff breeze. Once again, the voice spoke in her head, without recourse to her ears, but this voice was stronger, deeper.

"Then it is true. A little girl...." There was disgust in the tone, as though being forced to serve a mere human being was demeaning enough, but this was beyond endurance. Rhea had learned the danger of indulging in idle chatter with a demon, and came straight to the point.

"I want my mother to stop loving my father," she said. "I want things to be as they were." There was a barely noticeable pause before the demon answered her.

"Things can never be as they were, little one."

"I told that other demon, don't call me little one! My name is Rhea. Why can't they be?"

"Did my — colleague — not inform you, Rhea, that a wish granted is a relentless thing?" No, Rhea started to say, but then she recalled that he had said something like that.

"Yes, but so what? Aren't you more powerful than he?"

"I am. But we have our ethics." Rhea wasn't certain whether he was speaking of demons in general, or using the royal "we." Either way, it was damnably frustrating.

"You refuse to obey me?" she demanded.

"Give me another task, mighty and diminutive mistress, and I shall obey." Ignoring the irony of his address, Rhea thought quickly.

"Can you make my mama not have her baby?" It was certainly possible that the baby, being in heaven, was beyond the demon's control.

"Quite easily." Rhea felt a flood of relief. She wasn't certain she could have come up with another wish.

"Then do it," she commanded.

"As you will—"

"Wait a minute. That's not all."

"Then be quick. I have other things to do than stay here and follow the orders of a precocious five-year-old."

"You'll stay here as long as I want you to," Rhea reminded him, holding out the book slightly, as though it were physical proof of her contention.

"That is true." The demon's voice conveyed deep, quiet anger, and Rhea was sorry she had spoken so curtly. Still, she dared not try to placate him. He might interpret that as weakness.

"I don't want any brothers or sisters," she directed. "Not ever! Can you arrange that?"

"Yes, but your mother must suffer a bit of pain for it."

"I don't see why," Rhea said in a voice that was almost sulky. "But it's perfectly all right with me."

"As you will, so mote it be. And now, Mistress Rhea, may I take my departure?"

"First, I want you to hold me harmless," Rhea instructed. There was a moment's pause, and when the demon's voice came to her again there was fresh anger in it, together with a new respect.

"You have followed all the requirements properly. I cannot—"

"I still want you to hold me harmless. Swear it!" She still felt a tinge of apprehension about talking to so powerful an entity in this peremptory manner, but she was also beginning to enjoy her position of authority. To a child of seven, it was as heady as wine.

"Very well," the demon asserted. "I hold you harmless for summoning me."

"Now and for all time," Rhea reminded him, tapping the book with a tiny pink thumb.

"Now and for all time."

"Good. Not get back where you came from." She felt his absence instantly, and with it a potent sense of relief. Still, it wasn't quite the painful relief she had felt the first time.

I'm getting used to this, Rhea thought, and began to hum a little tune as she cleaned up the basement.

It was swift in coming. That morning, as Rhea still lay, half dozing, in her undersized bed, she heard a scream, intense and full of fright. It was muffled by the walls of the house, but it brought her to a bolt upright position. She sat listening, her heart pounding, forgetting her wish for the moment. Then she heard a hubbub of voices somewhere and she thought, Mama.

For just an instant she felt terror and remorse, but then she knew the sweetness of power. Even her mother, she thought, even that serene and potent being she had always tried so hard to please, was helpless against the powers she, Rhea, now controlled. She didn't want to hurt Mama, or Daddy either, for that matter. But from now on things would be different in the house. Indolently, she rose and put on the robe that lay across the chair near her bed, then inserted her feet into her slippers and, opening her door, went out into the hall.

"Is she bad hurt?" The voice belonged to one of the servant girls. Rhea saw them gathered about the foot of the stairs, looking like a gaggle of jackdaws in their black dresses and caps. The butler was trying to pick up Mama by the shoulders. "I've always said those stairs were treacherous steep," the same maid asserted. There was a strained, almost hysterical tone to her voice.

"Will you stop your jabbering and help me with the mistress, girl?" the butler demanded. His voice was shakily imperative, his face, visible to Rhea in profile, florid and bulging with veins. Two of the maids instantly gathered about Mama's feet and lifted her. Together with the butler they carried her up the steep stairway. Mama was wearing one of the new frilly dresses she had bought recently, and that Daddy always made such a fuss about. As her head twisted, her eyes fluttered open for a moment, falling upon Rhea. The gaze of the two females, woman and child, locked for a moment, and Rhea thought crazily that her mother seemed to know that she had had something to do with all this. Rhea herself didn't understand the connection between her mother's fall and the elimination of her unborn sibling, but she assumed that there was some relationship between the two matters. Nor did it occur to Rhea that the expression of sudden fear and loathing in Elaine Carter's eyes was a response to something she had seen in her daughter's. But the look made Rhea's heart race until she told herself that she was being silly. No one could possibly suspect a little blond-haired girl of such nefarious doings; and certainly no one could prove it. All these thoughts flashed through Rhea's mind in an instant. Then her mother was gone, down the hall and into her and Daddy's bed chamber.

A doctor was summoned, and soon afterward Daddy arrived, huffing, from his office, where he had been doing some sort of work. Rhea felt sorry for him when she saw his expression. She almost knew remorse for what she had done, but then she remembered that he only felt that way because it was Mama, and if it had been she, he probably wouldn't even have come home from his old office.

"In God's name, what has happened?" he demanded of the butler, ignoring Rhea's presence. Rhea had dressed in one of her nicest dresses, and combed her own hair with especial care for the occasion.

"Mrs. Carter had a fall, sir," the butler said. "She appears to have lost her footing on the stairs, near the top, and to have fallen all the way to the ground floor."

"Is she all right, man?" Daddy demanded, waving his fists about in a nearly comical way. His face was so red that Rhea was frightened that he might get sick himself. Then the butler did something Rhea had never seen a servant do before. He touched his employer, placing his hands on Mr. Carter's shoulders and looking directly into his eyes.

"The doctor is with her now, Mr. Carter. But surely the lady will be all right. We are all praying for her."

Lionel Carter forcibly calmed himself and stepped back, nodding vaguely. For the first time he became dimly aware of his daughter's presence, and he went to her and picked her up, holding her close to give and receive the comfort of body warmth. Her tiny arms encircled his neck and she hugged him tightly, and he began to cry. At that moment the door to his bed chamber opened and a tall, graying man stepped through. He looked at Lionel for a moment, then closed the door behind him.

"Mr. Carter?" he inquired with grave formality. Lionel nodded rapidly. "May we retire to some place of privacy, sir?" He looked directly at the child in Lionel's arms. Lionel put her down.

"Daddy —" Rhea said, but he patted her on the head and shook his own, and led the doctor down the stairs, those treacherous stairs, and to his private study. Suddenly the entire house seemed graven with animosity. If it had killed his wife, he thought, choking back his sobs and blinking at his tears, he would burn it to the ground, and build her a monument in its place. It took him three tries to find the knob, but finally he managed to open the door and usher the physician into his study.

"Will you have some brandy, Doctor?" he asked, courteous from habit. The doctor shook his head. "Please sit. Do you mind if I —?"

"Certainly not." Lionel poured himself a drink and stood staring down at the man, who seemed nervous now, though he must be adept at hiding such emotions. "First of all, let me assure you, Mr. Carter, that your wife will not die from this accident." Lionel felt such a flood of relief that he broke into audible sobs, his large frame shaking and quivering from them. The doctor looked mildly embarrassed, but sat quite still until his host had regained his composure.

"She is with child," Lionel said timidly. The doctor shook his head.

"No longer, sir. I'm sorry. There was simply nothing to be done."

Lionel took himself behind his desk and sat, laying his head on the blotter and crying uncontrollably. The doctor made as if to rise.

"Perhaps another time, Mr. . . . ." But Lionel raised a hand and waved it blindly, still crying, still seeing the salty tears soak into the blotter. The doctor resumed his seat. A minute later Lionel raised his head and stared blearily at the man.

"I am sorry, Doctor. I don't mean to —"

"Please. I understand completely. Perhaps I could give you something —"

"No, no. May I go to her now?"

"First I have more to tell you." The doctor hesitated, as though unsure of the wisdom of his course. Then he shrugged as Lionel stared at him in bewilderment. "It is not possible to be certain at this time, Mr. Carter, and I sincerely hope that I am mistaken. But I seriously doubt that your wife will ever be capable of — of bearing you another child." Lionel stared at the doctor for a moment, dumbstruck. Suddenly the doctor came up out of his chair and stood before Lionel almost like a supplicant. "You already have a child, Mr. Carter. A beautiful little girl. You should be grateful that God has been so kind —"

"Kind?" Lionel heaved himself upright and leaned across the desk, his knuckles grinding into the blotter. He could feel the dampness of his own tears. "Kind, sir? God is —" He caught himself just short of blasphemy, gouging his upper lip painfully with his lower teeth. "May I go to my wife now, Doctor?" he asked in a graveled but controlled voice. The doctor looked at the clock on the mantel, then fished a watch from his vest and checked it against the larger timepiece, wound it a turn and replaced it.

"I have administered a mild opiate. It should not have taken full effect as yet. But try not to tire or excite her." Lionel moved around his desk and toward the door. His hand was on the knob when the doctor spoke again. "And please try to remember, Mr. Carter," he said tiredly, "that she is not in full possession of her faculties. She may say things that she would never — Please keep it in mind."

Rhea was still standing in front of her mother's door. Lionel felt a stab of anguished tenderness for the child, standing such a pathetic vigil. He took a moment, bending down and placing a hand on her tiny shoulder.

"I am going in to see your mother now," he said softly. Her eyes were emotionless, and he admired her. It must cost the child dearly, he thought, to contain her own grief so totally for his sake. His hand tightened on her shoulder as he thought that the doctor had been right. They were fortunate, he was fortunate, to have such a child. "She must rest now, dear, but you may see her later." He paused, and she looked at him for a long moment before nodding.

"Yes, Daddy."

"When I come back out, you and I — We shall spend some time together, Rhea. Perhaps have a cup of chocolate. Would you like that?" She smiled, such a brilliant smile that it wrung his heart. She was truly an indomitable child. He couldn't imagine where she got her courage. Surely not from him. Doubtless from her mother.

He kissed her, hugged her, and then hurried into the bed chamber.

The drapes had been pulled closed against the bright sunlight. Elaine lay on the bed, in one of her new nightgowns, the covers pulled up under her breasts. She looked so peaceful it was as though he had come to join her there. Her lashes rested, long and graceful, against her cheek. As he moved quietly toward her, she opened her eyes and smiled. The smile trembled like a frightened thing and fled as she seemed to remember. Lionel pulled a chair near to the edge of the bed and sat. He kissed her gently on the cheek, which seemed unnaturally warm against his lips, then took her hand and held it tightly. Her own grip was astonishingly strong, her gaze searching.

"I lost our child," she murmured. He tried to speak, nodded instead. "My darling, I'm sorry," she said. He crossed her lips with his finger.

"Dearest, I love you." He choked on the last word, looked away from her. Why, when a man most needed to lend strength to his wife, did he have to seem so weak? Her hand tightened even more on his fingers.

"Do you? Lionel, tell me truly, do you love me yet? Even now, when I've failed —"

"Now! he said sternly. "Now, Elaine, there will be no further talk of failure here. You have succeeded brilliantly in making me happier than any man has a right to expect."

"But I was so evil to you for so many years." She made a vain attempt to sit upright, contorted her face in pain and lay back, her forehead suddenly beaded with perspiration.

"Lie still, please," he begged. "You'll harm yourself."

"Lionel, please forgive me," she pleaded. "It was an accident. I didn't do it purposely, I swear."

"But of course not! Of course you didn't. I'll hear no more of this!" He remembered the doctor's admonition. She was not in possession of her faculties.

"Lionel, I'm sorry," she wept, holding to him, staring into his eyes hysterically. "I'll make it up to you in a thousand ways, I swear. I'll give you a dozen children, a dozen fine sons to carry on your name, if only you'll let me try! If only you won't hate —" She stopped abruptly, staring at his face. Lionel was aware of the stricken expression he presented to her, but he could do nothing for it. He tried to look away, but she took his face in both her hands and twisted it back again. "Lionel, what is it? What more is there?"

"You must rest now." He pulled her hands loose and pressed them together, kissing them. They were as rigid as marble.

"No, I must know! What more is wrong?" Lionel closed his eyes, shook his head rapidly.

"The doctor," he said. "He may be wrong. He said so himself. And we shall find other doctors. The best in Europe and America, I swear it." When she broke in, her voice was unnaturally calm and intense.

"Lionel, you must tell me. What did the doctor say?" He grabbed her up in his arms, clutching her, forgetting her injuries for the moment.

"The doctor says that you — that we can have no more children." Her breast swelled against his cheek as her breath caught. "No more children — ever!" he choked. "But we still have each other. My dearest, I still have you, and that is all I care about, you must believe me."

"Then I can give you nothing," she said in a voice suddenly gone languid and furry. The opiate was finally overcoming her despite her emotions. He pulled his face back from her breast, looked into her eyes in shock.

"Nothing? How can you say that of yourself? You have given me so much. Your own dear self. And my daughter." But she seemed not to have heard him. She lay back against the pillow, her eyes drooping closed.

"Nothing," she repeated mindlessly. "And less than nothing. A child not even your own."

It took a moment for Lionel to absorb his wife's last words. He sat staring down at her. Suddenly her eyes opened again, wide and terrified. She stared up at him with such clarity and comprehension that he knew instantly that her words had been true. She raised a hand, clutching at him, but he drew back.

"Darling, I didn't mean that! I — I didn't know —"

"What did you mean?" he demanded stonily.

"I meant nothing. Only —" He reached forward, stopped his hands just short of the grasp they might have made at her injured body. Even now he could not bring himself to harm her physically.

"Elaine, I will know what you meant," he said. "If you love me, then account for your words, Madam!" She stared up at him, her eyes overrunning. Suddenly her head shook from side to side, and then her entire body, until he thought she would injure herself further.

"It's true!" The words came out as though purged from her, and at their riddance she lay back, more tired than before. "It's true, my dearest," she sobbed. "Rhea is not yours. She is not your child." Then her eyes opened once again, and she looked at him with a fresh expression of entreaty. "But I didn't know then. I didn't know how much I loved you, how much you meant to me." He commenced to rise, and she clutched at his hand, holding it tightly against her breast. "Lionel, you do love me, please, you mustn't stop loving me. I can't live if —"

"I still love you, Elaine," he said with infinite tiredness. It was true, he thought with a grim humor. Some men must be born to be fools, for at this moment he loved her yet, despite the fact that she had left him with nothing. He took her wrist in his hard ironmonger's grasp and pulled her hand from his clothing. "Yes, I still love you," he said, rising. She stared up at him frantically, as though trying to look past his eyes, to see truth or falsity in him. "I love you," he said once again. "Soon — very soon — I shall demonstrate to you the extent of my love. Now you must rest. You must grow strong again, for me."

"Yes. Yes, I'll get well. For you." She lay back, but her eyes did not close yet. She stared at him. Lionel walked to the door and glanced back despite himself. Her lashes, finally, curled against her cheek, and her troubled breathing grew more placid as she drifted into the sleep of the drugged.

When the door opened, Rhea stepped forward. It had taken him so long, she had begun to wonder when he would come out, or if ever. He stood in the hall for a moment, standing with unnaturally stiff posture, staring straight ahead, though there was nothing there to look at. When she touched his hand, he looked down at her blankly for a moment. Then his hand jerked away as though touched by something slimy. Rhea fell back, because for an instant she was afraid that he might strike her. But his gaze grew blank, as though he no longer recognized her, and he turned and walked down the long staircase. She ran to the top step, looked after him. She wanted to follow, but his strangeness frightened her.

"Daddy?" Her voice was very soft, and he didn't hear it. He walked to the door of his study, groped for the knob and then went inside. Even from this distance she heard the key rattle in the lock. Hesitantly, she took a step downward, then another, then began to run. She lost her footing, caught at the bannister and righted herself, ran to the bottom, screaming, because she didn't know what he was going to do, but it must be something terrible. The servants were beginning to gather, and she tried to speak to them coherently, but she could only shriek. They assumed that the day's events had finally caught up with her, that the emotion that had been packed inside her was at last breaking through. One of the maidservants caught her up to comfort her and try to keep her from hurting herself. Rhea screamed the more frantically, trying to tell the fools that her daddy was in danger, that he —

They all stopped, stock still, at the sound of the shot. The report had no direction, no source, in the walls of the house, but Rhea knew that it came from in there, from her daddy's study. The servants stood looking at each other mutely for an instant, all of them too shocked to take action. Then, from upstairs, muffled by the door and walls of the bedchamber, they heard a harsh, drugged scream.

1955

Phillip

It took eight days for the studio to get back to him. Phillip had begun to wonder if he had overplayed his hand in Hatfield's office. The eight days were the most strenuous of his life, emotionally. There was always the possibility that Chuck would find out what he had pulled, and go into one of his fits of temper. The fact that no one at the studio contacted Chuck about the trick Phillip had pulled was the one encouraging sign until the phone rang on Tuesday of the following week. Phillip got to it just before Chuck.

"Mr. Stafford, please," a tart young female voice requested.

"Speaking."

"This is Mr. Carstairs' office, Mr. Stafford. Mr. Carstairs would like to know if you could have luncheon with him in his office tomorrow."

"Of course."

"Would twelve-thirty be all right?"

"Fine."

"Who was that?" Chuck asked when he had hung up.

"Claudia. She wants me to have lunch with her tomorrow."

Mr. Carstairs' office was smaller, more tastefully decorated and somehow more comfortable than that of Mr. Hatfield. Carstairs' secretary was a woman in her twenties, possibly less efficient than the dragon who guarded Hatfield's door, but more pleasant by far. Carstairs turned out to be a man in his early thirties. His desk held photos of a pretty woman and three cute little girls, together with a model of a North American F-86 Saberjet which Phillip assumed he had flown in Korea. On his wall hung a diploma from the University of Southern California. On his swivel chair hung an Ivy League coat. He was trim and tall, a neat if not striking figure in his pin-striped, tapered shirt.

"I've been looking forward to meeting you, Mr. Stafford," he said with a smile. "You made quite an impression on Mr. Hatfield."

"I was afraid I might have overdone it," Phillip said, returning the man's smile.

"From what I heard, you almost did. Listen, I ordered each of us a green salad and an open-faced beef sandwich for lunch. I hope you don't mind."

"Sounds just fine." Phillip lowered himself into a chair indicated by his host, who sat behind the desk. For the first time Phillip noticed his manuscript resting before the man.

"Listen, you've got a good script here. I guess you know that if we didn't think so, you wouldn't be here."

"Thank you," Phillip said noncommittally.

"Of course, Mr. Hatfield would never admit this, and he'd probably demote me if he heard me say it to you, but it's the best thing this story department has seen in three years. I'm authorized to offer you twenty thousand dollars for it right now." Phillip managed to keep from gulping. The most money he had ever had in his life had been eight hundred dollars, which he had taken with him to his first semester at the university. The budget on a film of this sort would probably run around a million. He concentrated on that in order to put the figure in proper perspective.

"That's not much, is it?" he asked. Before Carstairs could reply, there was a discreet knock at the door and their lunch was brought in. Carstairs was served at his desk, while a small folding table was set up for Phillip. When the waiter had withdrawn from his office, Carstairs thrust his fork into his salad and smiled at Phillip.

"Okay," he said, smiling in a way that made them compatriots. "Now I'll tell you how high I'm really authorized to go. Thirty thousand dollars cash and a contract for ten weeks at four hundred a week to do the revision."

"Revision?" Phillip stared at the man. "I thought you just said it was the best script to hit this studio in three years."

"As far as I'm concerned," Carstairs said with a mildly exasperated note in his voice, "it's the best script I've ever seen. In a way, that's the trouble with it." He leaned forward earnestly. "Look, we like everything about this script. I do, and so does Mr. Hatfield. We can see from this that you're a very talented young man. But some of your ideas are, well, too refined for a mass market. I doubt we could get this story past the censors, and if we did we'd catch hell from the National Legion of Decency and every Catholic Ladies' Sodality Society in the United States. It's going to have to be revised, and we trust you to do the revision because we can see that you're a good writer."

"What kind of changes do you require?" Phillip asked around a small morsel of lettuce.

"First of all, this stuff with the priest ogling women's legs. Oh, I know, a priest is a man like the rest of us, and if some babe's skirt hikes up he's going to look. But not in a Hollywood movie. In a Hollywood movie every priest is either Barry Fitzgerald or Charles Bickford, right? Second, there's this bit about his doubting he should be a priest. He can waver a little bit, especially when he's confronted with this moral dilemma. But not as much as you have in here. And the killer has to be a turd, and the other guy has to be likable, so people can feel happy when things are straightened out. A killer is a bastard. Always. That's why he's a killer."

"Really?"

Carstairs sighed. "Of course not really. But in a movie. Look, you've got to bend a little, Phil. All right if I call you Phil?"

"Sure."

"Well, you've got to give some. This isn't a novel you're submitting, Phil, it's a script for a film. Kids go to films. Little old ladies go to films. Sometimes even priests go to films. And we can't offend people." He shoved his empty salad plate away and went to work on his hot beef sandwich after lifting off the metal cover. Phillip followed suit.

"It'll make it a less effective piece," he said mildly.

"Don't I know it? But that's the point. A film can very easily be too effective. It can disturb people. And they don't go out to the movies to be disturbed. Am I getting through to you?"

"Sure you are." Phillip chewed on a piece of beef, hoping he was displaying just the right degree of reluctance. "I guess you know I can use the kind of money you're talking about."

"Can't we all?"

"Not to mention the chance to break in here." He looked at Carstairs meaningfully, making his statement a cue.

"Listen, if this script takes off the way we think it will, you could become a permanent fixture in our story department. And from there, who knows? A man with your talent and your balls could go anywhere. You could be a director, or even a producer. Hell, who knows? Someday you could be my boss." He smiled disarmingly. Phillip decided the time had come to capitulate.

"I guess I could make the kind of changes you want," he

said.

"Terrific. It's going to be nice having someone like you around."

Following the luncheon Phillip went to a movie, scarcely noticing what was happening on the screen, vaguely aware of the mumbling from the sound track. Mainly, he wanted to kill time until Chuck would be at work. Then he went back to the apartment and packed his things. He supposed he could afford to stay at a hotel for the time being, until he found a better apartment somewhere. When he was packed he went to the dresser in Chuck's bedroom and took the script. If Chuck had thought to make a protection copy it could mean trouble, but Phillip didn't think he had.

He checked into the Statler that evening and ordered dinner sent up to his room. Then he went into the bathroom and began tearing up Chuck's script, one page at a time, and flushing the strips of paper into the Los Angeles sewage system.

1976

Janet

She had only the vaguest idea of what she had expected, but certainly nothing so ordinary and normal in appearance. Janet's idea of a psychic had always been that such a person was at least ninety percent showman. Thus she had had some obscure idea that Mrs. Baker's house would be an exercise in theater of the occult, a Gothic backdrop for the show that would be performed there. Perhaps one of those gingerbready things that abounded in certain parts of L.A., with porticoes and gables and maybe some Cupids carved into worn and cracked wood. Instead she found herself before a stucco edifice, modest in appearance, with a paint job that was at least a year from the need to be refreshed. The lawn was freshly manicured and obviously watered. The windows sparkled with recent scrubbing, and parked in the drive before the two-car garage were a Datsun sedan and a Volkswagen camper.

When Janet pressed the doorbell she heard the chimes from deep inside. They didn't play the funeral march, or a bar of some somber Bach fugue. They just chimed, pleasantly. Somewhere inside the whirr of a vacuum cleaner stopped. She waited a moment, then decided that someone inside was waiting to find out whether the chime had really sounded. She pressed the button again. A moment later the door opened and a woman looked out at her.

Once again she noted the ironic dissimilarity between that which she had expected and that which she found. The woman wasn't old, as she had assumed, but really quite young, perhaps in her early thirties. She wasn't foreign-looking, or gypsy, but an ordinary-looking housewife type, more than usually attractive, and dressed in blue denim pants and a terrycloth top. Several wisps of light brown hair protruded from under a yellow bandana that had been knotted about her head. Her eyes were her best feature aside from a trim figure and slender, tapering legs; they were large and neither blue nor brown, but a deep shade of gray, and at the moment they stared blankly at Janet as though the woman thought she might be the census taker, or a salesperson of some type.

"Yes?" she asked in a pleasantly throaty voice, her tone courteous but just a bit impatient.

"I'm Janet Stafford," Janet said almost timidly. She had begun to think she had approached the wrong house despite the fact that the name Baker was stenciled on the mailbox at the curb. Her eyes widening, the woman looked at her wrist, in a futile attempt to check a watch that wasn't there. A narrow red mark indicated that the watch and strap had been there recently.

"Oh, my God," the woman said, rubbing her wrist and still looking at Janet. "Is it that time already?" She stepped back, opening the door wider. "Come in, will you, Mrs. Stafford?" Janet stepped past her into a pleasantly furnished living room. The couch was rather modern-looking, and the rest of the furnishings, two easy chairs and some tables, were more traditional, but the overall effect was pleasing. The carpet was shag, a deep sea green that coordinated with lighter green paint on the walls. Pictures were hung all over the place, some family photographs and a large reproduction of a painting over the couch. Janet had seen it in department stores. Some wild horses running across a plain, with the title beneath: *Free as the Wind.*

"I could come back another time," Janet offered.

"Don't be silly. It's my fault." She thrust out a large but graceful hand, which Janet accepted. "I'm Yvonne Baker, by the way, in case you haven't guessed. Tuesday is my usual day for house cleaning, but it kind of got away from me this week. I hope you'll overlook my appearance." Janet had dressed up a bit for the occasion. She was in a short gray dress, with alligator shoes and bag, and she had worn a gold chain bracelet that Phillip had bought her before they were married. Now she felt absurdly overdressed and a bit boorish on account of it.

"You look just lovely," she said automatically.

"You're the soul of tact, Mrs. Stafford. How about a cup of coffee? I have a pot on the warmer right now.

Janet allowed herself to be conducted to a small kitchen, bright and spotless, with a narrow table in front of a window that overlooked a fenced backyard. A tree grew in the middle, from which hung a swing made from an old tire, and she thought she saw, at the edge of the window's range, a dilapidated doghouse. Plants lined the window sill, all green and tender looking.

"Have a seat, Mrs. Stafford," Yvonne said. She plucked two mugs, one yellow and one red, from a mug tree next to the stove. A huge Chemex pot rested on a warmer with a stub of candle burning under it. "You take cream and sugar?"

"No, just black, please."

"A girl after my own heart," Yvonne said, splashing some strong black coffee into the two mugs. "I always say, if you're going to gussy up your coffee that way, why not drink hot chocolate and be done with it?" She grabbed an ashtray from the sinkboard and placed it in the middle of the table. Janet realized that somewhere along the line she had already decided she liked Yvonne Baker very much. In fact, she envied her somewhat, her simple, secure, middle-class life. Even when Janet had come to Hollywood all full of dreams, she had believed that this was the kind of life in store for her, and now she felt as though she had missed something.

"I guess you want to know something about me," Yvonne said. "By the way, may I call you Janet?"

"I wish you would."

"My friends call me Von. I can't hang up a shingle like a doctor or an attorney, so people have to be told about me. I have this gift. I don't know where it comes from, and I don't pretend to understand it. I've had it from childhood, and it works. I can't remember when it started any more than you can remember the first time you opened your eyes and saw something. I think I was four or five years old before I realized that everyone didn't have the same ability. I remember, dimly, wondering why people went to places when something bad was going to happen to them." She shrugged and took a sip of her coffee, then made a face because it was too hot. "You don't have to believe me. Nobody does at first. But I'm never wrong. Not once in all my life," she said with a touch of sadness. Then she smiled. "I'm like the Greek seer in mythology who wasn't popular because he always told people the truth."

"I can't remember his name either," Janet said.

"I could probably make a fortune at this if I could just master the trick of telling people enough of the truth to keep them convinced, and then feed them a line. But I can't do that." She took another swig of coffee and found it more to her liking. "You're not just a bored housewife, are you, Janet? I mean you're here because something is happening in your life. Right?"

"Yes, that's right." Janet looked into her coffee cup, took a drink from it.

"Well, there are two things you'd better know about me. First, as I said, I'm never wrong. I knew when my hasband was going to propose to me, I knew when I was going to get pregnant, both times, I knew the first one would be a boy and the second one a girl, and I knew when my husband would die." Her voice quivered a bit on the last clause. She must have seen something in Janet's face, because she made herself smile. "Oh, yes. Even before I met him."

"Oh, my God! You must have loved him, very much."

"I'll say. Now, I've developed a technique. I always ask my new clients this question. If I see something bad in your future, do you want me to soft pedal it? I don't mean lie. Just soft pedal. Or do you want it unvarnished?" Those deep gray eyes were looking straight into Janet's. "I won't think less of you either way, Janet."

"I — I guess I want it unvarnished."

"I thought you would. And that's the way you're going to get it. Now, the other thing you need to know about me is this: I can see what's going to happen, but there my power ends. I'm like a man with a powerful telescope. He can see things you can't, but he can't control the things he sees. So if you've come to me for help, you can have your money back, and no hard feelings."

"Can I change what is going to happen?"

Yvonne shrugged. "Sometimes. But it's very, very hard. Things have a way of working out to the same ending no matter how hard we try to stop or change them." She took two swallows of coffee. Janet had the idea that Von was giving her an opportunity to absorb the things she had just been told. "Are you sure you want to go through with this?"

"Yes," Janet said. Von's eyes took on a different look the moment she heard the answer. There was a new excitement about the woman, an air of anticipation. "I'm not very brave," Janet explained compulsively. "Don't get the wrong idea. I'm scared to death of what you're going to tell me. It's just that not knowing is even worse."

"All right," Von said. "Step into my office. Bring your coffee, Janet." The two women rose and Von led the way through a narrow hallway and into what had been intended as a bedroom. It was unfurnished except for a small round table and two armless chairs. Von took the farther chair from the door. Janet looked around at the room. It was carpeted in a dark color, though she couldn't make out the exact shade because there were thick curtains on the windows. She pulled out the remaining chair and sat, nervous and apprehensive. She had the thought that it wasn't too late yet. But she sat. It was then she noticed the chain bracelet lying on the table.

"I'm certain that I'm going to get a strong signal from you,

Janet," Von said, picking up the bracelet. "Will you give me your hand, please?" She reached across the table with her left hand, and Janet extended her right. There was a mild sensation of static electricity, not the snapping kind, but a sort of buzz of power as their skin touched. Von smiled reassuringly. Then she closed her eyes and began to speak.

"Some simple background to begin with, just so you won't be inclined to doubt me. Your full name is Janet Louise Perry Stafford. You're twenty-nine years old, and I never would have guessed it." Janet smiled, but Von wasn't looking at her. The woman's eyes were still clenced shut. "You have two daughters, ages six and eight. You've been living in Los Angeles since you were eighteen."

"May I ask something, Von?" Janet asked with a surge of courage that surprised her. Von opened her eyes, still holding onto the bracelet and Janet's right hand.

"Of course."

"You told me that you knew when your husband was going to die even before you met him. So how come you have to go through all of this — well, this, with me?" She half expected anger, but Von only shook her head slightly.

"I knew when my husband would die because that was part of my own future. I could do the same with you, but first I'd have to know you intimately, and this is a whole lot faster."

"Oh." Janet felt bested, but not satisfied.

"Still not convinced?"

"Forgive me, but this stuff you've told me is all common information. You could have found it out —"

"You and your husband had sexual intercourse exactly eighteen times before you were married," Von said quietly. Janet gasped and tried to draw her hand away, but the other woman held to it tightly. "I mean, on eighteen separate occasions. He wasn't your first lover, but he was the first to make you climax, and he accomplished that on the first try. That was when you thought you fell in love with him, but real love came later. Your first lover was a school teacher in your home town." Janet felt a sheen of sweat on her forehead. She wanted to stop the woman, but she couldn't find the breath to speak. "You're as normal as Huckleberry Finn, but there was a time back there when you could have developed a crush on another girl, whose name was Diane —"

"All right!" Janet sucked in some air. "All right," she repeated. "That's enough."

"I'm sorry, hon, but you asked for it. You want me to go on?"

"I'm not sure. Yes, go on."

"Okay. You're here because your husband hasn't made love

to you in over five weeks and it's got you scared to death." Janet felt her teeth cutting into her lip. It was very close now. In a few moments she would know what she had come here to find out, and she wasn't certain she was prepared for it. "You have good reason to be scared, hon," Von said. Her eyes opened again and she looked straight at Janet. "He hasn't been faithful to you in the past, you know. In fact, I hate to say it, but he's something of a bastard, and he's been screwing everything in skirts, if you'll pardon my French." Janet looked straight back at her.

"I know that," she said. Von shrugged.

"You're a better man than I am, Gunga Din."

"I just want to know if I'm going to lose him."

"You've already lost him."

"No!" Janet pulled her hand loose from Von's grasp and half rose from the chair. She stopped herself just in time, just before she would have slapped the woman across the face. Von was looking up at her calmly, with an irritating expression of sympathy.

"I'm sorry, Janet. You said you wanted it unvarnished."

Janet fell back into her chair and laid her head on the table. She stayed that way until she was all wept out. Dimly, she was aware of the front door opening and someone clumping through the living room.

"Mom?" a voice called. Von left the room quickly, and in a moment Janet heard her engage in a quick exchange with someone who had a young masculine voice.

"Go find something to do," she said finally, and a moment later the front door opened and closed again. By the time Von returned, Janet had composed herself. "You want the rest?" Von asked, standing over her and crossing her arms. "Or is that enough?"

"What more can there be?"

"I don't know, but I had the feeling there was something else, something big, just before you pulled away."

"I think I've had enough for one day," Janet said. Von leaned down and put an arm around her shoulders.

"I think you're probably right." She stood back and Janet started to rise. Then she sat down again, heavily.

"Damn it, I have to know it all," she said. Von Shrugged, but there was that air of excitement about her, as though she were curious to get a better look at something she had only glimpsed. She took her place at the table again, picked up the bracelet, and took Janet's hand, which had turned cold and clammy.

"Your husband never loved you. He only married you because you added an appropriate touch to his life, and he knew he could control you easily." She was silent for a moment, as though perusing some page printed on the underside of her eyelids. "Oh,

Jesus, he's a bastard," she said. "But he'd have stayed with you for the same reason he married you, at least for a while."

"Then why am I — Why have I lo—lost him?"

"Because he's met someone else, and she's got him snagged but good," Von said with some satisfaction. Her eyes were closed hard, clenched like tiny fists.

"Someone else? But who? Do I know her?"

"No, I don't think — no. Not yet."

"Well, who is she?" Janet had the idea that if she knew the competition, she might be able to fight, to change things.

"Goddamn, I don't — I keep getting a confused picture of the bitch. Tall and short, and big and small, and blond and black-haired, and—" She stopped suddenly, clenching her eyes even more tightly. Then her whole being seemed to go rigid. She drew back into her chair, breathing in a loud, wheezing manner. "Oh, God. No!" She shrieked. Her eyes suddenly opened, and she looked straight at Janet for several seconds without seeming to recognize her. Then she yanked loose, dropping the bracelet and jumping to her feet so quickly her chair tumbled over behind her. "Get out!" she screamed. "Get away from me!"

"Von, what's the —"

"Get out now! Please. Oh, please!" She started to cry almost hysterically. Janet rose and started to leave, then turned back to the distracted woman.

"I want to know what you just saw."

"No! I won't tell you any more. I'll send back your money. Anything you want, only please don't ask me any more questions, please!"

The woman's fear finally communicated itself to Janet. She turned and ran out of the room, turned into the living room. She remembered that she had left her purse in the kitchen, almost didn't stop for it, then ran in, picked it up, and made for the front door.

She raced the Jaguar's engine the way Phillip had told her never to do, jammed it into reverse and squealed out of the drive, narrowly missing a parked Volkswagen. The tires squealed again as she jammed down on the accelerator pedal. She had never driven so wildly in her life. She had always been an excellent driver, and it was astonishing that she didn't have an accident now, or get a ticket.

By the time she reached Beverly Hills, she was a little calmer. She clenched the wheel until her knuckles hurt, and her palms smarted. When she pulled into the garage she thought grimly, Well, whatever Yvonne Baker saw, it wasn't an accident on the way home.

1812

Rhea

At the age of fifteen Rhea Carter had metamorphosed into a breathtakingly lovely young woman. All the promise of her childhood's beauty was fulfilled, and doubly so. The long, silky curls had lost neither their luster nor their softness, and her skin seemed not to have altered by an atom since her birth. Her eyes were identical to her mother's, deep blue with tiny flecks in them, for the person fortunate enough to be looking when the light was exactly right.

But there was more than beauty to her attractiveness. Though she had always behaved as the soul of decorum, and her virginity, like that of nearly all girls of her age and class at that time, was firmly intact, there was a subtle air about Rhea that caused respectable old ladies to whisper behind their fans with expectant disapproval. No one could define the difference between Rhea and other girls her age. It was a compound of many simples: something in the way she walked, or moved, or turned her head; a look deep in her eyes; a touch of suggestiveness in her voice, even when she spoke of the most innocent matters. These things were noticed by members of her own sex and greater age, and occasionally by her peers, at least those endowed or encumbered with acumen beyond their years. Men of all ages and grades adored her without stint or discrimination. A single look and they were smitten. The older men fancied that what they felt for her was an avuncular affection, except in the rare case of a real gentleman, as honest with himself as he dared not be with others. Younger men yearned for delights which they suspected she could give them should she so chose, though many of them were too scantily educated in carnal matters to have more than the most sketchy understanding of those pleasures. Many of them dreamed about her, and left clues to their nocturnal fancies to be washed off of their bodies.

For the first several years after Lionel Carter's "pistol accident" as friends discreetly called it, there had been a sufficiency of callers to the Carter house. A plurality of them were men. Rhea had noted them looking about the place with a prospective air, as though they half expected to come into possession shortly. Very few paid a second call, and only three or four of the men possessed the fortitude to return more than thrice. Rhea remembered a particular afternoon when two of them, bearing flowers, had called simultaneously. They looked at each other across the parlor as though it were a dueling office.

They were very presentable looking men, turned out in fine clothing, with glittering buckles on their shoes and well powdered wigs, but Rhea, watching unseen from the doorway, knew how pathetic was their cause.

This was a full two years after her father's suicide (for she never thought of it in any other way, leaving disingenuousness to the adults, who were more practiced in it), and her mother was still caught up in a love as futile as it was insoluble. Eventually, a maid arrived to accept the flowers they had brought, and to tell them that Madam was not receiving callers for the immediate future. Visibly irritated, the two gentlemen had brushed past Rhea without notice.

"She must have really loved the old fool," one of them said. They were comrades now, defeated in the same honorable endeavor and no longer, therefore, adversaries.

"A damnable waste, if you ask me," muttered the other man. He was shorter, stockier, and perhaps a few years older. His clothes, on closer inspection, revealed signs of careful mending.

From that day Rhea decided that even had she been able, she would never revoke her wish. It was far more comfortable to have her mother live on in perpetual, musty grief, than that the house of Carter should pass under the sway of such a master as one of these.

Rhea continued at Mr. and Mrs. Cameron's school until she was old enough to move on to a finishing school, and then chose the Talbott Academy, a selection quickly ratified by her mother, who had nothing to do with her daughter except to support and avoid her.

As for Rhea herself, once she had accepted her father's suicide, and sublimated the fact that she was the proximate cause of it, and once she had reconciled herself to the fact that her mother was never going to like her, life went on much as it had before. It was a comfortable existence, because the servants, sympathetic to this unwanted half-orphan, spoiled her a bit.

At the Talbott Academy Rhea was regarded with something of the awe usually accorded to a two-headed frog. As a young woman capable of reading and writing she was unusual; there were a few others whose parents had been so daring as to allow the inculcation of such knowledge in their daughters, but even the teachers at the academy couldn't read Latin or Greek.

One of the few girls of Rhea's acquaintance who could read, and who was able to converse on matters more intellectual than clothes and social gatherings, was Theresa Dalrymple. Theresa was in no wise Rhea's equal mentally, and she recognized this fact, making for a fairly firm basis for their friendship. Theresa was a year older, a quiet, refined, and vaguely pretty girl whose intense feelings were always carefully clothed in decorum. By nature submissive, she was an ideal friend for the firm and determined Rhea. It was more a relationship of superior and subordinate than a normal friendship, but this was long before the age of the amateur psychiatrist and *Popular Psychology*, so no one suspected the attraction that probably lay at the basis of their affinity, least of all its principals.

Rhea had never taken an interest in men, partly because she found them incredibly juvenile and dull, and partly because, since they took too much interest in her, there was no challenge to them, as there was to a mathematical equation or an uncommonly complex Greek sentence. It was just five months before her sixteenth birthday that she met the one man who, during her youth, would show her polite indifference. It would have been far better for him had they not encountered one another, and they would probably not have if it hadn't been for Theresa.

"Please, just this once, Rhea," the supplicant begged. Rhea, in her year at the Talbott Academy, had never attended one of the carefully chaperoned social events permitted the girls. She could think of nothing more enervatingly boring than to be imprisoned, under the watchful eye of several dusty virgins, with a platoon of witless young men who would eye her like a piece of mutton they couldn't afford to buy.

"If you'll come with me this once, I'll never ask again, I vow," Theresa persisted. The previous three balls had given rise to this same importuning on Theresa's part. She had met a young man who captivated her, and the feeling seemed mutual. Though she had never mentioned it, Rhea was certain that her friend contemplated marriage, once she was of a proper age, and assuming that this rustic lothario could work up the nerve to ask for her hand. A touch of jealousy she could not acknowledge consciously, coupled with the irritatingly monotonous begging of her friend, finally dissolved Rhea's resistance.

The ball was to be held at the Cosgrove College, a small institution then enjoying a short-lived popularity among young men of means in the area. Situated a convenient six miles from the academy, it served as the scene of all the mixing of the sexes for the Talbott girls.

Rhea's first sight of a social event of that nature provided only a moment's interest. She had barely been convinced by Theresa that she should not bring along a book to while away her time. The decorations, scanitly applied and without great invention, seemed the sort of thing in which a child might delight. As Rhea passed into the hall, she could not begin to understand the air of excitement that seemed to radiate from her companions, any more than she had been able, a few years earlier, to understand their immersion in the delights of hopscotch.

And the young men seemed part and parcel of the place: fairly decorative in a meretricious way, but with no admirable function. She looked forward to an evening of intense boredom, punctuated by the irritation of turning down offers of punch and dancing companionship from these bumpkins.

That, largely, was the way the evening proceeded. Young men flocked around her, pleading for her partnership in a reel or minuet, proffering crystal glasses of punch or morsels from the table, demurely wrapped in laundered napkins. Now and then she accepted food or drink from one or another, mostly because it amused her to see the look of disappointment in the faces of those whose offerings had been refused. Once she even agreed to dance with a darkly handsome young man, only to find that his conversation filled her with as much ennui as did the sitting. It tickled her that the other girls would have liked to drive her from the hall with her clothes afire, but this delight seemed hardly worth the wasted time.

Halfway through the evening Theresa finally made it through the pack of young supplicants. She had a man in tow, a man who appeared slightly older than the others, or perhaps only a bit more quiet and mature in manner as well as larger physically. He towered over his contemporaries, and his chest was deep and broad. Although Rhea possessed what would have been considered an unseemly knowledge of sexual proceedings (gleaned from her Latin books), she herself had never before felt the quickening of sexual attraction; but now it was instantaneous. The man stood there, looking slightly embarrassed, his massive, rather rugged face nearly blank with the effort to hide his abashed reaction to this meeting. When Theresa introduced them he barely looked at Rhea, and she had the feeling that he would have preferred to go back to the dance floor with

Theresa.

"Rhea, I'd like to introduce Raymond Wakeling. This is my dearest friend, Rhea Carter."

"Your servant, Madam," Rayond Wakeling said, bowing slightly from the waist. Rhea nodded from her chair, suddenly aware of her own body, the simple white frock she was wearing, the casualness with which she had tended to her hair that evening. She wished that she had it to do again. Theresa was looking up at her gentleman's face expectantly.

"I should be most honored, Miss Rhea, if you would bestow upon me the next dance." There was a reluctance in the request that intrigued Rhea as much as it irritated her. She could tell from Raymond Wakeling's voice and bearing that he would prefer to be turned down. She rose from her chair gracefully.

"The pleasure is mine, Mr. Wakeling," she said. A chorus of groans from the other males brought a slight flush to Mr. Wakeling's cheek, but didn't seem to gratify him, or to compensate for the loss of several minutes of his chosen's companionship. For the first time in her young life, Rhea determined to compete for something. Certainly a skinny little wallflower like Theresa should offer no real problems.

The dances of the day did as little to stimulate conversation as any other form of intercourse. When they were properly done, only hands touched, and to be the partner of a beautiful woman meant little more than prestige, since partners met one another only slightly more frequently than other participants. Circuits were made about the room, as though those who had composed the dances were determined to encourage mingling but not intimacy. Still, Rhea managed to work in a word here and there.

"When Theresa spoke of your attractiveness and good qualities, Mr. Wakeling, I was inclined to believe that she had given herself to exaggeration. I am happy to find that my opinion of her judgment was faulty." This as they orbited each other twice, their hands touching. Wakeling blushed at the frank compliment, but it was not unusual even for those staid days. He nodded, obviously at a loss for words, and moved on to the next young lady, who appeared to have been awaiting the opportunity with relish.

As she moved about the floor, greeted by each partner with glee and relinquished to his successor with reluctance, Rhea cast a discreet eye upon Raymond Wakeling. His own eye, considerably less discreet than hers, crept repeatedly back to Theresa, standing on the sidelines and beaming in naive satisfaction at her coup in bringing together the two people who, other than her immediate family, meant the most to her. Theresa's trust and openness were gratifying to Rhea, since they made the girl more vulnerable to the kind of subterfuge which she intended; but Mr. Wakeling, it seemed, would require a more concerted attack.

They met again in their circuit as the dance terminated. He bowed, obviously relieved that he could get back to his known quantity. Obviously, Rhea thought, his seeming lack of interest in her stemmed from insufficient self-confidence. Before he could take his leave, Rhea smiled at him in her most tantalizing manner.

"Is it not deemed proper in the circles you frequent, Mr. Wakeling, for a gentleman to offer a lady refreshments when they have danced together?"

"I —oh, certainly, Miss Rhea. What would you like?" He seemed contrite and a bit nonplussed by his breach of etiquette, but still reluctant to spend more time apart from Theresa.

"A glass of punch, I think, and perhaps a morsel of something. I find myself a bit faint." She took her own cue, placing her hand lightly on his arm as though for support. He looked more concerned, as though apprehensive for her health, or perhaps merely anxious at the thought of having an ill woman on his hands.

"Right away, Miss Rhea, of course." He started to move away. She gripped his arm lightly.

"Please bring it to the veranda, Mr. Wakeling. I find myself a bit breathless as well." Her eyes supported her words, but the message seemed lost upon him.

Rhea made her way to the veranda as the next dance began. There were no unoccupied males to bother, since this was the reel and all hands were occupied with it, including, Rhea noted with satisfaction, Theresa Dalrymple. One of the chaperoning dowagers stood at the door, eyeing her like an untrustworthy prisoner. Rhea smiled once and ignored the old woman, moving as far from her as possible. The night was warm and scented with the myriad fragrances of spring. As she waited for Raymond Wakeling to arrive with her snack, Rhea mapped out a simple plan.

She knew there were certain gestures or movements on her part that excited men and emboldened them, and now she wished she had been more assiduous in cultivating them. Still, it must be a simple matter to take a man away from such a goose as Theresa, with her milk-and-water personality and her mediocre looks. Perhaps forthrightness would turn the trick. At any rate, she didn't see what she could lose by the attempt; she hadn't made any visible progress so far.

He made his appearance at long last, a cup of punch in one white-gloved hand and a plate with a slice of cake in the other.

"Forgive my tardiness, Miss Rhea. I wasn't certain of which veranda you referred to." He proffered the cake, and she accepted it. "I selected something sweet because such things offer a quick resuscitation of energy. Sugar, I mean to say. One learns these things in military training." Rhea allowed her eyes to widen, and she leaned forward, balancing the cake on one hand and gripping his wrist briefly with the other.

"You are a military man! How fascinating, Mr. Wakeling. And exciting." He blushed with pleasure, and Rhea thought that at last she must be making headway with him.

"Hardly that, ma'am. I mean to enter law once my formal education has been completed. I am a lieutenant of militia, nothing more."

"Nothing more indeed! I find it exemplary that a young man accepts the responsibilities of his social station in such a manner. Particularly in these parlous times, with England behaving so piratically on the seas." His brow furrowed at this reference. "Oh, not that I know of such things, certainly," she assured him. "I have only heard—"

"It's only that I don't like to think about such matters, Miss Rhea," he explained.

"You wouldn't welcome the opportunity to defend your country? The children? And us women, so utterly dependent on the valor of young gentlemen?" She nibbled at the cake, regarding him from under lowered lashes.

"Oh, well," he replied, somewhat flustered, "If war should come, then surely I should go with my unit. However, I do not hold with the common notion of war as the noblest of pursuits. My maternal grandmother has been a widow since 1776 on account of a war. A just and necessary one, no doubt. Yet she remains widowed. And now, ma'am, if you'll take my arm, I shall conduct you inside. I hear the reel ending, and with your consent I should like to rejoin Miss Theresa." Rhea moved slightly to her right, to the railing where she had placed her glass of punch. Facing Wakeling, she leaned back, allowing her breasts to thrust forth provocatively. The move took her from the chaperon's line of sight.

"And if my consent is withheld?" she asked in a voice only slightly teasing. She was looking directly into his large black eyes, and he fidgeted.

"Miss Rhea, you make me awkward. I —"

"Perhaps I don't wish you to rejoin Theresa. You see, Raymond, I find you uncommonly attractive."

"I — I hardly know what to say." He twisted clumsily, as though his clothes had become uncomfortable. "This statement speaks well for your generosity, but not for your judgment, ma'am. With all these young gallants at your feet —"

"I don't want them. They bore me."

"I'm sorry. Surely one will presently appear who will not

bore you?"

"He has already appeared." She looked at him so directly that he twisted away his gaze, as though afraid his eyes might be seared.

"Miss Rhea," he said in a tone so measured she was certain he was choosing his words singly, "this is a most flattering revelation, and one I shall treasure to my last day."

"But?" She hoped the interruption would fluster him the more, but he was set on his course now, and hardly seemed to hear her.

"However, the instant affection I felt for Miss Dalrymple on our first meeting has — has —"

"Ripened?"

"Has developed into something deeper. Something quite durable."

"But surely not impregnable."

"Impregnable. Precisely the word for which I was groping. Thank you." Rhea continued to regard him, her eyes as wide and uncompromising as musket barrels.

"Then you are really rejecting me in favor of Theresa Dalrymple?"

"That is to put the most uncomplimentary shade on it, ma'am."

"But that is the sum of it." He stood quite still for a moment, clearly miserable in his discomfiture. Then he nodded once shortly and offered her his arm once again. "You idiot," Rhea said. He reddened, but his gentlemanly training saw him through.

"As you say, ma'am. My arm."

"I prefer to remain here, thank you," Rhea informed him in a voice as cold and as sharp as a sawtooth. The arm was withdrawn smartly, and he bowed from the waist.

"May I fetch your wrap, then?"

"You may go to hell, sir!" she hissed. Beyond him the chaperon moved with a rustle of thick petticoats and a flash of black gown, apparently having sensed that something was amiss in what had seemed a simple tête-à-tête. Wakeling fell back a step as though she had threatened to strike him with something lethal. His eyes widened and a nervous tic appeared in his cheek. He bowed once more, then turned and strode from the veranda with stiff, martial tread.

Rhea stood looking after him, filled with a mortification she couldn't remember having known previously. The chaperon regarded her with concern from across the veranda, perhaps wondering what action this situation called for. Tears of rage overflowed Rhea's eyes, and she turned her back on the crone to avoid her ministrations.

You swine, she thought, trembling. *You vile snake!* In that moment she hated Raymond Wakeling more than she had ever hated another.

And yet she wanted him.

In her reading of matters erotic, the whole matter had seemed silly to her, grotesque and silly from all that she could gather about the actual proceedings. To experiment in such an awkward, ludicrous physical exercise had never occurred to her. Now, for the first time, she was determined to learn the gratifications of sex. With no direct knowledge of the pleasures involved, she still was determined that Raymond Wakling and no other would insert himself in her.

Be certain, my superbly sculptured friend, when you are mine, you shall writhe for this night's doing.

1812

Rhea

Liber de Malo had rested on a shelf in Rhea's room at home for all the years since her father's death. For some time she had been afraid to use it, or even to read it, and there had been no cause to do so. Rhea's life was a reasonably comfortable one, since her mother had retired from the world into her nunlike existence. Her studies had always kept her interested, and she had no need of friends. There was plenty of money, or so it had seemed to her. Rhea's interest in worldly pleasures had not yet been quickened. The few things she had desired had always been forthcoming with little or no effort on her part. Beauty, intelligence, and a limited access to her mother's fortune had made demonology a superfluous commodity until she met Raymond Wakeling.

There was an inherited hardness in Rhea which had seldom been called to manifest itself. Now it surfaced, truncating the period of maidenly weeping and accelerating Rhea's turn toward purposive action.

The remainder of the week went by draggingly. It was all Rhea could do to endure Theresa's monotonous raptures over Raymond Wakeling, but she managed to seem cheerful, and for the first time in their relationship sought to strengthen their friendship. She didn't always elect to go home for the weekend, there being little there to attract her, and less of a scholarly and concentration-aiding atmosphere for the pursuit of her studies; but this weekend she made an exception, to the slight relief of the school staff, who found her presence slightly unsettling for reasons they could not have recounted themselves.

The school kept its own coach for the purpose of providing safe and convenient transportation for its young charges to and from their homes. Since there were more girls than coach, it was necessary to conduct two trips on those weekends when all or most girls took leave. Rhea had hoped that she and Theresa would not ride together, but her luck didn't hold to that extent. At least she was spared, by the presence of so many others, the necessity of tolerating her friend's incessant chatter on the subject of Raymond Wakeling.

At midnight, after a most careful rereading of the requisite chapter, Rhea repaired to the Carter basement with candles, chalk, and the blood of a chicken which she had had to purchase herself, there being no freshly slain fowl in the kitchen at the moment. She brought the book along for a ready reference, and as a physical assurance that she was not going through a childish and meaningless ritual. Emotional self-defense had required of Rhea that she metamorphose her earlier experiences with demons into a murkily recalled fantasy, with the result that she no longer remained certain that any of it had occurred.

She set about the rites with greater care than before, but with greater efficiency as well, and even after doublechecking all her precautions, she was ready to call forth her infernal servant in less than a half hour. The setting, with the flickering candles and smeared blood, and the intricate design on the floor, resuscitated her repressed memories sufficiently to produce a slight shudder of apprehension. In steely voice she read the Latin words not from *Liber de Malo*, but from a sheet of fine stationery on which she had carefully transcribed them. This was a new ritual to her, since she had decided to summon not one of the demons with whom she had done business in the past, but another, the mightest described in the pages of the volume.

The instant she had read the words, the paper in her hands burst into flames. She felt the heat of it, but was not burned. The sheet was consumed before she could drop it, as the candles flickered once, then resumed their steady illumination. Her heart thumping crazily, Rhea looked up slowly, with uncharacteristic anxiety. What she saw startled her, and then, belatedly, frightened her, more than could have all the horrific, slavering demons of hell.

Before Rhea stood Raymond Wakeling, dressed precisely as he had been on the occasion of their single meeting, right down to the white gloves he had worn. For the first time, and the last for a good many years to come, Rhea yielded to her dismay to the extent of falling back two steps, emitting a gasp that barely missed becoming a shriek. Her nightdress was clammy against her skin. The man in the chalk prison stepped forth, as though to leave its confines.

"Stop!" she ordered with an authority born of terror. The man stood his ground, smiling. In the instant of her recoil, he seemed to have grown just a bit taller and more massive. "What possible justification do you have for assuming such a form?" she demanded, and he laughed at her.

"Merely a jest, ma'am," he assured her, bowing from the waist so that his uppermost parts nearly extended past the barrier she had provided. 'A humorous way of demonstrating that I know already what you wish of me."

"Then grant it and be gone!" she hissed.

"Now, Miss Rhea. Do you reject the lover for whom you have already demeaned yourself?" Rhea flushed with embarrassment and anger.

"You are not he," she reminded the demon. He laughed again, apparently with genuine and discomforting amusement.

"No," he granted. "I am not that pathetic fool."

He cannot leave the figure I have drawn, she thought. *He cannot.* And she grew bolder through this self-reminder.

"I wish no further conversation with you," she said, managing to inject a note of contemptuous dismissal into her voice. "Give me what I summoned you for and then leave me."

He bowed once again. "As you wish, Miss Rhea, of course. Yet we must observe the form, ma'am. Tell me precisely what it is you wish." She had thought this out in advance, remembering the near calls and actual disasters of a decade earlier.

"I want Raymond Wakeling — the Raymond Wakeling I met this past week, and with whom I danced — to love me, totally and irrecoverably. I wish him to be mine on any terms I may chose, and to be helpless in the face of his need for me." The effigy of her true love bowed once again, with a touch of mockery in his grave obeisance.

"As you wish, Miss Rhea, ma'am. You have been served by us before. In the light of the consequences, are you certain you desire me to do this thing?" These ominous words caught Rhea unaware, and she trembled, her chin working once wordlessly before she took herself in hand.

"Quite certain." This time he did not bow, but looked at her with condign gravity.

"As you will, so mote it be, little miss. However, I must warn you. My power is greater by far than the power of those you have summoned before. It is not limitless. What you have wished, in the words you have expressed it, can be granted to you only by Him Who Must Be Obeyed."

That name stirred a vague recollection in Rhea's mind. She had read of a creature called He Who Must Be Obeyed in *Liber de Malo*, in the final pages, when she was a child. The name had repelled her, and she had rejected the chapter without bothering fully to understand it.

"I can do this for you," the demon in Raymond Wakeling's form continued. "Raymond Wakeling will indeed fall in love with you on your next meeting. His love will be as potent as you have described. He will become an even more wretched creature than he is." Here the demon's voice took on its former mocking tone. "He will grovel before you as a slave, in the hope of any crumb of attention you wish to bestow on him. He will be pitifully grateful even for your anger and contempt."

"But?" Rhea urged shortly. The demon sounded like an adult describing an approaching outing to a child barely out of her infancy. No one had spoken thus to Rhea within her memory, and it roused her resentment.

"But," the demon said in a tone only slightly more serious, "should the two of you ever be separated by more than fifty miles' distance for more than two weeks' time, the charm will be terminated. And no power will ever restore it."

"That sounds silly to me," Rhea said petulantly. The demon conferred upon her another of his sweeping bows.

"I do not make the rules, Miss Rhea, ma'am. Unfortunately," he appended in a slightly ominous tone. "Do you accept these provisions?"

"First clarify them to me. Are you telling me that if I should be separated from Raymond for more than a fortnight, or by more than fifty miles—?"

"You may be separated by the earth itself for thirteen days," the demon said a trifle impatiently. "You may stay away from the dolt for all your life, and still hold him captive. Only if you are separated by more than fifty miles for more than two weeks' time will my power cease to serve you. Once the charm has been broken, this man will doubtless hate you with infinite intensity for all his life. That is only human. Or so I am told."

"If Raymond will be enslaved by love for me, why should he leave me for so long?"

"Miss Rhea, I am only describing the laws and limitations which govern me, and the way in which they pertain to your command. I am not saying that Wakeling will leave you for a fortnight. Nor am I guaranteeing that he will not."

Rhea stood for a moment, irresolute. She had had two previous experiences with infernal spirits, and knew that her own wishes could be turned against her in literally diabolically clever ways. Still, she knew from common sense that a man fanatically in love could be controlled. Even should she grow bored with Wakeling temporarily, a likelihood she could not grant, it should be simple to keep him in Philadelphia without seeing him until she desired to do so. He would be hanging on her wishes, she thought with excitement.

"Very good," she said. "I agree to your conditions."

And the demon vanished, leaving behind only a whisper of a shred of a chuckle.

1975

Yvonne

A conscience was something she couldn't afford, Yvonne Baker told herself. She repeated this dictum a thousand times after her terrifying meeting with Janet Stafford. She had lived with fear all her life, fear of things she knew were coming, like Stan's death. She had become inured to fear, as a chronically ill person becomes inured to pain and inconvenience. Not that she had known of every little event that was coming. That would have been unbearable. She had looked away from the details of her future, glimpsing only the big events, too massive for her gaze to avoid.

This was the first time she had ever refused to honor a tacit contract with a client. It was simply too much. More than she was prepared to involve herself with. Anyway, she told herself again, it was not her concern. She had refunded the woman's money, plus something to cover her gasoline and time. For all the good it would do her.

Could a moral obligation be eliminated that cheaply?

She had started smoking again, something she had given up long ago, when she had forseen that it would kill her otherwise. Didn't that in itself prove that the future could be changed, if you tried hard enough? And didn't it mean that she owed Janet Stafford her shot at changing it? She could leave this bastard to his richly deserved fate and go away to live her life any way — But would she do that? For the first time in her life Von couldn't get a clear picture of what a person would do, of what the consequences would be if she acted. She was forced to make her decisions the way most people did, almost blindly, and she hated the experience.

She eyed the telephone.

It seemed to squat like some kind of troll, mocking her, as though the holes in the dial were ten grinning eyes. She left the living room, lighting a cigarette, and entered the kitchen, where she poured herself another cup of coffee, then, with a forced thoughtlessness, laced it with bourbon. How many times had she done that today? And it wasn't even noon. She sipped the scalding brew, then walked across the room and picked up the kitchen phone. Putting down her cup, she dialed swiftly.

"At the tone —"

She chuckled to herself dryly, hung up the phone, and looked at her coffee again.

You know you're going to do it, she told herself. Why prolong the torment?

She picked it up again, dialed the number Janet had included in her letter. It rang twice before a maid answered. *Fancy schmancy,* Von thought.

"I'd like to speak to Mrs. Stafford."

"I'm sorry, ma'am, Mrs. Stafford is not feeling well, and has instructed me --"

"It's urgent," Von said in her most peremptory tone. "Tell her Yvonne Baker is calling. She'll speak to me."

"Oh, of course, Mrs. Baker. Just one moment." The alacrity with which the maid yielded could only mean that her instructions had included a rider expecting calls from Von. That made her feel all the guiltier.

"Hello? Von?" The voice was barely recognizable after four days and nights of strain. Stifling a fresh stab of conscience, Von launched into the subject immediately.

"I called to tell you that I'm sorry about the other day. And to say that if you want, I'll tell you what I saw." For a moment no sound came over the wire. Then Von heard Janet crying. "There's no time for that," she said, punishing the other woman for her own remorse. "Can you come over here?"

"Yes, of course, certainly I can. When?"

"As soon as possible. Right now. If you're sure you can stand this."

"Oh, Jesus, Von, I can stand anything but this—not knowing."

"All right, hon." Von's door chimes sounded. "Listen, someone's at my door. You get over here. I'll have some coffee on."

"All right, Von, and — oh God, thank you!"

"Sure, hon," Von said, feeling all the guiltier for Janet's pathetic gratitude. She hung up and went to the door in quick step. "Yes?" she said when she had opened it. She was confronted by a young woman, probably in her early twenties, a girl more striking-looking than beautiful. She had long black hair that hung down her back, and eyes that were blue green. She wore a white dress, short for the present fashion, but quite attractive on a woman with legs like hers.

"Mrs. Baker?" the girl asked.

"That's right."

"I hope you don't mind my intruding on you —" The girl looked past her into the living room.

"Well, actually, I am in something of a hurry, Miss, uh —"

"Carter. Rhea Carter. Please, this won't take long. It has to do with Janet Stafford." Von stared at her for a moment, suddenly wary.

"I just sopke to Mrs. Stafford," she said, placing a foot against the door to keep the girl from pushing her way in should she decide to try. All of a sudden something seemed strangely familiar about her. But the girl made no attempt to enter. Instead, she sighed, and her face showed a deep and apparently sincere relief.

"Oh, then you're going to help her?"

"Well — if I can."

"You have no idea what a relief that is, Mrs. Baker. She's been in such a state since your meeting. I finally managed to extract your address from her, and drove here from Beverly Hills to ask you—"

"Oh. Well, come in for a moment then," Von said, stepping back. Not many friends would go to such lengths, she thought. Janet Stafford must be a pretty decent sort to attract such devotion. Von had forgot for the moment that the girl seemed familiar. "Would you like some coffee?"

"No, thank you. I'd just like to sit down for a moment before I have to drive back up there, if you don't mind."

"Yes, all right." The girl sat in a chair facing the couch. Von took her cigarettes from the coffee table and plunked herself in the middle of the sofa, fumbling with a match until she managed to get it lit. "How long have you known Janet Stafford?"

"Oh, a long time. Years and years. All her life, really." The girl was smiling, and Von returned the smile with the first spontaneous one she had known in four days.

"I hope you'll forgive my appearance," she said. She was dressed in the same old blue jeans and top she had worn when Janet had called on her.

"Why, you look delicious, Von. You're really a very attractive woman, you know. At least you turn me on." She said it in such a matter-of-fact voice that it took a moment for Von to feel shocked. *I guess I'm getting out of touch in my old age*, she thought, and decided to take it as a joke.

"Oh, well, I'm sorry, dear, but you're not my type."

"You can't win them all," the girl shrugged. "Phillip Stafford likes me." Von looked at her sharply.

"How long have you really known the Staffords?"

"I told you. All their lives."

"That's not possible, is it?"

"No? Why not?"

"After all, how old are you?" Von took another drag on her cigarette.

"A hundred and seventy-nine." The girl said that as calmly and as literally as she had spoken about her physical attraction to Von. It sent a huge chill down Von's spine.

"I'm not in the mood for jokes, Rhea," she said. Rhea smiled back at her, brightly.

"Really? I'm always in the mood for them. When they're at someone else's expense." She had rested her elbows on the arms of her chair, and now her fingertips touched very lightly, moving in a circular motion that fascinated Von. It looked incredibly sensual, and she found herself growing breathless looking at it. "Right now the joke is on Phillip Stafford, and Janet. And their children. But particularly, at the moment, the joke is on you, dear."

"I don't understand. I—" Von's nostrils were suddenly assaulted by an acrid smell. Something was burning. She tried to remember if she had put down a cigarette somewhere, but couldn't. She started to rise.

"No, you won't get up, Von," Rhea said, still smiling her bright, friendly smile. "You'll stay right where you are."

"I thought I smelled something burning."

"You did. You do. Burning is such a horrid way to die, isn't it, dear? But quite appropriate in your case. You may as well get used it it."

"What are you talking about?" Von tried to rise again, but her legs wouldn't lift her. She stuffed out her cigarette in the ashtray on the coffee table and used her arms, but they wouldn't help either. She looked sharply at the girl sitting across from her, her knees pressed so demurely together. "Who are you?" she demanded. "Why can't I get up?" The burning smell was still there, perhaps a bit stronger.

"I told you. I'm Rhea Carter. I'm from Philadelphia. Right now I'm the woman who has taken Janet Stafford's husband away from her."

"No, that's not true! I would have known. Why didn't I know?"

"Because your gift has been cancelled, darling. It's no longer expedient to let you see things. You see, Von, we work for the same person. Only I know it, and you never have. You've been working for him all your life. It's no one's fault that you hadn't the imagination to make more of it for yourself. You could have had so much from life, so much pleasure, instead of the drab existence you've led. The price is the same either way, and now it's come due."

"Stop this! I want to get up!"

"No, you'll stay where you are. You haven't the strength to disobey me, dear, because you've been serving the Master for all your life, and after sucking at his tit for so long you are his."

"Please! Something is burning." She was covered with sweat. She could feel it between her breasts and between her thighs, but no amount of exertion would raise her from the couch.

"You bet it is. Look." Rhea made a gesture with her head, indicating a place on the carpet. A place in the middle of the floor was beginning to smolder. She couldn't see anything glowing yet, but smoke was rising in wisps.

"God damn you, let me up," she hissed, making a supreme effort. Still she couldn't move. Rhea laughed, exactly like a young girl who is having a gloriously good time.

"You're even more attractive when you're frightened," she said. "Frightened and helpless." Suddenly, catlike, she rose, looking startlingly beautiful in her white dress, with her long, lovely legs. Despite her terror Von felt a thrill of excitement at the sight. Rhea paced the distance between them, reached down and touched the bandana that bound Von's hair. Then she plucked it off and the light brown hair spilled over Von's shoulders. "Yes," she breathed. "Very lovely."

"Leave me alone. Please. Go away."

"Soon, darling. Not yet. Before you go to your just deserts, I'm going to give you a little taste of what you could have had. If only you'd had the sense." She began to open the buttons of Von's top, unhurriedly, one at a time. Von squirmed, tried to lift her arms, but they had become totally useless.

"Don't. Please don't do this." Rhea laughed throatily. She had opened all the buttons now, and she pulled the top out of Von's waistband, then pushed it back over her shoulders and pulled it free. It dropped to the floor. A moment later it was followed by the threadbare white bra Von had put on that morning.

"There. Now we can get to know each other a little better, can't we?" She reached back and with a quick, deft motion unzipped her dress, shrugged it forward and stepped out of it, and her loveliness was set off by the black lace panties and bra she wore. She took off the bra. "That makes us equal. Except you're still wearing your pants. We can't have that." Reaching down, she opened the button at the side of Von's pants, unzipped them and stood upright. "Take them off," she commanded.

"No, don't, please." The sweat on Von's face was mixed with tears now. But she was struggling out of her pants. Suddenly her legs were competent enough to lift her barely clear of the couch. In a moment she wore only her panties.

"That's fine. I'll take care of those, darling," Rhea whispered. She sat down next to Von and peeled the panties off of her. "Now," she said with a gentle push, "just lie back, dear." Her hands were already working intimately, expertly. Von's head fell back on the arm of the couch, her lips parted and moist. Somehow the pleasure had become a part of the terror, one emotion, one sensation, incredibly intense. She continued to plead with Rhea, but she could tell from the girl's laughter that she knew her victim no longer wanted her to stop. She bent down and kissed Von on the mouth, then the throat, then the breasts, while her hands continued their work.

Von had never been noisy about sex. Even with her husband she had never proclaimed her pleasure loudly. But this was too intense to hold in. She strangled and gargled and finally shrieked as Rhea's mouth replaced her hands.

"Now, you see? That's what it could have been like for you all the time, honey." She was already dressing, quickly and efficiently as though she were at home, and late for work. Von was aware of the burning smell, and that it had grown hugely in the past moments. She opened her mouth to scream, but was unable to make more than a muted strangling sound. Rhea zipped her dress and stood looking down at her victim, still smiling gaily. The smoldering spot had sprouted flame, and it rose slowly until it crackled two feet above the floor. "I could let you get dressed, I suppose," Rhea said thoughtfully. "But it won't make much difference when they find what's left of you." The flame was spreading. Von couldn't look away from it, and the heat was beginning to burn her skin uncomfortably. Rhea walked through a narrow lane that had not yet burst into flame, and immediately behind her it ignited. At the door she turned.

"You do make a lovely picture lying there like that," she chuckled. "And now, I really must run, darling. Thank you for asking me in and — everything. It was nice." She opened the door, turned for one last look into Von's pleading eyes. Her own eyes twinkled mischievously. "What is it those Christian fools say on their bumper stickers? Oh, yes. 'Have a nice forever'."

1812

Rhea

To Rhea, sex was a plaything. Other girls of her age knew nothing of its delights, or even of the rudiments of the act itself. To mention such sordid matters to one of them would have been regarded as a breach not only of propriety, but of morality. In such matters ignorance was considered a mark of breeding. They would learn the particulars, to their undying regret, on their wedding nights.

Having perused, at Mr. and Mrs. Cameron's school, various ancient manuscripts written by pagan geniuses, Rhea had learned enough of sex to be able to take the lead with Raymond, who was little better off than she in the matter of direct experience. His gentlemanly training would have balked at the thought of actually enjoying carnal pleasures with a well brought up young lady, except that the drive of his passion for Rhea, which had sprung upon him with the bewildering speed and overwhelming ferocity of a giant cat, made him helpless before any demand she might care to make upon him.

Their first encounter took place in a house owned by his parents, not far from his college, which they made available to him in order to relieve him of the necessity of coming home when his studies were particularly demanding. His father, a former sea captain, had also entertained the unspoken hope that his son, whose backwardness in such matters had become a source of fretfulness to the old man, might use it to further his education in non-academic pursuits. Wakeling *père* had no reason to believe that his dream was being fulfilled, for Raymond was terribly shy and extremely moral even for the age in which he lived.

He began his relationship with Rhea, therefore, nearly as ignorant as a child. Rhea's book learning, and the natural inclination she proved to have in such matters, saved them from the hours of travail that often accompany encounters between virgins.

The house to which he brought her was unkempt, since it was not being attended by servants. Dust was everywhere, and Rhea, already certain after two days of Raymond's slavish attention, relieved some of her own nervousness and entertained herself by rebuking him sharply for having brought her to such a place. She even toyed with the notion of having him clean the house personally before proceeding with their tryst. Only her own eagerness to discover what she had been missing for fifteen years restrained her. Rhea was already learning the pleasure of cruelty.

He was wretchedly nervous and knocked lamps over, rapped the edge of the door with his boot's toe, bumped into furniture, and even into Rhea herself once. He was far more embarrassed than he had been with the one whore he had visited at the insistence of friends, partly because Rhea was a young lady of quality, and partly because he couldn't believe that she actually intended going through with this matter. Nevertheless, he undressed with alacrity because he couldn't bear to provoke another scolding, and then stood fidgeting in an agony of humiliation while she inspected him coolly.

The coolness was a façade. Rhea had never seen a naked man, and had had only the sketchiest idea of their construction, pieced together from her bawdy readings. This direct revelation was breathtaking, all the more so since she knew that this superb creature was her property in a sense more real than pertained in the case of the blackest slave in the Carolinas. Still dressed in her undergarments, she walked to him slowly, savoring the moment. For this instant she was fond of Raymond. She felt an overwhelming affection that was illogically but quite naturally mixed with her exultation at having him under command. Even the mild tang of sweat that clung to his skin excited her, and when the touch of her fingers brought his appendage to life, she nearly fainted with her excitement. It didn't look exactly as she had imagined it from the descriptions she had read, but it was close enough that her concept was retroactively modified to fit reality. For one thing, she had vastly underrated the size of the thing; and the ratio of sizes, between its somnolent state and this rigid wakefullness, quite overwhelmed her. She knew a mighty urge to drop to her knees and kiss it, fondle it, manipulate it, to feel more deeply the throbbing she detected through her fingertips.

She knew a mild and momentary qualm about being seen by

him without clothing, but nothing of the terrified embarrassment that ordinarily accompanies such premiere unveilings, partly because her intense sexual nature, of which she had never had the opportunity to learn before, drowned out such feelings, but mostly because, at the moment the apprehension occurred to her, she recollected the demon's promise. Raymond was laboring under a mighty spell. There was simply no chance that he would find her other than enchanting, even were she possessed of warts and a wooden leg.

Spell or no, any normal young man would have found her a bewitching sight. At fifteen, unlike many, she was a fully matured woman, who still wore the pink and white glow of childhood. Her breasts were not as large as they would ultimately grow, but they were fully rounded and tipped with pinkness. Her hips had taken on the contours that Nature intended, and the thatch of golden hair between her thighs promised a treasure of delight beneath its tangle. Her face was alight with passion, and the blond ringlets that framed it seemed to match precisely the muted sunlight that parted the drapes. Instinctively, as she rose to the tips of her toes to kiss Raymond, she parted her lips and moistened them with the tip of a tongue that promised intense sweetness.

Even in her state of excitement, it would have been too much to expect this callow boy to bring her to completion their first time. Still, he managed, while frustrating her, to make her all the more intrigued with the possibilities of this physical congress. By the time the light from the window had crawled up the wall and faded, leaving them nearly in darkness after four intense couplings, she made the acquaintance of the orgasm. To him it was already an old friend.

1976

Phillip

The one gratification in Phillip Stafford's life of late lay in the fact that Janet had stopped her *opéra bouffe* attempts at seducing him. There were moments when she would look at him across the table, after making a late night snack for him, and he would glance up just in time to catch an expression in her eyes of indecision, as though she couldn't make herself ask him something, or tell him something. There would be a kind of anxiety in the gaze, as though she were afraid, and suspected that he might be involved in her fear. It was a puzzle, but not one to which Phillip could devote any of his energies at the moment. He was too concerned with other matters. Mainly, he was concerned about the most recent evidence of his enslavement.

"I don't understand this, Mr. Stafford," the head of Personnel said, when Phillip called him in. "Why should you even concern yourself with such a trivial and routine matter?"

"I don't consider it trivial or routine when there's a chance to save the studio some money and sweep out some deadwood," Phillip returned. They were sitting across his desk, in his own office, where he was in charge of things more fully. The head of Personnel was a young man with a degree in management from some state university. At the moment he looked bewildered.

"But, sir, this man has been a faithful employee for thirty years. His job is all he has. In all those years he's only been out sick a handful of times."

"And because of that, he accumulated a good deal of sick time, which he has now exhausted. The studio owes him precisely nothing."

"Legally, that's true, sir, but what about the morale factor?"

"That's precisely what I'm thinking of. I don't want employees thinking that they can flout the procedures of this corporation. We have guidelines to cover such cases."

"Yes, sir, and allowances, written right into the corporation bylaws, for suspending those guidelines when, in the opinion of management —"

"I happen to be part of this studio's management, Brent," Phillip reminded the bright young man before him. His voice softened and took on a cultivated, ominous tone he had learned to use in special cases.

"I'm aware of that, of course, sir," Brent agreed, his own voice taking on a slight quaver. Then he strengthened it by an apparent act of will. "But I don't think Mr. Hatfield will agree on this matter." Mr. Hatfield was a vice president and Phillip's immediate superior. Phillip stared at Brent, absorbing the implied threat.

"Of course it's your right to go to Mr. Hatfield," he said. "You may even have your way, if you do. But keep this in mind. Mr. Hatfield won't be here forever. He's an old man. And when he leaves, it's likely that I'll be replacing him. I think that likelihood merits some consideration on your part, Brent." Brent just sat for a moment, looking back at Phillip, and Phillip couldn't help admiring the man's balls.

"I — I didn't mean to give the impression that I might go over your head, Mr. Stafford. I only meant to suggest that what you're asking isn't the usual policy of the studio in such —" He choked, licked his lips, and pushed his glasses up the bridge of his nose. "But, of course, sir, if you feel that strongly on the issue —"

That had been a week before. The janitor had been given the studio's ultimatum: return to work the next Monday or give up his job. He had elected to return, as Phillip had expected. Phillip saw him later that same day, going lethargically about his duties. The man had greeted Phillip with wan cordiality, so apparently no one had mentioned to him Mr. Stafford's involvement in his predicament. The thing about the incident that had astounded Phillip was the lack of concern he felt. There were no pangs of guilt, only the apprehension he had felt in advance, that when word of his part in the matter leaked out, it would damage his position, and for some weeks he studied the faces of other executives, looking for some sign that their attitude toward him had deteriorated. He found no such clues, and eventually relaxed. The only thing that plagued him after that was the thought that he had done this for Rhea, and that he knew, as he had tried to keep from knowing, that he would do anything for her from now on. And for a while it seemed that, even though he had capitulated, he wasn't to receive his reward. Then, three days after he had faced Brent down, his private telephone rang. It could be anyone, Phillip thought, but as he raised the receiver to his ear he knew better.

"Well, I owe you one, darling," she said in that tone, with just enough mockery to provoke him without giving him anything to justify a counterattack. A snappish answer rose to his lips, but he swallowed it with whatever pride he still had.

"When do I collect?" His own voice was peremptory, as though he were commanding her favors instead of pleading for them.

"Why, anytime, dear." She waited just long enough to tempt further pleading on his part, then, before he could speak, offered, "Right now?"

"All right," Phillip said, not even trying to keep the eagerness out of his voice. "Our usual meeting place?"

"Oh, I think you deserve something better this time, dear. Why don't you come over to my apartment?" He swallowed hard. The telephone receiver slipped in his fingers and he had to readjust his hold.

"Well, I have been promoted. I was beginning to wonder if you had a place to live, or if you just — evanesced — when you weren't manipulating me." She laughed throatily, as though she found the idea truly amusing.

"Oh, no, Philly, I assure you, my reality is very physical." She gave him an address in a better part of L.A. and hung up. Phillip stared at his Scotch, now mostly water, and tried to control the excitement in him. If he could ever conquer and control this woman, he thought, he would gladly sell his soul. Or whatever he still had of it.

1812

Rhea

It was a Wednesday afternoon, when they found time to meet at their usual trysting place, that Raymond turned up displaying visible agitation. At first she hardly noticed, responding with her usual mixture of amusement and scorn. He was always agitated at their meetings, anxious about pleasing her, dissatisfied with his appearance, frightened by the merest glance from Rhea. She soon noted, however, that there was something special about his state of mind on this day. He arrived late, for one thing, which he had never done before. Rhea, annoyed by his tardiness, had decided to make him suffer for it. When he finally burst into the bedroom, spotlessly clean now, she was lying on the bedspread, already nude. Even the sight of her nakedness, which usually captured his attention completely, seemed only to exacerbate his distracted state of mind. Quite dutifully, he stripped and lay down next to her, but his lovemaking was perfunctory, as though he were going through the motions of some merely mechanical duty. Rhea felt a stab of anger, the false emotion that covered her sudden fear. Had the spell been weakened in in some way? Had the demon broken his covenant? Had he never been bound to obey her, but only toyed with her desires? She thrust away Raymond's clumsy and lethargic hands and pushed herself up on the bed, leaning against the wall. It felt chilly on her back.

"What is the matter, you idiot?" she demanded. Her voice sounded petulant in her own ears, but she had grown accustomed to giving herself rein in Raymond's presence, and she didn't try to amend the impression. He stared at her, blinking, looking much like a little boy who has been reprimanded by his older sister.

"I'm sorry, darling. Really, I —"

"Tell me what is on your mind, then," she commanded. "Assuming you have a mind."

"I just received word that Congress has passed a declaration of war against England. President Hamilton is expected to sign it momentarily, if he has not already done so." He looked up at her as though expecting some response.

"In Christ's name, is that all! What has that to do with you and me?" For a moment she had feared that their affair had been jeopardized in some way.

"But don't you see, darling? I'll have to go. My unit will be activated. There's no telling where they will send us, or for how long. I may not see you for months, or even years." Rhea's derisive smile froze to her mouth. The fiend, of course, had foreseen this when he had made his supposedly meaningless stipulation. Suddenly Raymond buried his face between her breasts. She could feel the slight raspiness of his close-shaven cheeks. He always shaved just before coming to her, and splashed his face with expensive cologne, despite the fact that it was customary, in that time, for a man to shave but once a week. Her left hand clutched at his thick, muscled neck, and the fingers of her right hand grasped the luxurious, wild curl of his black hair in a proprietary grip. "Oh, Rhea," he sobbed against her flesh, "please promise me that you won't desert me. I shall think of nothing else but you. You must promise me that you will not reject me for someone else, or I shall kill myself, I swear it."

"No such promise is required, dearest," she said in a voice gone cold and hard. "For you are not going." He stiffened in her arms, gently drew away from her. His eyes were like those of a devoted animal.

"Not go? But how can I avoid it?"

"You will not 'avoid it' at all," she purred, and then exploded, springing to her feet and pacing the room like an enraged tigress. "You simply will not go. You're not some common backwoodsman to be ordered away. And I will not do without my pleasures for their petty little war. Do you hear me, I won't!" Her voice rose in pitch and volume until it became the shriek of a thwarted child. He stared at her with a look of real fright.

"But, darling, you must let me go," he said in a tone at once reasonable and placatory.

"Oh, must I? Since when have you taken to telling me what I must do?"

"But if I refuse I shall be disgraced. My family —"

"What care I of your family's reputation?" she demanded rashly, not stopping to consider the bearing of the matter on herself. "What care I for national honor, or freedom of the seas, or any of those idiotic slogans?"

"My father's business would suffer grievously —"

"Then he had better find another source of income," Rhea hissed with perverse satisfaction, taking surcease in his discomfiture. Raymond started to rise, looked into her face, and contented himself with sitting on the edge of the bed. The powerful knots of his muscles, the thick black hair that covered his arms and chest, excited her, and she moved toward him almost stealthily.

"Darling, please, you don't understand. I am an officer, and must go with my men."

"From now on, Raymond, I shall decide what you must do." Her voice was calmer now. The charm had not weakened. If anything it had waxed stronger with the passage of time. She stopped, standing scarcely a foot in front of him.

"Rhea, please don't do this to me. I can't make such a choice, dearest —"

"But I insist that you make it, Raymond. What if I tell you that there will be someone else if you leave? That I shall find another man, bed him within a week, and wed him in a month? That if you are indeed gone for a year, you'll return to find me with another man's child in my arms? What then, Mr. Wakeling?" She stepped closer still, widening her stance so that her feet bracketed his, and looked down at him with imperious pleasure. He actually quaked with his misery, and tears boiled from his dark eyes. "Well?" she pressed with relish. "Make your decision, young Mr. Wakeling. Time is not abundant. Once I dress and leave this place, you'll not see me again, except to pass me on the street. As I stroll with my husband." She was bluffing. Still, it was a bluff she played with serene confidence, for she knew that he dared not call it.

He sat there, tense and hunched, his neck craned back so that he could stare up into her uncompromising eyes. His jaws worked convulsively, as though he were trying to find words. She had never seen such misery in a face before, and for a moment her affection for him almost overcame the pleasure she felt in exercising such power.

Impulsively, his arms circled her hips, drawing him to her in a hard jerking motion. She felt his cheek and temple against her abdomen. Her fingers tangled in the thickness of his hair and she pushed his head back, turned it toward her, and then with deliberate slowness drew his face between her thighs. For a moment he was still, but then the movements of his lips and tongue, and the greediness of his hands grasping her buttocks, told her he had made his choice and his surrender.

"There, there, Raymond," she chuckled softly as physical and emotional pleasures coursed and merged in her. "You see? There never was any decision to make, was there?"

An hour later she lay in the crook of his arm, one tiny hand resting on his penis. Filled with the silky confidence that often follows an exceptional coupling, she relived the afternoon's triumph in her mind as he lay next to her, evading reality through sleep. The recollection of how he had crumbled before her ultimatum warmed her, so that she kissed him lightly on the lips, not disturbing his slumber. He looked so incredibly beautiful lying there, like any of the Greek gods she had read about in her old manuscripts. And he was totally hers. She had been foolish and weak to believe that she depended on a magic spell to hold him. Of course she had required the help of the demon to break him away from that weak and silly infatuation he had entertained for Theresa, but now that he had tasted the delights she could give him, he would be unlikely to return to any other woman. By this time the poor lamb had all but lost his identity, submerging it in her own. He wouldn't know what to do, how to live, without her.

Disengaging herself from him, she rose and walked to the window. Opening the draperies a bit, she looked out on the street below. A husband and wife strolled by, arm in arm. For the first time in her young life Rhea envied such people their conventional intimacy. Well, let the poor boy go off and fight his war, she decided. They would announce their engagement before he left, and she would portray the brave young virgin facing the uncertainties attendant upon having a soldier fiancee. But there would be no uncertainty. She possessed the means to see that no harm came to her Raymond.

He stirred on the bed, making a soft snorting sound, and she looked at him with rare and genuine tenderness.

There were other matters to consider. If she was to wed this man, it would be more comfortable if they were able to maintain their prestige — and their fortune. The money that she, as Mrs. Raymond Wakeling, would one day command. It would be hard, doing without these afternoons, but once they were married she could keep him in her possession always. And it couldn't be that long. She might even arrange for him to sustain a little wound; just enough to see him safely and honorably home. Lieutenant Raymond Wakeling, wounded in battle against the enemy, she thought. That should content his family's meddlesome friends and customers.

Yes, Raymond, you were right, she thought. You'll have to go with your men.

Still, she hardly regretted their confrontation on the issue. It had proved to her the terrible power she wielded over him, a power that surely could not be weakened, much less disrupted, by anything so trivial as time or distance. It was so right between them. How could he ever be anything but hers? Their momentary opposition must also have demonstrated his position to Raymond himself, if he had entertained any comforting delusions in the matter. She was certain he would never trouble her again.

At that moment life seemed as luminous to Rhea as the sunlight that warmed her naked body through the window glass. Behind her, she heard Raymond shift on the bed again, and when she turned he was sitting up, looking at her with an expression like a sheepish question. The penis that had lain limp and exhausted in her fingers moments before was rousing itself. The sight of its growing stiffness excited her so that she laughed deep in her throat.

"Of course, darling," she purred, moving to him languidly. "Why not?"

1812

Rhea

Dear Miss Carter:
    There are certain matters of such delicate nature that they should be discussed in person and in private, and should never be put to paper. This is more true when there is no trust, and no reason for trust, between two human beings. However, as the content of this letter comprises matters which I cannot contain further, and which I must say before I can rest, and since distance precludes any possibility of saying them to you in person, the mails are my only recourse.
    The things which occur between man and woman can be beautiful and wholesome, ma'am, or they may be perverted. They may be constructive and palliative, or they may be wounding and pernicious. They may be natural, or they may carry the foul stink of hellishness about them. The affair that until recently obtained between you and me was of the worst possible sort. As a grown, rational and presumably Christian man, I cannot eschew my part in matters, nor my responsibility for the consummation of this unsavory liaison. Were these not enlightened times, I should suppose, as our ancestors would have, that I had been possessed by some malign spirit, and incapable of governing my emotions, or indeed my actions.
    As a Christian, ma'am, I could forgive you for causing me to take liberties to which no gentlemanly bachelor is entitled; I could

pardon the patent delight which you took in manipulating and belittling me in my own eyes; I might even overlook the perverted practices which you visited upon me, and which must bear their stamp on my body to the grave, and upon my soul through all eternity. But for endangering, and causing me to endanger, the one pure and lovely affection of my life, I can offer you, ma'am, only a deep and cordial hatred that will endure so long as there is life in my breast. I implore our Lord Jesus Christ to expunge it from my soul so that, should we encounter one another in Heaven, I shall not foul that splendid place with this horrid resentment.

Concurrent with the dispatch of this letter, I am posting one to Miss Dalrymple. Rest assured that I wish to tell her no more of the odious deeds we have shared than a decent young female would wish to know; which is to say, nothing. However, it is only fair to warn you that I shall, in future, tell her anything that I believe may enlist her sympathies or resuscitate the affection she formerly felt for me. I am astonished to think that I once considered myself worthy of that affection. You have proved, and helped me to prove, that I am not. Nevertheless, I shall plead for her forgiveness, and should she offer her affections anew, accept them and strive to approach worthiness as one attempts to prove worthy of God's love, saved from the futility only by the grace of the Giver.

I feel no obligation to you for what has occurred between us; it was at least as much your doing as mine. I thank God there was no issue from our abhorrent dalliance.

I am eager to be finished with this, and shall say no more but that you are to regard me as a stranger in future, for I should find your presence, or even the mention of your name, supremely repugnant. I abhor you, and should sooner embrace the foulest demon in hell than to allow your shadow to fall across me. Any letters you may dispatch to me will be destroyed unopened, and should you ever attempt to force yourself into my presence, I cannot vouch for my restraint.

I remain,   Your most humble and obdt. svt.,
                             Raymond Simpson Wakeling III

The sound that erupted from Rhea the first time she read Raymond Wakeling's last letter to her was less a scream than the wail of a hideously wounded animal. She threw herself upon her bed, clutching the crumpled note paper to her breast, and kicked and churned without volition, her body possessed by an emotion she had never known before, even at the death of her father. Her fellow students ran to her room to see what was the matter, as did the matron in charge of the dormitory, but no one could approach her, with her flailing and kicking.

Eventually she subsided, huddling on her bed, against the corner of the room. There was agitated discussion as to what action might be appropriate. Some favored the summoning of a physician, but eventually the matron surmised that the letter which Rhea clutched to her breast had something to do with her state. All attempts to convince Rhea to give up the letter, however, elicited only snarls and threatening clawing gestures. The matron was unsure of the proper course prescribed by such a situation. Eventually, as Rhea fell into normal weeping, the crowd of girls drifted gingerly away, and finally the matron did the same, intending to suggest that Rhea be sent home for the duration.

The first thing Rhea saw, when she returned to her home that afternoon, was her mother's face, ghostly but still lovely, regarding her from the window of the master bedroom. The instant Rhea saw it, the face vanished behind fluttering curtains. Rhea wished to see that face once more, wished that she had a mother of the sort other girls took for granted, a mother to whom she could go with her troubles and despairs. She had been a little girl the last time she had wished for such a thing, and it had got her nothing but grief, because she hadn't the wisdom to make her wish in the right terms.

The situation that pertained, nonetheless, was that her father was gone and she had never had her mother. For once Rhea's own strength was no comfort to her, and she knew the ache of being unloved. The thing Raymond Wakeling had felt for her hadn't been love. He had thought so because his senses were clouded; she had thought so because she wished to think it.

She entered the house, giving her hat and wrap to a servant, and climbed the stairs to her room. There she took off her clothes and lay on the bed, staring at its canopy.

The demon had known what would happen, certainly. But could she blame a demon for being what he was? She would have to be smarter, that was all. She would have to wish for things that couldn't turn sour because they would be subject to her ownership with no requirements of deeper values or commitments.

For the moment, blessedly, her body craved no carnal pleasures. Her despair at the loss of Raymond obscured and deleted purely erotic demands, but she had learned enough about herself to know that those demands would return, perhaps stronger than ever. Even in this, the demon had had his jest. Well, there must be other men who could satisfy such needs as well as Raymond Wakeling. For the rest, she could live without love.

There were certainly compensations to be had for her status. The diamond hardness of her temperament would see her through. And the demon would do her bidding. Outsmarting her once would hardly extricate him from that necessity, whether he liked it or not. Only in future she must see to it that her bidding reflected wishes with which she could live.

And for the moment there was one thing which she could not countenance: the thought of Raymond living with that milk-and-water little bitch who had been mooning over him these past weeks. Rhea to no extent shared Raymond's doubts as to the reply he would receive to his letter: Theresa Dalrymple would welcome with alacrity the opportunity to resume their relationship. She wouldn't even be enterprising enough to make capital of his position.

It was intolerable to think of such a stupid and characterless little girl marying Raymond, living with him, sharing his bed, making love to him, perhaps even enjoying some of the practices that he and Rhea had discovered together. Better anything than that, she thought as she drifted into an exhausted sleep. Better that he should die. . . .

"Well, child, and what would you have of me now?" The middle-aged man before her bowed slightly over a protruding belly, and his eyes twinkled with mischievous delight. The demon had chosen to take, this time, the portly form of her father.

"You, sir, are a foul fiend," Rhea told him in a tight, quiet voice. The demon bowed once again, lower this time, and his eyes twinkled even more merrily.

"What can I say, child? There you have me." Rhea could not avoid smiling. It was her first fleeting smile since receiving Raymond's vengeful letter. She had to remind herself that this being was the root of her predicament, that he was as evil as he was potent, and that his intelligence was formidable. He stood ready to destroy her the instant she let down her guard.

"The charm that bound Raymond Wakeling to me has been terminated," she said. He nodded, still smiling, and crossed his fingers over the comfortable belly, mingling them with a gold watch chain that hung there. "He hates me, as you prophesied." The demon's countenance assumed a sympathetic expression, but he didn't reply. "You knew this would happen."

"I could hardly have prophesied it otherwise," he said reasonably.

"You know perfectly well what I mean. This foolish war, and its inevitable consequence. You foresaw it all."

"Hardly inevitable, child. You were warned. You should have prevented Raymond from attending the war."

"Then he probably would have gone to prison for desertion. Either way I'd have lost him."

"Not necessarily. A woman of your wit could have found ways around these little problems, had you not yielded to a hubristic and, if you'll pardon me, rather fatuous overconfidence. Still, I think you're better off without the man. A dolt."

"He intends to marry Theresa Dalrymple."

"Now *that* is a perfect match!"

"Never mind that. He has written her a letter, begging to be reinstated in her graces."

"It will be delivered tomorrow morning. It was detained, owing to the exigencies of war. Do I surmise correctly you wish me to prevent the marriage?"

"Is there no chance at all that I may have him back?"

"Oh, no, child, none at all, none at all. Don't torture yourself with such hopes."

"Then I wish you to prevent not just the marriage, but his continued existence." The demon frowned.

"His death? That is what you wish of me?" There was a mild flavor of reproach in his eyes and his tone, as though he had expected something more imaginative from her.

"Yes! Kill him. Don't let her have him, even for a moment."

"If that is your command," the demon shrugged, "I hasten to obey, of course." He looked at her, the same distant, almost sad, reproach in his eyes. Rhea returned his gaze. Why should she be concerned with the opinion of her harbored by a hellish creature who had already tricked her so foully? Still, his disappointment in her was a barb.

"But?" she asked finally. He smiled in the flickering candlelight.

"Far be it from me to criticize, child, but from a girl of your obvious intelligence, and the talent for mischief which I sense in you, I had expected — better."

"I confess I do not understand you. What more can I wish for either of them than his death?"

"Oh, Rhea, Rhea, this man has wronged you. He has written terrible things to you, left you with the ache of unrequited love. He has denied you all but the solace of revenge. And the worst you can think of doing to him is to send him to — heaven?" The last word was spoken with distaste. "A man who is allowed to live on, but in bitterness and despair, might be tempted to turn from his God, and thus damn himself forever. Yet, it is for you to command and me to obey, child."

"Wait!" Rhea snapped. The demon regarded her quizzically.

"I was not about to leave."

"Don't kill him." Rhea began to pace before the rotund figure in the pentagram. He looked at her expectantly. "Keep him alive. I want him to live for a long time. Let him become an old, old man."

"A centegenarian, if you wish." Rhea barely heard the words. She continued to pace, thinking with furious speed and fervid acuity.

"Let him continue to love this pusillanimous creature, if he likes, and she him.

"Love can be painful. It is one of our best weapons, when used properly."

"Yes, yes. But prevent the marriage." He looked slightly disappointed again, and she amended her command "Or let them marry or not, as they wish. Only see to it that they can never consummate their petty little love. See to it that he can consummate his love with no woman, ever again." The demon bowed, this time with evident respect.

"Now that," he said dryly, "is more like it."

"What, precisely, will you do to him?" Rhea asked, ceasing her pacing and regarding him with an unfamiliar mixture of apprehension and anticipatory relish.

"Tomorrow, very early, there will occur a skirmish between Lieutenant Wakeling's unit and a small British force. A minor thing, soon forgotten in the great churn of history. Very few casualties will result. But Mr. Wakeling, poor man, will be struck by a stray musket ball, actually aimed at another. A frighteningly imprecise weapon, the musket, eh?" He paused, clearly enjoying her impatience. "At any rate, this particular piece of lead will sever a portion of Mr. Wakeling's anatomy which delicacy forbids me to name."

Rhea gasped, stepping back a pace and shuddering at the thought of it. The demon looked at her questioningly.

"You wish to recant your command?" he asked, a note of sternness creeping into his voice. She looked at him with an unwavering gaze.

"I do not," she said steadily. Once again he bowed, and there was a quality approaching awe in his voice when he replied.

"You are truly my mistress, whom I obey willingly. And now, if you have no further need of me, my dear, I have preparations to make."

Early the next morning, having convinced all concerned that she was well enough, and that it was her wish, Rhea returned to the academy. The morning mail was being distributed to the girls when she arrived. She waited a bit, placing her wrap in her room, and then, humming a little tune beneath her breath, took herself in languid fashion to the room occupied by Theresa Dalrymple. Theresa was alone for the moment, her roommates being occupied elsewhere. As Rhea looked in, she was eagerly reading a letter, tears of joy streaming down her face, which had become pale and lined in past weeks. Rhea remained silent, letting the girl enjoy her little, meaningless moment. Finally, Theresa looked up to see her standing in the doorway, her arms folded across her breasts, leaning against the jamb in a deliberately insolent, almost loutish manner. Theresa's face lighted in an uncharacteristically triumphant expression, which Rhea answered with a smile that was almost gentle.

"Do you want him, dear?" she asked in a tone so soft that Theresa had to strain to make out the words. Then her voice became a serpentine hiss. "Well, you can have him!"

1976

Janet

She had never been much for taking action. That doubtless accounted for a good many of her personality traits, Janet thought. She wasn't a women's libber, and had always felt an antipathy toward such women, probably because they intimidated her. She had happily given up a fairly promising career for marriage, choosing a man who was accustomed to taking charge. His money had assured that any decisions visited upon her, including those of motherhood, would most likely be simplified, routine. Twenty-nine was an advanced age for making so profound a change in oneself, and it didn't come naturally now that the need to act had been thrust upon her.

Yvonne Baker's death had shocked her more than her own mother's had, years before. It could have been a mere coincidence, the fact that the woman had been killed just after her call to Janet. But how did one explain the fact that she had lain there, as though in a stupor, until the flames consumed her? The paper had reported various theories, advanced by the fire department and the coroner. One was that something in the carpet, upon combustion, had emitted an anesthetic gas which had kept Von from feeling or hearing the flames, or perhaps a poisonous gas that might have killed her, mercifully, before the flames had crept to the couch. There was some indication, from the crisped remains, that she had been lying on the couch naked, and the coroner's report had implied a suspicion that she had been an alcoholic.

None of that explained the woman's terror at whatever she had seen in Janet's future, or the fact that she had finally decided to tell her about it. It didn't explain the fact that she had sounded sober and lucid when she had called Janet. And it didn't explain why she would have made that call and then taken off her clothes, lain down on the couch in her living room, and burned to death.

There was one other matter that pulled tantalizingly at Janet's consciousness. A neighbor of Von's had been reported as having seen a woman at her door just before the fire occurred. At that time, of course, Von had been fully dressed. The neighbor wasn't certain whether the woman had entered the house, and she couldn't describe her very well, having seen her only from behind. But she did say that the woman was dark-haired, with a good figure, probably young, and had been wearing a short white dress.

There was surely no reason to suppose that this mysterious and possibly mythical woman had anything to do with the paramour of her husband, the woman whose image had been so mixed up in Von's reading (blond and black-haired, tall and short . . .). Still, the connection was there, in her mind, insistent, ineradicable.

The possibility of hiring a private detective occurred to Janet, but such an action was repugnant to her. She had been brought up to believe that one did one's own work. Even dirty work.

And so it was that, a week after Von's death, in a rented car, Janet found herself taking up a station across from the studio, where she sat for three days running, from the time Phillip arrived until the time he left, moving to a nearby coffee shop for lunch and dinner. She remembered, from some old film in which she had played a bit, the technique of laying her money on the counter while she was eating, so that she could leave without delay if it should prove necessary.

On the fourth day, just before she would have gone to the coffee shop, Phil came out of the exit reserved for management. He turned to the right, his low-pressure tires squealing on the pavement, and almost disappeared before she could meld into traffic and follow.

Keeping him in sight without getting too close wasn't as easy as she had imagined, and finally she allowed herself to close the distance a bit. He seemed immersed in something, perhaps his destination, and she counted on that, hoping he wouldn't notice her.

On the freeway traffic was light, so she kept in the right lane to be certain she could get off when he did, and followed at a greater interval. They were in West Los Angeles before he gave a flick of his right-turn signal and cut across two lanes to reach the next offramp.

After that he moved slowly, hugging the right curb, as though looking for an address. He turned twice and she almost lost sight of him. Only the distinctive look of the Rolls Royce's rear end prevented it, as she saw it duck around a corner. Janet slowed, so as not to crawl up too close behind him, then eased around the corner. He was already parking in front of some exclusive looking apartments. He didn't stop to lock his car, which was unusual for him, but moved through the archway leading onto the grounds of the apartments almost at a run. Janet couldn't see another parking space nearby, so she parked in a red zone.

By the time she reached the apartments he was gone from sight. She stood, indecisive, until she noticed a sign near the gate that announced, "APARTMENT FOR RENT — TWO BEDROOM UNFURNISHED." That would be her license to prowl about the place, she decided. She could always say that she was looking for the manager's office, or that she just wanted to see what the place looked like before deciding.

The apartments were two-story, splayed out from a central axis, with the entrances arranged so that none was visible from any other within two hundred feet. Trees and masses of foliage furthered the privacy of the tenants, and an artificial brook ran its convoluted course back and forth through the grounds, making itself visible from each window of every apartment. Tiny footbridges with rope railings crossed it at strategic points. Somewhere people splashed in a pool, and she glimpsed a handball court's wall above the trees.

Well, whoever she is, she's no office girl, Janet thought. Unless he's paying the rent.

And then she almost walked into him.

He was standing at the door of one of the apartments with

his back to her, waiting with stiff impatience. She had no idea of how long his girl friend had kept him waiting there, but he showed no sign of intending to turn away. Janet doubted her own judgment for a moment, doubted that it was he at all, but he was wearing the beige suit he'd had on when he had come out of the studio, and she recognized his shoes, the style of his hair. Seeing him there, waiting to be admitted to his mistress's apartment, made it all too real, and tears sprang to her eyes. She turned and walked away, suddenly frightened that he might see her. Before she had covered ten feet, she heard the door open and a young woman's voice say something in a light, mocking tone. Phil's grunting reply sounded sulky, but she recognized the tightness that came into his voice when he was sexually excited. She hadn't heard that quality in his voice for a long time, and it made her cry in earnest.

She found a wooden bench near the brook and dropped onto it, her knees letting go all at once. There was no hurry, she supposed. He would be there for a while.

Oh, God, she thought, why can't I hate him even now? It isn't fair that I love him so much.

After watching some birds searching for bugs in the grass, she tried her legs. They supported her, and she went back to the door of the apartment. Let them find her, if they would. But the door was still fast, the drapes drawn. Naturally. She took her little address book and pencil and examined the card over the doorbell.

R. CARTER

Rita? she wondered. Rhoda? Rosemary? Well, there was time to find that out. And ways to do it, she supposed. Perhaps she should have hired a professional after all. The tawdry details of this work were getting to her, making her despise herself more all the time.

Except that now she was getting mad. She had only fooled herself consciously about her husband's fidelity. Underneath the thinnest shell of self-deceit she had known that he was, as Yvonne Baker had finally put it, a bastard. But now, having her nose rubbed in it, she felt the urge to go in there and beat the hell out of both of them.

That urge evaporated when she remembered the things that

had prompted her to follow him here. Something about this woman, quite possibly, had put that ring of sheer terror into Yvonne Baker's voice.

She wrote down the address, then stood for a moment. The entrance was shaded, and she felt a slight chill. For a moment she thought she heard something from inside, something soft and sibilant, a shuffling sound. But that was impossible. The door was thick and heavy, surely proof against anything more quiet than a scream or a pistol shot. The sound had resembled laughter, a chuckle, distant but amplified, and on second thought it hadn't seemed to come from inside the apartment at all, but from the air about her. Janet hugged herself for warmth, and moved away.

1976

Phillip

Unlike his wife, Phillip Stafford entertained no scruples in the matter of hiring his dirty work done. Furthermore, twenty years of pulling his way to the top in a competitive business hadn't left him without discreet and reliable contacts.

The sign on the door read, WALTER LANKERSHIM — INVESTIGATIONS. There was no eye painted on the glass, no "We Never Sleep," as there would be in an ancient movie. The building was middle-class, and on the low side of that, the kind of place rented by many different businesses, some of them semi-legitimate. On one side of Walter Lankershim's office was an escort agency, and on the other a mail order school for writers. Phillips opened the door and entered.

There was an old but well-polished desk with a manual typewriter resting on a shelf that swung out from its interior. He had half expected to see a leggy secretary there, but instead a man in a wrinkled shirt that was either white or some very pale color was hunt-and-pecking through a pile of papers, copying everything with great care. He finished the particular piece he was typing, then looked up. Fortyish, with a bushy moustache and a half-day's growth, he at least looked as though he had been cast for the part of the hero's partner, and should be wearing a worn shoulder holster.

"Can I help you?" He looked at Phillip like a man taking inventory, noting his clothes, his posture. He straightened up and turned from the typewriter, evidently deciding that this client merited some attention.

"I want someone's background traced," Phillip said. The man cocked his head to one side like an inquisitive and alert watchdog.

"Why?"

"Bill Ryan said that wouldn't matter."

"You know Bill?" He sounded more interested, but not less careful. "How's that daughter of his? What's her name? Miriam?"

"The last I heard she was dead, and had been for eight years." Phillip allowed his displeasure to show through. He was always impatient with games like these, and a bit insulted. As though he wouldn't check out something that obvious if he were a phony. But the man smiled, cocking his head to the side once more.

"Okay. My name's Lankershim. I intend to check with Bill, by the way." He rose and offered a strong hand. He was taller than he had looked behind the desk, perhaps because he was very slender, even skinny. He was almost as tall as Phillip.

"Phillip Stafford."

"Come on into the inner sanctum," Lankershim said, opening a door near the desk. "I have to do my own typing now because my secretary quit last month to get married." *Or was laid off because you couldn't afford her salary*, Phillip thought.

The other room was furnished in early Sears Roebuck, with a framed picture of some bottles on the wall to his right, a medium-sized window across the room, and a desk with two extra chairs, unmatched and very lightly padded.

"Have a seat, Mr. Stafford." Lankershim eased himself into the swivel chair behind the desk. "Can you tell me anything about her?" That caught Phillip in the middle of sitting down, and he hesitated, glancing at the man before he touched the scanty cushion.

"How did you know it was a woman?"

Lankershim grinned broadly. "I got it right, didn't I? Goddamn, I'm getting better all the time. You just seemed to me like the kind of man who, if he had troubles at all, would have them with a woman. What's she trying to do, make you marry her?"

"No, nothing like that. Do I have to tell you about — our relationship?"

"It would simplify matters. I'm not asking out of idle curiosity or prurience, Mr. Stafford. Obviously, the more I know about this woman, the better job I can do. And for less money."

"I'm not concerned about money." That was something Phillip would never have said if he'd been in his usual frame of mind. But whatever this man charged, it would be worth it if he came up with some information that could be of use.

"Well, can you tell me where she lives at least?" Phillip withdrew a slip of paper from his pocket and, rising, leaned across the desk, dropping it on a worn and stained blotter. Lankershim glanced at it as Phillip dropped back onto the uncomfortable chair.

"The address will help," he said with a touch of dryness. "But the name may be a phony. Do you think you can get me her fingerprints? On a glass, maybe?"

"I — I don't know. I thought that was what I was paying you for," Philip said irritably. "To take care of that sort of thing."

"Okay." Lankershim shrugged. "It's just easier if we work together, that's all. Since you're not concerned with the money, we'll do it your way. But it will take longer, you realize."

"Oh. I'll do what I can." Phillip wished he hadn't come to this place. It had been a futile idea. What had made him think there was anything he could learn about Rhea that would give him a handle on her? She was probably invulnerable, as she seemed.

"Look, Mr. Stafford, let's not play around this thing. If you want my help, it's to your benefit to tell me about it. I can do you more good that way, more quickly."

"All right." Phillip could feel his control slipping away as he launched into the story, taking it from the beginning. He had never felt this way before, had never had any less than total mastery over himself. That had been one of his chief weapons in both business and personal relationships. He had always felt some contempt for those, including the great mass of humanity, who showed their feelings to others. But now, as he went through the story of his disintegration since meeting Rhea, and the things she had made him do, tears rolled down his cheeks and splashed to his collar. His voice was almost unintelligible at times, and he had to repeat himself. Finally he got it all out, and then fished a large white linen handkerchief from his hip pocket, wiped his face, and blew his nose noisily. Lankershim was regarding him without expression.

"It's not an unusual story," he said. "It's just rougher on you than most men because you're used to having your way with women, if I read you right."

"But why should she make me do these things? She doesn't stand to gain anything from it."

"Maybe she's cracked. I don't know. Maybe she's setting you up psychologically for something. I take it you want to know about her background because you think it might give you something to use against her." Phillip nodded, not yet in full possession of his voice. "It may work, but there's no guarantee. Have you thought of going to the police with this?"

"Oh, no. No, I don't want the police brought into it. Bill said you were discreet."

"The suggestion was a way of covering myself. Now that it's out of the way, I'll take your job, but since you're obviously so rich, I'm going to soak hell out of you. A hundred a day and expenses, just like in the Phillip Marlowe novels. Is that agreeable?"

"Yes, that's fine," Phillip said quickly.

"How soon can you get me that fingerprint?"

"Well, I'm not certain. I only see her when she calls. And besides, I'm not sure I could — I can —" He looked imploringly at Lankershim, who finally took pity on him.

"All right, forget it. I'll go over and get it off her doorknob some evening." Phillip bit his lip.

"Is that legal?"

"Don't sweat it."

"All right. But bear in mind that she's not stupid. She's the cleverest woman I've ever met."

"That should make it more interesting." Phillip fumbled for his pen and checkbook.

"I guess I should give you something on account. Will five hundred dollars suffice?"

"Sure. Fine," Lankershim said coolly. *Probably thinking of all the bills he could pay with it*, Phillip thought. Lankershim walked around the desk and placed a hand on Phillips's shoulder. Such familiarities usually irritated Phillip, or actively disgusted him, but for once he found the gesture comforting. "Can I call you at the number on the check, by the way?" he asked.

"Yes. No." It was his home number. "Wait a minute." He took out his pocket secretary and scrawled his private office number across a page, tore it out, and handed it to Lankershim.

On the street he felt a bit better. He was back in action at least. Lankershim might actually find something out for him. And even if he didn't, Phillip reasoned, he was only out a paltry five hundred. It was good to be on the offensive for a change. He saw a cocktail lounge a few doors away and headed for it.

1840

Rhea

While in her thirties Rhea had left Philadelphia, and all those puritans and busybodies who had known her, and moved to New York, which was already, by then, the financial capital of the United States. She had almost forgot Raymond Wakeling, though she had seen him occasionally on the streets. He had turned himself into an embittered old man. Theresa Dalrymple had announced, upon his return from the War of 1812, that she intended to stand beside him. Their engagement had been publicized, preparations made, but on the eve of the wedding the intended bride had developed a mysterious malaise, and had had to visit relatives in North Carolina. Preparations for the wedding had been quietly dropped.

Shortly afterward, both of Raymond's parents had died, and the fortune he inherited did little to restore his zest for life, though the passing of his mother and father allowed him greater freedom to drink. He had thrown himself into manly pursuits, mainly hunting, and in 1817 had fallen from a horse, sustaining a bad fracture which had resulted in a permanent limp. In 1818 Theresa had returned to Philadelphia for a visit, on the arm of a new husband, a distant cousin from the southern branch of the Dalrymple family. By that time Rhea herself was an orphan and in control of the fortune she had inherited from her mother.

She had already launched herself on a career of sexual adventures which would earn her an unsavory reputation in her native city. Her youth and money had insulated her from the worst consequences of such a reputation, but the fact that she was not received in the finest houses sometimes rankled.

For a while she considered moving to a southern state, where she could buy some slaves and land and perhaps go into the planting business. The idea of owning slaves attracted her for some reason she couldn't explain even to herself. But in the end she elected to move to New York, which seemed a more cosmopolitan city than most in America. Her fortune, which had grown thanks to sensible investments, would keep her in relative luxury wherever she decided to live, and as for owning slaves, she had found a way to enjoy that gratification without paying a cent.

In New York she bought a huge house, bigger even than the family mansion which she had closed rather than sold, hired a staff of servants, choosing them as much for a taciturn and uncurious temperament as for their efficiency, and had settled down to a new life. It was then 1828, and Rhea Carter was thirty-two.

She looked to be in her early twenties, a quality of sustained youthfulness she had inherited from her mother; and so, for a while, the advancing years meant little to her. The few men she found desirable who refused to succumb to her considerable physical charms and acquired sexual competence were induced to develop a potent affection. She used the powers of darkness seldom, and with restraint, but she saw no reason why such powers should be allowed to lie unutilized.

Those men, possessed of unusual integrity or character judgment, who shied away from a woman of Rhea's stamp despite her looks, were the least fortunate of her paramours, for once brought under an obsessive charm they had nothing left when Rhea tried of them. They were useless to other women, wives or prospective wives. Most of them died early, suicides or victims of careless accidents.

By 1840 Rhea had noticed that she was winning more and more of her lovers through the intervention of supernatural forces. At first this puzzled her, until she realized that she was now well into her forties, and that the men whom she found attractive, youngsters in their twenties, while perhaps not averse to a casual fling with a lovely if mature woman, were naturally drawn to girls their own age. That was when she began to think more and more about the calendar, and to fear the obdurate march of her age. And that was when she decided that she, of all women on earth, was in a position to do something about it.

"Well, and what can I do for you today, my love?"

It was her old friend, the demon who had castrated Raymond Wakeling for her. This time he had taken the form of a recently discarded lover who had turned to drink when he finally realized the futility of his love, and had died under the wheels of a beer wagon on the east side of the city. Rhea smiled at his choice of guise.

"Louis' hair was just a shade darker, I think," she said, and raised her glass in a mock salute. She had set aside a special room for such visitations, and forbidden it to the servants. The demon returned her smile and his hair darkened.

"How is that?" he asked, walking to the very edge of the pentagram. He always did that, and very casually, as though he expected her to give him permission to depart from its confines.

"Better. I have a task that even you should find an interesting challenge."

"You want to have an affair with President Jackson," the demon ventured. Her laughter was a derisive snort.

"That overbearing fool! I'd have to burn the sheets afterward."

"Well, let me see," the demon mused, his eyes twinkling. "You want me to put Raymond Wakeling's appendage back in place so you can have a nostalgic try with him." Rhea manufactured a scowl, but couldn't maintain it.

"Forget that dolt," she ordered. "What I want has nothing to do with a man. Not directly with any particular man, at least."

"Ah, this is a novelty," the demon said with apparent interest. "To my recollection you have never asked anything of me that dealt with matters other than the heart."

"You know very well what I mean to ask of you," Rhea snapped. "You always do."

"Not this time, little mistress. I have deliberately neglected to look into your mind. Occasionally, I like to be surprised. Of course, if you wish me to—" Rhea poured herself a fresh glass of wine.

"Never mind. I don't mind telling you." Her heart was pounding, and her blood felt hot in her veins. Even wine didn't help, and she had to concentrate to keep her hand from shaking as she placed the glass on the arm of her chair. The demon looked at her attentively. "I want you to make me young again," she said. Then, without looking at him, she rushed on. "Not a child, of course. Early twenties should do just fine." Finally, she forced herself to look directly into his eyes. They were still twinkling, and for a moment she thought she had been apprehensive for no good reason. This demon had never failed her in anything in all the years she had made use of him. Then she saw that he was shaking his head, and that a wry smile had taken possession of the face he had assumed. It looked out of place there; Louis had never had the imagination to smile wryly about anything.

"So, you have finally begun to notice the advance of the years," he chuckled. "The curse of humanity, little mistress."

"Never mind the ironic comments," Rhea said, feeling a burning sensation along her skin. "Just perform your assigned task and be on your way." He was shaking his head again.

"No, little mistress. For once you have asked something that is beyond even my powers."

"Don't try to gull me. There is nothing beyond your powers. If you can arrange for a musket ball to blow off Raymond Wakeling's cock, you can smooth my skin and rejuvenate my circulation." Her anger was born of fear and disappointment. She who had enjoyed ultimate power, to die like anyone else, from old age?"

"There is no deceit in me at the moment, little mistress, for there is no need of it. To do as you ask would be a simple matter, were I allowed. But this power has been reserved by Him Who Must Be Obeyed. Were I tempted to grant your wish, the consequences would be disastrous for me, and for you as well." Rhea's legs tightened, and she had to fight to keep from leaping to her feet.

"And who is this personage of whom you are so solicitous? It would seem that you are afraid of him." The demon threw back his head and laughed. She thought he was laughing at the idea that he could be afraid of anything, but then she realized with chagrin that his laughter had been occasioned by her show of naivete.

"Only the most abysmal fool in the three worlds would fail to show trepidation at the thought of Him Who Must Be Obeyed."

"He is a mighty spirit?" she asked. Suddenly the demon's countenance lost its humor.

"His power is to mine as mine is to yours, little mistress. His intelligence is to mine as mine is to Raymond Wakeling's. Even this only suggests the gap between us. It does not describe it."

Her hands fluttered, picking at her skirt, rubbing the surface of her glass. Damn! She hadn't been fidgety within her memory. "Does He Who Must Be Obeyed have a less ponderous name?"

"Many. He has been given names by every culture of men as he has made himself known to them. I think you know some of his names."

"I have never believed that such an entity existed," Rhea said with irritation. She had not liked to think about it, in truth.

"He exists, as I exist."

"And only he can make me young again?"

"Let us say that on our side of the fence, he is the only one with that power." Rhea allowed herself to rise from her chair and pace. The demon watched her respectfully, with only the barest hint of his ironic twinkle.

"And how do I go about summoning this august demon?"

"He Who Must Be Obeyed is not a demon. He is to demons as men are to apes and monkeys. As to summoning him . . . ." He threw back his head and laughed more uproariously than before, as though the absurdity of the suggestion had only now commended itself to him. "One does not summon the great engine of evil, ma'am. If he wishes to come to you, he will do so."

"And can I command his power as I do yours?"

"Does his name suggest that he is subject to human orders?"

"Cease this display of jocularity at everything I ask," Rhea snapped. The demon frowned.

"Then I suggest you cease indulging in absurdities, little mistress. Now. You have given me a command which I cannot obey. Will you either give me another command or your permission to withdraw?" Rhea stepped very close to the demon. Only the single painted line of the pentagram's border separated them, and she saw the quickening of interest in his eyes, the working of his fingers, as he hoped that she might cross that protective border. She smiled coldly into the face that now filled her vision.

"Then go," she granted. "Until I need you again." For the moment he did not vanish, but smiled once more.

"You may go," Rhea said. "You may go where you belong." And suddenly she was looking at the wall behind the place where he had stood.

She sank into her chair and buried her face in her hands tiredly. For the first time in her life she felt old, though she was not yet in the middle of her forties. It was a premonition of years to come, the tiring of her body. She downed her wine and poured another glass, then drank half of that. It warmed her but did nothing to lessen the feeling of despair in her breast.

When one deals with demons, she thought, one must expect cruelty.

She wondered if she should have taken the demon's offer, and requested an audience with Him Who — with Satan. But the thought of it made her a child again, reviving the fears she had felt when first she had looked upon a demon in the basement of her father's house in Philadelphia. Those creatures, until she had learned their ways, had made a mockery of every command she had given them, using their intelligence, superior even to her own, to turn her fondest desires into a sour brew. How could she hope to deal with such a being as this? He would cheat her of whatever years she had left, spirit her off to his own domain and do — she didn't want to think of what he might do to her.

No, it was better to grow old, to cling to her life as best she could. It was a pretty good life, after all, and she had no reason to think it would grow less enjoyable just because she was amassing some years.

And so for the next few years Rhea contented herself with the compensations of a gracefully lovely middle age and the powers of the hellish hosts who had long been her servants. She plucked out the first silver strands that intruded among her golden locks and then, as they grew too numerous, took some satisfaction in the fact that they had chosen to grow in very striking veins, thick streaks that adorned her head like ribbons, and in their color, which was truly silvery and not the filthy gray that is the inheritance of many middle-aged women. Her face remained lovely, taking on the interesting quality that usually accures only to men, while retaining its former beauty in a slightly altered form. She looked in her mirror often, screwing up her courage to do so, and knew a momentary respite of her apprehensions each time, and then drank wine to keep from thinking of the days that lay ahead, when even her superb cells must bow to the relentless demands of the calendar's pages.

And so it was that in 1846, as President Polk signed the declaration of war against Mexico, Rhea looked forward with outraged frustration to her fiftieth birthday.

1975

Walter

In all of Walter Lankershim's life there was nothing that excited him more than an interesting case or a pretty girl. And since the matter of Phillip Stafford offered both, he encountered little difficulty in offering it his undivided attention. Before leaving Los Angeles, he stopped by his office to call the number that his client had given him.

"This is Walter Lankershim, Mr. Stafford," he said in reply to the cautious hello that greeted his first ring. "I have something to report."

"What is it?" The crystal clarity of their connection seemed to amplify the tightness of Stafford's voice, and Lankershim reflected almost sadly on how easy it would be to string this particular customer along and take him for a bundle, if that were the kind of private detective he had been.

"First of all, are you certain you want me to take a chance on alienating this lady?" he asked.

"What do you mean?" The tightness was supplemented by something approaching panic.

"Well, I had to wait until she left her apartment before I could do my thing," Walter said. "So I got a look at her. That's very fine merchandise. I wouldn't mind being led to my destruction by something like that."

"You're welcome to the experience," Stafford replied in a

voice that expressed relief and the asperity that often accompanies it. "What do you have to report?"

"Well, a little contact of mine at the L.A.P.D. ran her thumb print through the F.B.I. files for fifty bucks. It'll be on your expense account under miscellaneous."

"All right. Get on with it, please." They were always in such a hurry, Walter thought. Always eager to spoil his moment. But he spoke with deliberation, stretching things out just a fraction.

"Well, to begin with, her name isn't Rhea Carter. It's Susan Black. She's twenty-eight years old, and she's a lot richer than you are, if you don't mind my bluntness." There was a silence at the other end of the line that could have been stunned or merely wary.

"Inherited?" Stafford asked finally, and Walter chalked him one up for quickness.

"That's right, but not family. It's a weird story. In 1970 little Susan, or Rhea, or whatever you want to call her, got out of college and went to work as a private secretary and sort of manager for a woman here in L.A. Her employer was a wealthy spinster of thirty-five, reportedly a striking looking woman who had moved here from San Francisco at the age of twenty. Nobody I talked to knows much about her origins, but she had a pot full of dough, and was something of a recluse except for her servants, her boy friends, and an occasional girl friend. At least that was the rumor. About the girl friends, I mean." Walter shifted the phone from his right ear to his left and leaned back in his swivel chair, draping one long leg over the corner of his desk. If Stafford was impatient, he kept his silence. "So then," Walter continued, lighting a Marlboro from a pack on the desk, "little Susan moved into the house. There were some rumors, backed up later by the servants, that the lady and her manager were more than employer and employee."

"Shit. If that woman is a queer, I'll eat your shoes."

"Well, she could be a bi. Apparently that's what the old babe was. Or she may have just been accommodating a generous boss. She was extremely well paid, and the other servants weren't. Not above the usual scale. Then, about a year after this happy little affair started, Susan's employer suddenly died. A massive coronary occlusion, according to the coroner. And up pops a will that nobody knew anything about except her and her lawyer. Signed and witnessed a week before she died."

"Leaving everything to Rhea," Stafford stated rather than asked.

"Except for a few small bequests to the servants."

"How much did it come to?" Stafford asked tiredly.

"After state and federal taxes, about three million." Walter waited for some comment, then continued. "So, whatever she's after in your case, I'd say it's a fair bet it isn't money."

"All right." Pause. "What's the next step?" Walter hesitated, not certain he should tell the rest to his client. Then he took a last drag on his cigarette and stubbed it out in his beanbag ashtray.

"There's more," he said. "I checked on Susan's background. Nothing. She was an Orange County girl. Graduated from Pacifica High School, where she was a cheerleader and very well liked. Went on to Cal State Fullerton, majoring in social science, which makes it odd that she took a job as a glorified stenographer. Usual cadre of boy friends and two steadies while she was in high school, none in college. Very conventional."

"Yes?" Stafford said, finally yielding to his own impatience.

"So I decided to check out the employer herself. Get this. Fifteen years earlier, it seems she got out of a San Francisco high school and moved down here to become an actress. While she was here she worked part-time for a forty-year-old woman who was vacationing from San Francisco. Then, suddenly, she gave up her career and went to work full time for this gal. There were some whispers about their relationship. Then the employer, Elaine Arthur, died and left her fortune to the girl." In the silence that followed, Walter lit up another Marlboro and dropped the match into his ashtray.

"All right. I repeat my question: what next?"

"I want your authorization to drive up to San Francisco on expenses and question Miss Arthur's butler. He's still up there, retired from what I could gather."

"Look, this is all very interesting, but I don't see what it has to do with the case you were hired to investigate."

"I don't see what it has to do with it either, but it's a weird series of events, and my detective's instinct tells me it has something to do with it. That money seems to have a curse on it, don't you think? Twice in a row women have died in early middle-age and left it to younger, beautiful women. Neither of those women ever married, and neither has Susan Black, or Rhea Carter, or whoever you want to call her. Each time there has been at least a hint of a lesbian relationship, though the young girls seem to have been as normal as dew on a rose up to that time. Now something screwy is defintely going on, and I'd like to know what it is. I think you should want to know, too."

"All right. But I hope it isn't a wild goose chase."

"If it is, it won't be the first one I've been on. That's ninety percent of this business, Mr. Stafford, and you have to wade through a lot of it to get a little paydirt."

"I understand. Why don't you fly up?"

"I'd rather have my car. It's only a day's drive."

"Do as you think best, and keep in touch."

"I'll do that."

After hanging up, Walter stubbed his cigarette in the ashtray, then picked up the pack and dropped it into his shirt pocket. He put on his jacket, emptied the ashtray into his wastebasket, and pocketed it. He thought of the .38 Special in the right hand desk drawer, rejected the idea. This wasn't that kind of case. It was just the most interesting thing he'd ever been paid to investigate.

As soon as he was well clear of the city on Interstate 5, Walter turned on his CB radio. In a moment he had contact with a trucker up ahead.

"What's your twenty, ol' buddy?" he asked.

"Twenty miles north of Shakey, ol' buddy," the trucker replied, using the CB slang for Los Angeles. "What's yours?"

"About ten miles behind you. Can you give me a ten-thirteen?"

"The weather's sweet, the road's clear, and Smokey is nowhere in sight. You can put the pedal to the steel." Walter ten-foured the trucker's message and accelerated to seventy. Ten minutes later the trucker spoke his call sign.

"Ten-four, ol' buddy," Walter said. "You see Smokey?" He kept the needle on seventy, waiting for the reply. When there was none, he keyed up again. "Come on back?"

"No Smokey, old buddy. I just passed a real quality beaver hikin' right on the edge of the freeway, if you're interested. Come on back?"

"Good stuff, huh? Come on back?"

"I only got a quick look, but she looked U.S.D.A. Prime. I'da given her a ride myself, but the comp'ny's been crackin' down on that. Back?"

"That's thoughtful of you, sixteen-wheeler. I'll see what I can do about it. Ten-four?"

"Roger. This is Big Sixteen, ten-four and ten-ten."

Walter steadied the wheel with one hand and eased his wallet out with the other. There was a folded twenty in one of the pockets, that he kept for just such emergencies. He laid it on the seat next to him, stuffed the wallet back in place, then unfolded the twenty so it would be conspicuous. A few minutes later he saw the girl. She was wearing flared denim pants and a red top, and she carried a pack of some sort. It looked like army surplus. Long, light brown hair was bunched under a blue bandana. Her ass should have been a national monument, and when she turned to look in his direction, he saw a face that couldn't be over nineteen. She jutted out a thumb, jerked it professionally. Walter braked to a stop. Maybe the journey could be made as interesting as its purpose, he thought. In the rear-view mirror, the girl was coming at a dead run. He reached across and opened the door so she could slide in. A face with skin that glowed *sans* makeup, perfectly formed lips and wide brown eyes. Under the tight clothes her body looked superb. She was breathing a bit heavily from the run, and he was certain she wore no bra. Walter checked the side-view, flipped the turn signal, and pulled into the lane.

"Don't you know that walking on the freeway is illegal?" he asked with a smile, keeping his eyes on the asphalt.

"So's attempted rape." Slightly breathless, her voice alone was enough to give a man a hard-on. She slid down in the seat and rested her knee on the dash. It lent her a coltish look as sexy as it was charming.

"How's that?" he asked.

"The last guy who picked me up. The damned fool would have made out if he hadn't got rough. I can't abide that." She looked out the window a moment. "I'm not hard to get along with," she said casually. "And riding's better than walking." She glanced at the bill lying between them and smiled. Walter was a little sorry he had put it there now. It seemed unnecessary under the circumstances, but a small loss. His hands were cramped and slick on the wheel, and it took concentration to keep the car straight. "What do I have to do to deserve that?" she asked.

"Just not be hard to get along with, I suppose."

"Super." She picked up the twenty and slipped it into a little pocket on her top. It was a bowling shirt, with a penguin printed on it. The material was stretched tight across her breasts. "Now maybe I can afford a place to sleep tonight that won't have rocks in my cheeks."

"Where —" Walter cleared his throat and tried again. "Where you headed?"

"San Francisco."

"That's where I'm going. You have friends there?"

"Never been there. That's why I'm going." She was inspecting the scenery again. They pulled up through the pass, and Walter's ears started to pop. He wished just once he'd remember to stock up on chewing gum before starting this trip.

"Why don't you save your money and spend the night with me?" he offered. "I was planning on going halfway tonight and getting a motel."

"It's a deal, mister." She laid her head against the door and closed her eyes. "What's your name?"

"Walter."

"Hi, Walt. I'm Brenda." Her eyes still closed, she reached across her body and offered him her hand. Walter shook hands with Brenda. The softness of that cool, moist hand made him wonder if he should stop at Bakersfield.

1974

Rhea

Two years before Walter's San Francisco trek, Rhea sat in the basement of a Satanic church. The place was done in flat black paint, with black enamel trim. One wall had been excepted from this rule: at the end of the room, the wall was a bright red, actually crimson. A raised dais rested near that wall, bearing a black podium on which had been painted the effigy of a snarling dragon in red, doubtless from the same can of paint as the wall itself. On each side of the podium stood two chairs, in which young girls sat, bracketing the priest.

The priest was a tall man in a red robe and a hood thrown with studied casualness back behind his neck, revealing a Telly Savalas head. The narrowness of his eyes was emphasized by carefully applied makeup, and his cheeks had been darkened to make his face appear pinched and pointed. He had a deep rumbling voice which he had obviously learned to use in some commercial public speaking course. The fake drama of the whole thing had kept Rhea near the edge of laughter through the evening, and the few other meetings she had attended. But even the finest satire could grow tedious if it ran too long. She was thankful that the priest was just winding up his sermon.

'Health, wealth, the pleasures of the flesh, dear friends. These are the rewards Satan promises to his faithful followers. And he promises them to you now, and here, not in some mythical world to be revealed after you are safely dead and unable to testify to others regarding its authenticity. Join the winning side — worship Satan — and see your most exciting fantasies come true. See your enemies smitten, and your years multiplied." The candlelight flickered across his face, aided, for practical purposes, by the few electric lights which had been turned on for this meeting. The people sat spellbound, for the most part. The girls on the dais brushed back the sleeves of their black robes and applauded, cueing the audience, who followed suit. Rhea applauded, too. The priest raised his hands gently for silence.

"And now, my friends, before we adjourn for the night, my brothers in Satan will pass among you to accept your offerings, while I offer prayer for the benefit of all who are here in the Master's name."

Two men, one young and one middle-aged, passed through the audience with collection baskets on long wooden poles. Change clinked, here and there a bill rustled. Rhea dropped in a five-dollar bill. The show had been worth it. The priest droned some uninspired prayer entreating Satan to protect those who were here in his sacred name and to smite the enemies of all true believers. Rhea stifled a yawn. Her endurance had been stretched at this meeting. It was time for the farce to end. The people began to gather up their belongings and make their way to the door as the prayer terminated in perfect synchronization with the collection. Rhea slipped the shoulder strap of her alligator bag over her shoulder and rose, making her way to the exit.

Her car was parked on the street. Rhea slid into it and turned on the ignition. The Mercedes came alive, emitting a gentle and sonorous rumble. She sat in the car for several minutes, watching the other vehicles pull out while the workers closed up the church, locking the doors. One car, an old Chevy, whirred and churned and coughed. Finally the door of the old car opened and a thick, squat figure emerged hurriedly. Skirts jouncing, the woman moved toward the church, trying to get there before the building would be deserted. Rhea put the Mercedes in gear and pulled quietly onto the grounds, stopping directly in the woman's path. She pressed the switch on the door and the driver's side window whirred down. The woman stopped, looking at the car and at Rhea. She was in her early thirties, but could have passed for forty. Gray hair protruded from under her hat. Her figure was dumpy and unappealing, and her skin looked sallow even in this light.

"I couldn't help noticing you were having some trouble, dear," Rhea said sweetly. "Would you like a ride?"

"Well, I — I was just going to ask if I could use the phone inside, to call the auto club."

"Why bother them? I can drive you down to the coffee shop on the corner and you can call from there, if you want."

"Well, I —" The woman looked at the car again as though it fascinated her. "Well, if it wouldn't be too much trouble." She had a voice, Rhea noticed for the twentieth time, like a busy signal. She jounced around the front of the Mercedes and opened the right side door, sliding in. "God," she said. "I've lived in places that weren't this good."

"It's a nice car," Rhea agreed, setting it in motion and turning toward the street.

The coffee shop was a block and a half north of the Satanic church. It belonged to one of the smaller chains specializing in canned and dehydrated foods and adorable waitresses in miniskirts. Rhea tugged her companion toward a back booth, assuring her that she could call the motor club later. "There's no school tomorrow anyway," she reminded her. "It's Saturday."

A blond waitress in a short red dress perked up to them and asked if they wanted coffee. Both women demurred. Rhea asked for a menu while her friend ordered tea with an artificial sweetener. After perusing the menu, Rhea ordered pancakes and tea.

"What did you think of the church, Brenda?" she asked when the waitress had left them alone.

"So you know my name, too," Brenda said.

"Too?"

"Besides the fact that I'm a teacher." Brenda looked at Rhea with a tinge of suspicion.

"It isn't hard to find out about people, and I'm insatiably curious. At least about people I admire." The waitress returned with their tea. She set the metal pots before the two women, then fished some packets of Sweet 'n Low from a little pocket in her stiffly starched dress. Rhea noticed Brenda looking at the girl with a mixture of yearning and resentment. The waitress had a trim figure and legs that could have graced a calendar in a barber shop.

"And you admire me?" Brenda asked when they were alone again. She was tearing open her tea bag as though it were an enemy.

"Oh, I admire anyone who tries to do something about his or her problems. And who's broad-minded about solutions." Brenda had poured two packets of Sweet 'n Low into her tea and was stirring it after carefully wiping the spoon with a paper napkin from the dispenser. She had discarded one napkin and used the second one. Compulsively sanitary, Rhea thought, and filed the information away.

"And you think I'm that kind of person."

"If you weren't, you wouldn't be spending time in that ridiculous church." Rhea tore open a couple of packets of Crystal sugar

189

and emptied then into her own teacup, then poured the hot tea in and stirred. The waitress materialized again, smiling with professional friendliness, and leaned across the table to set a plate in front of Rhea. It bore three medium-sized pancakes, a paper container with a ball of creamery butter, and a crockery server with hot maple syrup.

"Will there be anything else, ma'am?"

"Why, yes," Rhea said. "I'd like some extra butter and syrup, please. Put them on the check." When the waitress was gone, she began to spread the butter across her pancakes. Brenda was looking at them the same way she had looked at the waitress. "Would you like some?" Rhea offered sweetly. "The evening's on me."

"If I ate that, I'd gain three pounds by morning," Brenda grumbled.

"Yes, that must be a problem. I've never had to worry about weight." The waitress came back, placing the extra butter and syrup in front of Rhea. Rhea spread the butter and lavished the pancakes with maple syrup.

"You've never had to worry about anything, to look at you," Brenda said with a touch of anomosity mixed with grudging admiration.

"Why thank you, dear. That's a sweet compliment." Rhea shoved a forkful of pancake into her mouth.

"What did you mean by that crack about my going to the Satanic church?" Brenda's eyes were boring holes through the space between them.

"It wasn't a crack. I simply meant that you went there, as did most of those people, because you've tried every other way to get what you want, and none of it has worked. You've become a little desperate. But that priest isn't going to get it for you either, Brenda. He's a charlatan." She speared another morsel of pancake and ate it.

"While you're revealing all this, why don't you tell me what it is that I want?" Brenda's tone was hurt and challenging.

"You want to be young and beautiful. You want men to fall all over you." Brenda picked up her black patent bag and started to slide out of the booth.

"Didn't anyone ever tell you not to make fun of people who are less fortunate than you?" she demanded. There was a teary shine to her eyes.

"You can have everything you want," Rhea said. "Very easily, too." The older woman froze, looking at her.

"How? You just said it was all a fake."

"That priest is a fake. He knows no more about Satan than you do. But Satan is no fake. Nor am I." Their eyes held for a long moment. Rhea could see that Brenda was still hesitant, reluctant to believe what she obviously hoped was true, and to open herself to a cruel joke. "You listened to that fraud for two hours tonight. And you dropped a dollar into the collection basket."

"You've been watching me closely, haven't you?"

"Why don't you listen to me for ten minutes? It won't cost you a nickle. I'll even buy you another pot of tea." Brenda sat there for a moment, staring into Rhea's face, searching for the merest hint of ridicule. She was breathing raggedly. Finally she slid back to her place.

"I'll pay for my own tea," she said.

1846

Rhea

Unlike most women of her day, Rhea Carter read the newspaper daily.

The Mexican ambassador to the United States was livid, in compliance with instructions from Mexico City. He was dutifully, and doubtless genuinely, angry with General Zachary Taylor of the United States Army, and particularly at President James Polk for allowing and encouraging the general to venture into Mexican territory. Many people were convinced that war with Mexico was imminent.

Aside from increasing her stock holdings in various munitions and explosives firms, Rhea Carter paid the probable onset of hostilities no heed. It was a Westerner's fight, she felt, and not likely in the least to discommode her in New York. Furthermore, she could see no reason why she should concern herself over the question of whether the United States annexed some land on the western coast of the continent. Certainly no place with such an exotic and foreign sounding a name as California could bear upon her life in any significant degree.

She was far more concerned with Roger Mead and his sister Charity. Roger himself was no problem. When she had met him he had quickly shown himself to possess an artistic temperament with very little talent to back it up. He had first moved in with her because he was convinced that his destiny was to be the first American painter equal to Titian and Michelangelo. Rhea had refrained from laughing at his pretensions because he was over six feet tall, dark complected, and blessed with dark brown eyes that seemed to snap sparks when he was excited. His features were masculine and sensitive at once, with a strong jawline and a delicately curved nose; his thick, wild black hair, that seemed to jut in every direction like bayonet grass when he hadn't combed it recently, was possibly the most exciting touch of all. When he made love to her she liked to tangle her long, slender fingers in that hair. There was a pulse in his scalp, and she had learned to gauge the extent of his sexual arousal by the frequency of that pulse.

He was twenty-three years old, and by far the most attractive man she had managed to attract in a decade. The obvious fact that he was using her as a financial stepping stone to the recognition he would never achieve didn't bother her much. At least he was with her because he wished it that way, and not through the offices of her cadre of demons. That, at least, was how it was at the beginning.

It was Roger's temper that doomed him. His temper and his stupid masculine pride, coupled with a bit of overconfidence in his charms. He had chosen to take offense at too many things, possibly under the gross misconception that this kind of impudent behavior would make him all the more attractive to Rhea. She was not accustomed to taking nonsense from men, and one night, during a particularly stormy encounter, he had cornered himself with a threat to leave. Rhea, equally enraged, had taken him at his word and ordered the servants to pack his belongings.

Roger, like many weak men, was possessed of an almost dangerous stubbornness that served to compensate to some degree for his lack of genuine strength. He would not return without some gesture on her part. For the first night she didn't care whether he returned or not. She lay alone in her bed, still angry with him, and subliminally rebuked herself for having lost her temper and taken his threat seriously. The next morning she was still irritated, but she missed him, too. It had been her first night alone in three months, and the unspent passions which she had become accustomed to relieving with Roger increased her irritability.

It was obvious what she must do if she wanted Roger Mead back in her bed without sacrificing her own independence. Still, she continued to wait, hoping that he would yield to the common sense of the situation. She wouldn't even demand an apology, she decided; only the gesture of his return. Two days later the gesture had not been tendered.

Approaching her fiftieth birthday, Rhea was still a woman of remarkable if increasingly mature beauty, and she was one of the wealthiest women in the city. Buying a lover would have been a simple matter. But with the perversity that marks a personality unaccustomed to external disciplines, Rhea convinced herself that she would be satisfied by nothing other than Roger Mead's dark and muscular frame sprawled atop her. By the third day she knew what she would have to do. It had been a foolish act of self-punishment, she decided, to wait this long.

Just before noon on Monday, Rhea repaired to her secret room, locking the door behind her and dropping the one key, on its silver chain, down the front of her dress. With swiftness born of long practice, she lit the candles and mumbled the incantation.

By one-thirty Roger was knocking on the door. She allowed her butler to see him to the parlor, and let him wait for two hours while she bathed and groomed herself. Nearly thirty-five years of experience had taught her something of the power of her demons, and she knew that, now that she had allowed herself to resort to that device, there was nothing she could not do to Roger with impunity.

He was already standing when she entered the room. She had put on a plain gray dress, almost ostentatiously uninviting, and had tied her silver and blond hair in a tight bun behind her head. Her only concession to physical appeal had been to splash on some tantalizing fragrance from Paris. He stood there with his hat in front of him, held low. She knew what he was hiding, and it excited her. Still, this was a time for restraint, she thought, and knew that her eyes were sparkling with the exhilaration she always felt when she was in complete control of another human being.

"So you've come back." she said coldly. He choked on his reply. "I suppose you expect to move right back in." Her tone offered no hope, and she saw his eyes take on a panicky expression.

"I — had hoped —" His voice, usually deep and mellifluous, was cracked with tension and emotion. Rhea sank into a comfortable chair, leaning back almost grandly. Roger started to sit on the sofa, but she stabbed a look at him and he remained on his feet, a supplicant.

"Can you think of one reason why I should have you?" His face reddened. She saw a spark of anger in his eyes, quickly extinguished by bafflement at this unfamiliar and overwhelming need that he felt. Rhea was still angry with him for having forced her to seek supernatural aid in bringing him back. Resting her elbows on the arms of the chair, she made a steeple with her fingertips. "If I do take you back," she purred, "it will be on my terms." His face was a deep crimson now. She knew he wanted to kill her. He lowered his gaze, making the long, dark lashes seem even more prominent. He nodded silently. "Did you hear me?" Rhea demanded.

"Of course, Rhea," he mumbled. "Name your terms."

"I have no intention of naming them. I prefer to keep them

open, and to amend them as I see fit." He nodded again, totally defeated, and she restrained the urge to laugh with delight. "And now," she drawled, "we'll begin with an apology. A properly sincere and abject once."

It had been six weeks since that satisfying day, and Roger had offered her no more trouble. Rhea had come to think of him as an attractive pet. In the bedroom he was more ardent than ever, driven by a passion far stronger than himself; and far more accommodating as well, since they both knew that his need for Rhea was far greater than her desire for him. The rest of the time she kept him in his garret, turning out indifferent paintings. It was the only way to keep him from following her about like a pathetic mongrel.

Then, three weeks after his capitulation, the letters began to arrive. He had received one occasionally in the days previous to the change in their relationship, but Rhea had never questioned him about them. She had been tempted to do so, the more since they were written on small sheets of fairly decent notepaper that carried a vague fragrance. They had stopped for a while after his short sojourn away from the house, then suddenly reappeared. Now, when the first one appeared on the letter tray one morning, Rhea opened it casually, read it and handed it across the table to fidgeting Roger.

"You didn't tell me you had a sister," she said in a mildly accusatory tone. He accepted the letter, held it in a tight, crumpling grasp.

"No? It must have —" He was looking at the crumbs of bacon on his plate. "I didn't think you'd be interested," he finished lamely.

"Did you not, dear heart?" Rhea spread maramalade on a morsel of toast and ate it. "Aren't you going to read your sister's letter, dear?"

"I'll read it later."

"I'll tell you what it says. She has learned that you've returned to that house you were wise enough to leave some weeks ago. She implores you to leave that terrible woman whose attentions can only bring you grief." Rhea paraphrased the letter only slightly. Her voice carried a mock dramatic tone.

"Please, Rhea. She doesn't even know you."

"It sounds as though she knows me quite well. Tell me, darling, are you going to take her advice?" He looked at her sharply. "You're free to go at any time."

"You know I'll never leave you. Not willingly," he amended.

"Well, that's entirely your concern, Roger."

And that was the end of it for a few days. Then another letter arrived, and two days later a third. They all said much the same, and the writing style was repetitious and unimaginative. Rhea began to feel annoyed. She had formed a mental image of the girl, slight and mousey, a born school teacher wallowing in the opportunity to take out her directive instincts on her handsome big brother. When the fifth letter arrived, she didn't even allow Roger to read it, but after scanning it herself in his presence tossed it casually into the fireplace. A hard swallow was his only protest.

During the second week of this hail of communiques, Rhea determined to have some fun at the expense of the Meads. The letters originated at a small town fifty miles north of New York City. One day she opened the current one at the breakfast table and read it, then looked across at Roger. She rose, gathering her white silk robe about her, and moved toward her writing table. She looked back, as though slightly surprised that he hadn't followed her.

"Come, dear," she said, and he approached, a frown of concern on his handsome face. "Sit down." She indicated the chair in front of the writing table and he sank into it, looking up at her with plain apprehension.

"Your dear sister has been so diligent in showing her solicitude, Roger," she said, stroking his hair in a patronizing manner, "that I think it only fair that we invite her to come here for a visit, so she can see firsthand that I am not the monster she conceives me to be."

"No!" His cry caused her eyebrows to arch. Roger's hands reached up supplicatingly, clutched at her waist. "Rhea, please leave Charity alone. She can't harm you. She's only a child, and concerned for me." He looked up into her uncompromising eyes. "I'll never leave you if that is your worry," he said, and then bit his lip as she smiled with genuine amusement.

"Worry?" She stroked his hair again, shaking her head as at a child. "Why, Roger, dear, I can't imagine anything that concerns me less." Suddenly grasping his hair, she twisted his countenance toward the quill and inkwell. "Now write."

He hesitated, expending what will was left in him. Then, as though it were something apart from him, a giant, fleshy insect, his hand crawled to the pen, plucked it free, and dipped it. His other hand pulled a sheet of notepaper toward him. Rhea began to dictate, but his reluctance showed in the wavery scrawl he produced. She tore the sheet from under his pen, crumpled it, and dropped it to the carpet.

"Neatness is a virtue, dear," she reminded him. "Start over."

Once again her voice issued crisply, composing for him a brotherly invitation to his sister. He wrote very slowly, his motions laborious but his characters neat and sharp. Rhea gave herself over to the task of composition, inserting humorous protestations of affection. She was thoroughly enjoying his chagrin, indulging herself. To her at this point it was only a game, but unknown to her, Rhea

Carter's life was about to take its most fateful turn.

1976

Walter

Victor Banks lived in a four-bedroom, two-bath home in Hayward, California. That was why it had taken so long to track him down, Walter thought with a touch of wryness. On the other hand, he had a client who could afford a lot of his time, and some extraordinary expenses, such as the twenty-dollar bills and the single fifty that had crossed the palms of some people in the search for Mr. Banks. Certainly Walter was far more honest about his expense account than most private investigators. For instance, he had been paying double occupancy rates at the motels, but only putting down the single rates on his tab. Brenda didn't come under the heading of a legitimate business expense. She just made the trip a lot more fun than it would have been alone.

Now she sat on a small Spanish-styled stool, with leather straps on all three sides, wearing the same blue jeans and a different top, and examined the books on Victor Banks' shelves. Victor Banks occasionally looked across the width of his generously proportioned living room at Brenda, particularly when she stretched a bit, reaching for a book, and her top was pulled up, revealing some smooth white skin. Walter stifled his annoyance at this display of interest in a girl he had come to think of as his, and fed his amusement. The amusement was laced with a soupçon of awe, since Victor Banks, by his own accounting, was eighty-two years old.

"Is your coffee adequate?" Banks asked in his very subtle

British accent. He was dressed in a pair of expensive old slacks and a silk smoking jacket. Bluish smoke hung heavily around his head as he puffed on a Churchill cigar. He looked remarkable for a man of his age. He seemed never to have lost a hair, and there was a lot of black left among the gray. His face was wrinkled, but his eyes were alert and clear, with whites that had only the slightest traces of red in them, right around the pupils. His hand was as steady as a surgeon's. "Would you care for a fresh cup?"

"No, thank you," Walter said, smiling at the old man.

"I hope there is nothing wrong with it," Banks said with what sounded like real concern.

"It's the best coffee I've ever tasted."

"Thank you." There was real pride in his voice. "You know, my employers always insisted that I make coffee for them every morning. I usually brought a cup to their bedrooms. And for meals, of course. That is usually not regarded as a duty for a butler," he finished with a touch of pomposity.

"You must have been an excellent butler," Walter said, not in the least averse to buttering the old man up a bit. "You've certainly done all right for yourself." He indicated the house and furnishings with a vague gesture.

"I have done all right for myself, yes." Banks looked past Walter as Brenda stood and stretched, reaching for a volume on the top shelf and tightening the jeans about her butt. "My last two employers were stockbrokers. With their advice, I was able to make some excellent investments." His eyes returned to Walter's for a moment, then flicked away as Brenda sat on the stool. Walter wished now that he had resisted her blandishments and left her at the motel, or given her some money to buy a few clothes, or sent her to the movies. But she could be a difficult woman to resist, especially when she nudged a man with those breasts as they lay in bed and said that she had never met an honest-to-God butler before, and they were an endangered species.

"I'm sure you did very well, Mr. Banks," Walter said, trying to win back the man's attention. "But the former employer I'm here to talk about is Elaine Arthur."

"Yes, of course, Miss Arthur." Banks took a puff on his cigar, leaning back in the leather couch, and looked at not much of anything, or perhaps the Rembrandt print on his wall. "Yes, Miss Arthur was — a most unusual woman." He smiled apologetically, as though it were an infraction on his part to talk about an employer, even one who had been dead and buried for more than twenty years.

"Eccentric?" Walter asked. Banks mused for a moment, as though examining the question with British caution.

"Yes, I suppose one might be justified in using such a word

to describe Miss Arthur. I say, you're not going to quote me on anything are you?" Walter shrugged. He had told Banks he was researching an article for *Gentleman's Quarterly*.

"Only what you give me permission to quote," he assured his host. "And, of course, if we use any names they'll be fictitious." That seemed to placate Victor Banks' conscience. He was glancing toward Brenda again, but Walter didn't look to see what she had done to capture their host's attention. He was beginning to think it had been a stroke of luck having her along. She had probably got him into the house, and just possibly the desire to prolong her presence was keeping the old fart talking.

"Miss Arthur had excellent taste, of course. The finest decorations, cuisine, all that. But she had her little quirks. A proper servant does not question his employer's quirks, Mr. Lankershim. One is not hired to invade one's benefactor's privacy." He pronounced "privacy" with a short "i".

"Certainly not," Walter agreed with some vehemence. "But now, after all these years, you might be able to tell us some of Miss Arthur's eccentricities. They would make interesting reading, Mr. Banks. And no one will know who she was."

"Oh, well, she had a little room upstairs. Or perhaps it was a big room. I don't know, because none of the servants was ever allowed there, and neither was any guest, so far as I ever knew. Sometimes Miss Arthur would retire to that room for a little while, and we knew that she was not to be disturbed under any circumstances. Once when I rose late at night to check on a faulty appliance, I passed quite close by that room, and I was certain I heard voices from within. Of course I didn't eavesdrop," he said, looking as though Walter had accused him. "But I couldn't help hearing just a few syllables as I passed. I could swear that what I heard was Miss Arthur's voice and that of someone else, a gentleman."

"Some people talk to the radio or TV set," Walter suggested.

"Perhaps." Banks didn't seem satisfied with the explanation. "She never married, you know. Although she could have had any or all of a dozen wealthy and distinguished husbands. Not that she did without masculine companionship, you understand. Miss Arthur had many gentleman callers. She was just a young woman when I entered her employment, and so the gentlemen were quite naturally young as well. But as she grew older, they did not."

"What sort of men did she favor?" Walter didn't really care about Elaine Arthur's sex life, but he had to sound like a reporter. Banks knocked the ash off his cigar into a crystal ashtray, and then regarded the glowing tip with sedulous attention.

"Oh, all kinds," he said. "She was quite — democratic in that sense." There was a touch of distaste in his voice. Then he put the cigar into his mouth and smiled at Walter.

"Were you with her until her death?" Walter asked.

"Oh, my yes. Quite a surprise it was. She was a young woman still, no more than forty-five if that, and probably younger. She died of some sort of virus. It was quite swift, a matter of two or three days. It must have affected her brain, because toward the end she wasn't quite herself."

"Not herself?" Walter tried to sound casual about the question but his pulse was quickening, and he felt that excitement that always came to him when some arduous mining began to pay off.

"Oh, just some delusions. Rather ungentlemanly of me to mention them, I'm afraid."

"Oh, I don't think that matters now, do you, Mr. Banks?"

"Well, I suppose at this remove —" He looked in Brenda's direction again. She was replacing the book and standing on tiptoe as she scanned the top shelf for another.

"Do you suppose I might have another cup of that coffee after all?" Walter asked. Banks smiled at him delightedly.

"I knew you wouldn't be able to resist it," he said, rising with astonishing agility and picking up Walter's cup. In a moment he was back. He placed a fresh cup of coffee on the arm of Walter's chair like the impeccably trained servant he had never ceased to be, then returned to his couch and retrieved the cigar from its ashtray. It had turned cold, and he lit it with a match from a plain white book.

"You were saying?" Walter asked. Brenda was safely engrossed in another book.

"What was I saying? Oh, yes. Miss Arthur's delusion. She had a young secretary for the last few months of her life. A strikingly lovely woman, hardly more than a girl, named —" He paused, then lowered his gaze, rubbing his forehead with four wrinkled fingers. "I'm afraid my memory isn't what it used to be." Walter knew perfectly well what the name of the secretary had been, but kept it to himself. Finally Banks looked up again, his eyes showing triumph and delight. "Oh, yes, Miss Platz. Sally Platz. Just out of secondary school, as I recall, though she had spent some time in Hollywood, in an abortive attempt at an acting career. A tall girl with auburn hair. People used to mistake her for Rita Hayworth. She lived in, as did the other employees." Something, a mere shadow of a memory, crossed Banks' eyes, and Walter knew he wouldn't speak of the suspected intimacy between Elaine Arthur and Sally Platz. "Well, Mr. Lankershim," he continued with a new note of vitality, as though glad he had caught himself before mentioning the unmentionable, "just before Miss Arthur died she fell prey to a very strange conception. Possibly no one would ever have known of it, if not for the one time when she regained her faculties, or what was left of them. I had gone into her room to see to her well-being, and she opened her eyes. Rather startling, the way she stared up at me. She grasped at my sleeve, as I recall, with rather astonishing vigor, and then she spoke to me. She seemed quite lucid, though it was obviously an effort to talk." He knocked the ash off his cigar and puffed at it once again. Walter restrained an urge to shake the story out of the old man. He took a sip of his coffee.

What did she say?" he asked. He noticed that even Brenda seemed to be listening to the story. Banks smiled, clearly enjoying his moment.

"She fancied that she was Miss Platz. She begged me to help her. Said that Miss Arthur had stolen her body." He resumed his inspection of his burning cigar. "Rather pathetic, what? Still, I suppose it's an understandable belief. Brought on, no doubt, by her fear of death, and her envy of a younger and healthier woman."

"No doubt." Walter finished his coffee and put down the cup, rising. "And now, Mr. Banks, I think we've taken up enough of your time."

"Not at all. Not at all. I enjoy guests. One must keep one's interests alive, mustn't one?" He glanced toward Brenda, who was replacing the book, stretching once again. "There is one other point that might interest you," he said to Walter. "Except for some bequests to the servants of long standing, Miss Arthur left her entire estate to Miss Platz. Miss Platz, of course, was astounded. She had known nothing of the will until the day it was read."

"Pleasantly astounded, no doubt."

"No doubt." He saw them to the door. "The human mind is a wondrous thing, is it not, sir?" he remarked, and his eyes showed old, old memories once again.

"How's that?"

"The day Miss Arthur revealed her delusions to me, her voice seemed altered. As though, unconsciously, she had taken on Miss Platz's—" He searched for the word. " —inflections." Walter stared at the old man for a moment.

"Yes, that certainly is strange. Mr. Banks, I have one more question, if it's not an imposition." Banks smiled encouragingly while Brenda fidgeted, bored now that she had been deprived of the library. "Do you happen to know how Miss Arthur came into her fortune?" Banks blinked.

"Oh, indeed no, sir. I should never inquire into such matters."

"No, of course you wouldn't. I just thought you might have overheard something. Whether it was inherited, or —"

"Inherited. Yes, I do recall, vaguely, that she mentioned that once in my presence. She was talking to a young gentleman at the time. She referred to it as a stroke of fortune, though I'm sure I don't know what she meant by that." Walter looked at the retired butler for a moment, then shrugged.

"Well, I guess it's my job as a journalist to find out."

1846

Rhea

To amuse herself, Rhea had the servants clean the house from top to bottom the day before Charity Mead's projected arrival. "I am expecting an honored guest," she told the butler, injecting into her voice sufficient irony to be certain he wouldn't miss it. Roger was present at the time.

Rhea had looked forward with relish to the meeting. She had a very clear impression of what the girl would be like. A mousey and intense little thing, no doubt, much like Theresa Dalrymple, before the latter had changed overnight from inane virgin to vapid matron. For that very reason Rhea was determined to play all the social games to the hilt, and to welcome Charity with an outward show of benign cordiality. Aside from her constant ragging of Roger, it would be the first thing she had done in years that might introduce some zest into her life. So she told herself, for having never lived without zest, she was as unaware of its presence as was primitive man of air.

On the big day she rose early, bathed, and donned one of her finest dresses, deliberately choosing one a bit more daring than was perhaps quite proper for such an occasion. The body of the dress was form fitting, and it was cut quite low in front. Since little Charity was convinced that her brother's keeper was an immoral woman, it seemed inhospitable not to support the conception.

As she was putting on the finishing touches in the form of a rather strong French perfume, Rhea became aware of some commotion in front of the house. She went to the window and looked down to see a coach at her curb. The footman scrambled down from his perch, opened the door and stood starchily. Just before dropping the curtain back into place, Rhea glimpsed a slender woman in a demure pale green dress emerging with graceful care.

She went to the room which Roger used for his painting. He was dabbing at a canvas. At her entrance, he looked around blankly, nervously. Rhea was beginning to grow a bit impatient with Roger, bored with the stultifying docility that had come over him. He had always been a weak and characterless man, but his pretenses of pride and integrity had at least been amusing, and a source of challenge. It was always this way when a man was enchanted: to begin, she was elated at having him at her beck, pleased to be able to relax and act any way she chose in his presence, relieved to know that there was no need for concern, since he would never have the strength to leave her, or even to go against her in any matter, however trivial. Then boredom, as the man's slavishness took on that debilitating sameness. They lost so much personality when they finally surrendered to their state. It was like watching the same play with several different actors all supervised by the same director. The face and figure were different, but there was no variety in the dialogue or incidents. Her boredom invariably led Rhea to increasing snappishness with the men, and prompted her to take whatever delight she could find in grinding them down still more.

Now she looked Roger up and down, noting his unshaven face and the wrinkled clothes he wore.

"Roger, my dear, stupid little man," she said in a mock sweet voice, "I cannot believe that I neglected to mention to you that this is the day on which your sister is due to arrive." She gave him a chance to reply, then went on in the same treacly tones. "Why on earth aren't you turned out to receive her properly, dear?"

"I — I don't wish to receive her," he mumbled in a poor attempt at defiance. Rhea shook her head in wry wonder.

"Darling, do you still delude yourself that your wishes are of any moment?" Closing the door behind her, Rhea advanced on him slowly. "If you wish to leave my presence forever, that can be arranged very easily. But I don't wish to hear of any other wishes from you, ever again. Is that clear?" This time she waited long enough so that he had to reply.

"Yes, Rhea, I — I'm sorry. Please make my excuses to my sister, and tell her I'll be there just as soon as I can.

"Yes, dear," Rhea said, reaching forward and patting him on the cheek in a patronizing show of affection. "Now put away your paint set like a good little boy, and bathe and shave and dress in your Sunday clothes, and then repair either to the parlor or the street!"

She turned her back on a fresh apology and left the room, this time leaving the door open. Stopping to check herself in the full-length mirror that hung on the hallway wall, and patting the hair piled splendidly atop her head, she walked to the stairs. The butler was just trudging up them. He stopped and bowed.

"Miss Charity Mead has arrived, ma'am," he said. "I showed her into the parlor."

"Fine," Rhea said, noticing three worn bags that had been placed in the entrance way, near the wall. "Place her bags in the burgundy room and see that tea is prepared." The butler bowed again.

"I have already given instructions regarding the tea, madam," he intoned in the sonorous and slightly offended voice of a professional, and went after the bags. Rhea smiled to herself, looking forward with a surge of exhilaration to the experience of reducing this simpering little girl to tears of frustration and self-pity. Hurrying to the parlor door, she paused and stood for a moment, assuming her most queenly posture, then opened the door and entered.

Later Rhea would realize that her first sight of Charity Mead should not have been a shock. Considering her brother's looks, there was no reason to suppose that the girl would be anything less than a beauty. Still, that she should be such a rare beauty as this could not have been foreseen. Roger was a common-looking creature next to his sister. She was tall and rather large for a woman, though her excellent posture gave the impression of slenderness. As she turned from the window to face Rhea, her full-bosomed body seemed to flow like a liquid, portions of it turning at different rates of speed, yet all of it remaining intact in a curious sort of unconscious grace. Her hair, worn in a braided bun at the back of her head, was of no precise color. Depending on where the sun struck it, it could be brown or auburn or perhaps nearly as black as Roger's. Her face, quite simply, was perfection. Features that were finely chiseled, fragile enough so that one might fear to touch them, yet with bold blue-green eyes and a mouth cut to generous, almost large, proportions. She had removed her hat, and held it before her like a bouquet. Without offering Rhea her hand she bowed slightly, her eyes seeming to take in the older woman instantly. They snapped like flint.

"You must be Charity." Her senior years and her experience in meeting people on better than even terms helped Rhea in concealing her astonishment at the vision before her. She spoke sweetly. "I've so been looking forward to meeting you." If she had expected this ploy to disarm her guest, Rhea was disappointed. The girl looked at her with that same combative expression. She didn't smile, but only nodded. Rhea indicated a wingback chair near the fireplace. "You must be exhausted after your journey," she said. "I've ordered tea sent in to us while we make friends." Here she stopped and smiled. "Then you will surely want to go to your room and rest until dinner." Charity stood for a moment, making no indication that she had noticed the gesture toward the wingback chair. Then she turned and walked there, sitting with that same remarkable grace. She moved like a trained mannequin, Rhea thought, and found that the girl's motions elicited a strange excitement in her.

She followed, sat in a huge horsehair armchair facing the wingback, spreading her dress about her with chaste elegance. "Your brother sends his apologies," she said, folding her hands in her lap just as Charity had done. "He was not ready to receive you. I'm afraid I scolded him rather severely. He's so like a little boy, don't you agree? And when he starts playing with his paints and brushes, some sternness is often required, I'm afraid."

"I fear I have never thought of Roger's work as 'playing,' Miss Carter." The girl's voice had a mellifluous quality that was soothing and exciting at once. One graceful eyebrow arched, and she smiled icily. "It is still Miss Carter, is it not?"

"Why, yes, dear, that's right." There was a soft, discreet rap at the door. "That would be the tea, I'm sure." Rhea called out permission to enter. A middle-aged maid brought in a heavy silver tray laden with an ornate teapot on a stand, some cakes, and all the paraphernalia appropriate thereto. She wheeled the stand between the two chairs and, with a perfunctory curtsy, took her departure.

"I trust your journey was a pleasant one, dear," she said with the same sweetness as before, pouring a cup of tea for Charity.

"I fear that the tenor of a journey is determined by one's expectations of the destination, Miss Carter." There wasn't the slightest quaver in the girl's voice as she spoke, nor did she reveal a sign of regret once the words had been uttered. Rhea smiled quite artlessly. The girl intrigued and delighted her. She couldn't remember when anyone had dared to address her in such blunt terms.

"I'm sorry it wasn't more pleasant for you. Sugar or cream?"

"Plain, if you don't mind."

"I don't mind at all, dear. I prefer things plain, too." Rhea handed Chairty the steaming cup. "Now you must have one of these cakes. My cook is a wizard at baking." She speared a cake and placed it on a small plate, then passed it over, setting it on the stand before Charity. Then she poured for herself and took another cake. "Now," she said. "We have observed the amenities. And we can talk."

"Miss Carter, I don't wish to quarrel with you. I've come to take Roger home with me."

"Fine. Tell him so. He is free to leave any time he wishes."

Charity looked suspicious. To give her some time to think, she took a sip of the tea, which was still too hot, and then a bite of her cake.

"I should like to leave with him tomorrow morning. If you've no objections."

"Why none at all. You have your brother to convince, dear, not me." Charity's expression hardened. Her delicate chin set, and her nostrils flared. It was like a ballet, Rhea thought with fascination, watching this girl's face.

"You don't think he'll come with me, do you?" she demanded.

"I know he won't. But, of course, you are free to make the attempt." The tea was far too hot to drink. Rhea set her cup on the table, nibbled at her cake, and then placed it beside the saucer. Charity was pensive for a moment, then apparently decided to try a different tack.

"Miss Carter, please release my brother to me." Tears formed despite the girl's best efforts, and it seemed to anger her. Nevertheless, she bottled up her anger and continued her earnest plea. "Anything you wish of me, I shall give, if you'll lift whatever spell you have over him." Rhea laughed fullthroatedly, enjoying the conversation more all the time.

"My dear, I don't know what kind of imaginative fiction you have been using to fill your time, but I assure you, there is no 'spell' involved. Your brother is in love with me, and for the moment at least it amuses me to keep him here. He is more intelligent than a Pekingese and capable of performing functions beyond the abilities of lesser pets." Charity merely stared at her for long seconds, and Rhea thought *At last! I've broken her armor.* The girl put down her cup.

"It is true," she breathed. "Everything I have heard of you. You are a foul and disgusting woman!" She looked pugnaciously across the tea stand, obviously expecting an equally hostile return from Rhea. The older woman sat quite still for the moment, exploring her options, then leaned back indolently in her chair, crossed her legs under her long dress and petticoats, and placed her arms on the arms of the chair, long slender hands dangling over the ends. She sat like the queen of a bawdy house, surveying the girl before her, and smiled.

"If you don't care for your tea, dear, perhaps you prefer to go to your room now and rest. I shall have a bath prepared."

"Madam, do you fancy I should remain in this house now? I shall find a decent hotel nearby."

"Don't be a fool," Rhea said, leaning forward and picking up her tea. She accomplished this without uncrossing her legs, and now, leaning back, set the saucer on her knee, steadying it with thumb and forefinger. "If you intend to rescue your brother from this foul and disgusting woman, it is only sensible to make the most of your opportunities."

Charity stood looking at Rhea with impotent rage. Her lovely features had gone a deep magenta, and her hands clenched repeatedly. Tears of frustration now ran down her cheeks in a free cascade. Then she turned and moved to the door stiffly, but without forsaking that fascinating liquid grace. With her hand on the knob, she turned. Some measure of control seemed to have returned to her.

"Miss Carter, I wish to thank you." Rhea allowed her brow to arch, an invitation to continue. "Before coming here, I had formed an impression of you, but I was unsure of its accuracy. You have proved my judgment sound." Rhea laughed with plain enjoyment.

"And I wish to thank you for proving me wrong, dear. You see, I had formed an equally sharp picture of you, as a mousey creature without the wit or character to afford me an instant of stimulation or amusement." The redness of Charity's face was Rhea's instant reward. Charity had to take several deep breaths before she could find her voice. During the interval Rhea sipped her tea.

"In that case, ma'am," Charity said, still slightly breathless, "you were indeed sorely mistaken!"

"Yes," Rhea said before she could effect her withdrawal. "I made the execrable miscalculation of assuming that weakness and stupidity run in the Mead family."

Alone, Rhea finished her tea and her cake, then indulged herself in another helping of each. Finally wiping her hands on a linen napkin, she rose and walked to the door. The hallway was empty except for one young maid carrying two empty buckets down the stairs. Rhea brushed past the girl and entered her own room. No doubt Roger was still dawdling over his shaving mug. Locking the door behind her, Rhea walked to the window and drew the drapes to cut down the amount of light in the room, then moved to the wall that separated her quarters from the burgundy room. She removed from the wall a small picture and placed it on the floor. Behind the picture were two small holes, drilled with skill worthy of the house, at precisely the distance that separated Rhea's eyes. She leaned forward and looked through into the other room.

This was a game in which she had indulged occasionally, on those rare times when she had allowed guests in the house; but now she felt a potent excitement, one which she only vaguely understood, and which she had not yet bothered to examine.

Charity sat in a Louis XV chair, looking morosely out the window. The wall covering seemed to complement her loveliness, as did the ornate furnishings. It was like looking at a lovely painting,

Rhea thought. Near the girl sat a brass bathtub, steaming with freshly poured water. Another maid had just emptied two more buckets into the tub and was withdrawing. Charity looked around at the sound of the closing door, returned her attention to the outside for a moment, and then, languidly, rose and went to the door, which she locked. She began to disrobe, tossing her clothes onto the canopied bed carelessly. Rhea felt her throat restrict with an unfamiliar passion.

It was yet the age of petticoats. For a woman, undressing was a major undertaking, consuming significant portions of an hour. Rhea remained riveted to her peep show with the patience of a waiting predator. She fairly gasped at the first sight of Charity Mead's fully exposed loveliness. The girl walked to the tub, raised one foot over the edge, and dipped in a toe with tentative delicacy. Apparently satisfied, she balanced herself by gripping the edge of the tub and hauled herself over it and into the depths of the water.

Rhea turned from the peepholes, leaned back against the wall, breathing in large, ragged gulps. Finally she walked to the bedside table and removed the cap from her decanter of sherry. She noted with amusement that her hand shook noticeably. Sitting in a convenient chair, she rubbed her thigh absently, through her clothing, and sipped at the wine.

During her childhood and her girlhood, Rhea had read, in ancient Latin manuscripts, about all varieties of sex, including those whch her own time considered to be aberrant and repulsive. She herself had not found the activities described at all repulsive, at least in the abstract, but merely silly and pointless. While she had indulged herself in a great deal of sexual dalliance since that time, she had limited herself to heterosexual encounters, and always with one man at a time. Never before had she felt the enormous magnetic attraction incited in her by this nineteen-year-old girl.

And she began to wonder what she had been missing.

1976

Walter

For once he had managed to sneak away without Brenda. Not that she was ever much trouble. It was just that Walter liked to work alone, particularly during the digging portion of the job — which was ninety-nine percent of the job of detecting anyway. As much as he enjoyed having her around (especially as she had proved to be an even better lay than she looked), he couldn't stand to have someone sitting next to him, no matter how patiently, when he was leafing through old newspapers or staring at microfilm by the hour. And to make matters worse, Stafford knew about her now.

It had happened the previous morning, his third day in San Francisco, when he had made the error of calling his client from the motel room.

"What's that I hear in the background?" Stafford asked. Brenda was showering, and had left the bathroom door open.

"That's just the water running for my tub," Walter assured him, and then told him everything he had learned, including all the information he had picked up from Victor Banks the previous day. It was just that a client could easily misunderstand things like that, as Stafford did a moment later when Brenda came into the room, singing to herself in a voice loud enough to carry over the wire.

"I think your tub is full," Stafford said dryly.

"All right, you found me out." Walter tried to make a joke of it. "I have a little company with me. But she won't be on the expense account."

"I'm not in the habit of subsidizing people's pleasure trips," Stafford said acerbically. And that went through Walter like a barbed arrow. He felt his blood pressure rise precipitately.

"Look, Mr. Stafford, if you think I'm here on a pleasure trip, then all I can say is, you don't know a thing about detective work. You don't dig up the kind of info I just fed to you and goof off at the same time." There was a moment's silence, and then Stafford's voice came back, taut as ever but controlled.

"All right. I'll have to trust you, I guess. As long as she doesn't show up on your expenses."

Walter didn't like to have that kind of strain between himself and a client, but he supposed that the confrontation had at least cleared the air a bit, and proved to Stafford that he wasn't dealing with one of his studio flunkies. Walter considered himself one of the few real professionals in the business, and he didn't intend to take any crap from a client, no matter how lucrative, or how badly he needed the money.

The best way to forget such an incident was to get to work. Walter had the rare facility of concentrating so completely on his task that he was incapable of worrying about anything else while engrossed in it.

On this particular day he was at the San Francisco Public Library main branch. A young, blond librarian had shown him to the microfilm machine and dug out the proper films: the San Francisco *Chronicle* for the two decades ending in 1950. The girl saw him seated, then leaned across and inserted the film in the machine. He caught a whiff of her perfume, felt the roughness of her tweed skirt. Librarians hadn't looked or smelled like that when he was a kid. He would have noticed, even at the age of six.

He took an hour and a half going through the first reel, which covered 1931. Then he asked the girl to come back and fit in the next cartridge. After that he caught on and put the film in himself. By the time he got up to 1940 he was only skimming the obituaries, fairly sure that he had started with too late a reel.

His belly was rumbling when he finished 1950, so he went out for some lunch, then returned and asked for the microfilms from 1921 to 1930. The girl with the tweed skirt was gone to lunch, but another woman (twenty years older, no breasts, brusquely competent) dug out the roll and asked Walter if he could load the machine. He told her he was certain he could.

October 16, 1925 contained something interesting. It was a piece about a woman named Loretta Mullin, who had died when her car went over a cliff near the beach. She was burned almost beyond recognition, but the authorities had managed to get some fingerprints for positive identification. Miss Mullin was forty years old, had never married, and left an estate of two million three hundred thousand dollars. That was all of the article, but it left Walter with a racing pulse. He yanked the cartridge out of the machine and carried it up to the main desk. The blonde was back, just peeling off a long tan coat. She smiled pleasantly, shaking her hair back from her face.

"Do you have films of any other newspapers from this year?" he asked. She looked at the capsule, pursing her lips.

"I believe our files of the *Examiner*, the *Call* and the *Bulletin* all go back at least that far, sir," she said.

"Could you check, please? I'd like to see them all."

"Certainly, that's what I'm paid for," she said, and moved off into the film archives, her perky little fanny flexing with each step. In a moment she was back with three rolls of film.

He ran the *Examiner* through first, but its story was practically a recap of the one in the *Chronicle*. It assessed Miss Mullin's fortune at "approximately two and a half millions of dollars," but that was the only divergence from the first story. When he read the story in the *Call*, he almost knocked over his chair.

" —Aside from some small bequests to her servants, Miss Mullin left her entire fortune of more than two million dollars to her secretary and companion, Miss Elaine Arthur —"

Walter gripped the edge of the microfilm machine and stared at the screen for a moment, waiting for his heart to slow to normal. He lowered his gaze and rested his forehead in his hands.

"Oh, shit," he whispered. "What the fuck is going on here?"

He knew he would go on with this, because it was his job, and the most baffling and therefore interesting one of his career. But suddenly, very suddenly, he was coldly frightened.

Finally, he fished some dimes out of his pocket and made three copies of the *Call* article. The Xerox sheets dropped into the bin and he picked them up almost gingerly. Then, almost as an afterthought, he placed the cartridge of the *Bulletin* in the machine and ran it up to October 16. He was glad and sorry that he had done so, because this article carried a human interest angle overlooked by the other three.

" —It is believed that Miss Mullin meant this bequest as a continuation of a tradition, since she inherited the fortune in 1906 under nearly identical circumstances, according to her butler, Mr. Franklin Swift —"

"Well, Christ!" It was nearly a wail. A thirtyish man in a plaid sport coat, sitting three machines away, looked at Walter oddly for an instant, then hastily returned his gaze to his own screen.

"Is it possible to rent a typewriter?" Walter asked the blond at the desk. She indicated a room at the other end of the main reading room. "How about some paper?" Surreptitiously, after glancing in the direction of the older librarian, she took some paper out of a drawer and handed it to him with a conspiratorial wink. Walter thanked her and retired to the room she had indicated.

He found four cranky looking machines chained to metal tables, with coin slides on the sides of them. Shoving a dime into one, he nearly pounded his fingertips raw trying to get through his report. He told everything he had discovered so far, then went back to the room with the microfilm machines, which also housed a duplicating machine. He made a Xerox of the report and left after asking his blonde friend for directions to the nearest post office.

On his way to his car, after having mailed one copy of the report and the newspaper articles, he wondered whether Miss Mullin had had the opportunity to tell anyone that her body had been stolen.

1847

Rhea

The Meads, brother and sister, had developed a common habit: they never looked directly at one another. Not that they were obvious about it. Perhaps, Rhea thought with amusement, they were unaware of it themselves. They treated each other's face in much the same way that a well brought up person would treat someone with a pair of torn trousers. When they had reason to address each other, their eyes simply slid away like magnets with identical polarity. Roger, she had noticed, generally looked at his sister's hair, or the line joining her hair with her forehead, while her eyes seemed to gravitate to his chin or throat. There was a very subtle formality between them when they spoke, unnoticeable to anyone who had not known them before, or who had no reason to look for such minutiae in their behavior.

Rhea found it all quite amusing. Of course they never spoke to one another of the things that happened at night, after the lamps had been snuffed and one or the other of them, according to her preference, joined Rhea in her bedroom. That first night, a year previous, Charity had gasped to Rhea, between bouts of intense lovemaking, "My brother must never know of this." Rhea, her passion momentarily expended, had chuckled, "Not know it? My dear, we are going to be a happy little family."

It was Rhea's first experience with lesbianism, and perhaps

simply because it was the first, it had brought her delights more intense than any she had known, passions more intense than she had felt since her affair with Raymond Wakeling. The passage of a twelve month had done nothing to diminish the passions or the delights, and while she knew that she would eventually arrive at a balance between this new aspect of sexuality and the heterosexual experience that had once been everything to her, she allowed the unending freshness of her mastery over Charity Mead to have its rein. She opted for the sister's favors over her brother's three nights out of four, and had done so ever since that first night, the first night that Charity had spent under her roof.

On that night, after prolonging dinner unconscionably, in a spirit of pure deviltry, she had tossed off her third glass of wine and forked the two wretched siblings on her glance.

"Your sister must be exhausted after her long journey, Roger," she said. "Why don't you see her to her room? Before retiring to you own." As she had expected, he greeted this cryptic notice with mixed response. He was doubtless relieved that his sister wouldn't see him going into his hostess' room; and he was devastated at the thought of spending a night away from Rhea. Both responses entertained Rhea, but she was anticipating with relish the real entertainment of the evening: looking in on Charity once again as she disrobed for bed.

When she locked the door to her room and removed the picture from the wall, she found that Roger had done more than see his sister to her room; he had joined her there.

"Oh, pooh!" Charity said, her deep, clear voice coming through the tiny openings with satisfying clarity. "Rhea Carter is an odious woman, but I can't believe she would dare to harm me physically."

So, Rhea thought, her amusement edged with anger, little Roger has undertaken to caution his sister against me. He would pay for that, she promised herself.

"You don't know her as I do, sis," Roger said, his stronger voice penetrating with even greater resonance. "Sometimes I believe she has found a way to tap the core of evil itself. And it has given her powers beyond our imagination. Even now, though I hate her, I want to be with her. I feel that I have life and vitality only when I am in her presence. Oh, I can't explain the feeling." Suddenly his voice took on fresh vigor, grew audibly louder. "And I don't want you to learn it firsthand. I insist that you leave this house tomorrow morning, and I pray that will not be too late."

"Miss Carter has invited me to remain, and I intend doing so for as long as necessary, regardless of whatever danger you imagine for me. Unless you leave with me."

It was Roger's warning to Charity that planted the germ of the idea in Rhea's mind. Until then she hadn't thought about doing more with Charity than dangling her brother's helplessness before her like a bauble. But with Roger's panicky admonitions, Rhea began to entertain a new intention, one of which she was not fully conscious just yet.

When her brother had gone, stiff with frustration, Charity stood for a moment, her right hand held slightly in front of her at waist level. Then, gradually, it dropped to her side. Then, her shoulders slightly rounded, she walked to the curtained window. After a moment she reached behind her and began to unbutton her dress.

Once again Rhea felt that enormous excitement as Charity removed layer after layer of her clothing. When the girl stood naked, so vulnerably unaware of her hostess' scrutiny, and rubbed vaguely at her waist, Rhea felt such an overwhelming desire that her knees almost failed her. More than she could remember having wanted anything, she wanted that body. She had to touch that pale, transparent skin, to stroke those soft rippling breasts.

Charity walked to the bureau, where the servants had placed her clothes, and took out a nightgown. Then she walked back to the bed, nearly in a daze, and lay down without bothering to turn down the covers, or even to put on the nightgown. Lying there she was like some classic, erotic work of art.

With shaking hands Rhea replaced the picture over the peepholes. Then she walked to the door, tried to open it, took out her key and unlocked it. She walked down the hall, pausing for a moment before Charity's door before she continued to her secret room, and the pentagram she had painted on the floor.

Ten minutes later, fortified by a glass of sherry, Rhea walked to the door of the burgundy room. Without hesitation, she unlocked it with her master key, entered. Charity still lay naked on the bed. The oil lamp on the bedside table burned, throwing a pale yellow light over the girl's body. She had fallen asleep, but the sound of the closing door caused her eyes to open. She lay there, looking at Rhea with a dazed expression. Then, suddenly, she sat bolt upright, crossing her arms in front of her breasts.

"Madam, really!" she protested. "You could at least knock before —" She broke off as Rhea turned her key in the lock. Her eyes widened, and she drew back slightly as though afraid the older woman meant her some physical injury. Possibly, in that confused instant, she recalled her brother's warning and prepared to defend her life. "What are you going to do?" she asked in a tremulous but slightly defiant tone as Rhea advanced on her.

"Quiet, child," Rhea said in a soothing tone. "I mean you no harm, and you will not resist me. No, don't draw away." Charity looked at her like a terrified and paralyzed animal, but she remained rooted. Rhea stopped at the edge of the bed, reaching out and releasing the girl's hair from its binding. It fell freely down Charity's back, looking almost blond in this yellow light. Charity gasped, darting a hand back as though to catch it, revealing one soft, fragrant breast.

"Lie back, child. Yes, lie back." As Rhea's face lowered to hers, she turned away. Then, reluctantly but ineluctably, she faced the older woman again. Her mouth opened slightly as Rhea kissed her. Her lips, her breath, her tongue, were mild and fragrant as a baby's. Her hand clutched at Rhea's wrist to push it away, then froze as Rhea's fingers played over her breast. Rhea sat on the edge of the bed and laid her cheek against the girl's, burying her face in that superb garden of hair. Lightly, she touched Charity's ear with her tongue, and then said in a husky whisper, "I have never done this before, child. We shall learn together."

After that night their relationship had grown at a fierce clip. Rhea, naturally and instinctively, had taken the position of tutor, despite the scantiness of her own knowledge of lesbian sex. Her extensive background in heterosexual lovemaking had combined with her natural sensuality to cause her to learn with astonishing speed. Dimly remembered passages from the works of Petronius and other Roman poets had reinforced her educability. As to Charity, caught up in a passion that left her gasping, unable to quit Rhea's house or to resist her advances despite the intensity of shame she knew even at the height of arousal. She learned like an avid pupil, responding to Rhea's lead, picking up instantly on every new technique and answering it with the precise countermove, learning without being taught the trick of being at once submissive and aggressive, responsive and imaginative.

As had been the case with every man whom the demon had bewitched for Rhea, the girl's passion for and dependence on the older woman grew by the day. After a year she had reached the stage where she trembled at Rhea's slightest glance, and Rhea was certain that there had grown up an unwilling animosity between brother and sister flowing from the fact that each night they became rivals.

It was precisely one year past Charity's arrival at Rhea's home that the three of them sat in the parlor. Rhea, her chair drawn before a crackling fireplace, browsed through the evening edition of the newspaper, reading of the war in Mexico. To her left in a padded leather chair sat Roger, pretending to read a book, though his eyes kept wandering to Rhea's face.

At dinner that night one of the servants had brought in an elaborately decorated white cake with a single pink candle. In ornate curved lettering it bore Charity's name. The servant set it down in front of the girl, who looked at Rhea with eyes widened by wonder.

"But what is the occasion, Madam?" she asked. Rhea smiled.

"Have you forgotten, dear?" She reached across the corner of the dining table and squeezed Charity's hand warmly. "Tonight is the anniversary of that first night — when you came to live with us." Charity's face blazed a deep red, and she lowered her gaze to the cake.

"You should not have — troubled yourself, Miss Carter."

"Not troubled to commemorate such a joyous occasion?" Rhea asked with a teasing lilt in her voice. "What nonsense. Now you must cut the cake."

Now, two hours later, Charity sat at her feet, skirts drawn chastely about her, one slender shoulder pressed lightly against Rhea's skirts and, through them, her calf. The gown which she wore was low-cut, chosen and purchased by Rhea. It was not at all the kind of thing the girl could have been induced to wear a year earlier.

Rhea finished the article that had mildly interested her and folded the paper, laying it on her lap. Outside, a horse clopped along the street, drawing a creaky wagon as the clock on the mantel struck ten. Noting that Roger was in the midst of sneaking a glance at her, Rhea leaned forward, allowing her paper to slip to the carpet with a whispering sound and, reaching down, slipped her hand inside Charity's bodice to caress, briefly, one soft breast. Charity's head swiveled impulsively toward her brother, and their eyes met for the first time in months, only briefly, as the girl's nipple stiffened in Rhea's palm. Then Charity looked up at her. She was clearly flustered and embarrassed by this unwonted boldness on her mistress' part. But her body strained toward Rhea, and the breast seemed to flow around her fingers like jellied putty. Rhea leaned forward and kissed Charity's hair lightly.

"Go to my room now, child," she said softly, but loudly enough so that Roger could hear. "I shall join you in a moment."

"I — Yes, Madam." Rhea slipped her hand free and Charity rose shakily. The intense ruddiness of her face was pleasing, and Rhea decided that embarrassment, like sexual arousal, was becoming to her little friend.

As Charity moved with hasty grace from the room, Roger laid his book face down over the arm of his chair and looked with timid reproach at Rhea. This was the third night in a row that Rhea had chosen sister over brother. She considered the utterance of some *mot* that would rub salt in the boy's wounds, then decided to ignore his unspoken rebuke. Flushed as she was with triumph and sexual anticipation, the mixture of feelings made her feel odd somehow, different from the way she had felt on previous occasions. There was a slight dizziness, a lightness in her brain. It was not an unpleasant sensation, but it was unsettling if only for its unfamiliarity.

She rose and moved toward the hallway, picking up a silver candelabrum. The rest of the house, save the bedrooms, was in darkness. She spoke to Roger without granting him a glance.

"The serv—" Her words sounded furry in her own ears, and she spoke them again, more carefully. "The servants have retired, dear. Please put out the lamps." He looked at his knees for a moment before acknowledging the softly worded command.

"All right." He rose leadenly.

"There's no hurry, Rog— Roger," she said, noting that it grew increasingly difficult to keep her speech clear. "Stay up as long as you like."

"Thank you, I'm rather tired," he said sulkily. "I think I'll take my book to bed."

"Please yourself, dear." Her speech cleared momentarily, stilling the concern she had begun to feel. The room seemed uncommonly bright, or more precisely her vision seemed to have grown more intense. The floor felt soft under her feet, and it appeared to tilt slightly, like a ship's deck at sea.

Shifting the candelabrum to her left hand, she gripped the bannister with her right and began to climb the stairs with slow, deliberate steps. At the head of them she could see the door to the master bedroom slightly ajar, and through the opening Rhea caught sight of some quick, silken movement, reminding her that Charity was there, undressing for her. She tried to hurry, and in that instant the stairs seemed to tilt dangerously. Gripping the bannister more firmly, she cried out, a growling sound that was meant to be Roger's name. A fuzzy iris of dirty gray closed in from the periphery of her vision, making a tunnel through which she saw the door to her room. The candelabrum slipped from her fingers and clattered to the carpeted stairs. Vaguely she hoped that it would start no fire. Then all was blackness, and a distant cry of horror in Roger's voice, and the cottony pain of her forehead striking the edge of the stairs.

She woke to see a wrinkled, masculine face hovering over her. It was a strange face, and she felt a momentary stab of reasonless fear. Then she became aware of Roger and Charity hovering in the distance. She was lying on her bed. Undoubtedly she had been carried there by Roger or one of the servants. Stupid thing to have happen, she thought, irritated at her own weakness, and tried to sit up.

It was as though her mind had been disconnected from her body, though still imprisoned in it. Or as if she had forgot how to control her muscles, and couldn't remember. Nothing responded. She tried again, harder, and felt a flicker of response in her legs. The face that hung over her, looking magnified and reminding her, for some reason, of the demons whom she had summoned so many times, displayed concern.

"Now, now, dear," he said, speaking very distinctly, as though she might not understand plain English. "Don't tire yourself."

Stop talking to me as though I were an idiot, Rhea tried to growl at him, but nothing came out. Her jaw muscles refused to function. She couldn't speak!

"You've had a stroke," the man said. "I'm Doctor Harris, and I was brought here by one of your servants. Now you must rest." He patted her shoulder gently. Rhea wanted to push his hand away, and to tell him to keep his hands to himself. For the first time in her memory, she felt a fierce panic well up in her. Her eyes widened, and the doctor patted her shoulder once again. Then he turned to Roger and Charity.

"I fear there is no more that anyone can do for her tonight," he said, "except to undress her, cover her, and see that she remains warm and comfortable until morning. I'll look in again tomorrow." He looked at Rhea once again, frowned and shook his head. "We know so little of these matters," he said.

"Will she recover, Doctor?" Charity asked in a hushed voice, as though she thought to conceal the question from Rhea. They were all such ninnies, Rhea thought. The doctor shrugged.

"From all our knowledge in such matters, it is possible. The stroke seems to have been fairly severe. Still, in time, with patience and considerable application on her part, she may recover her powers of motion and speech, at least partially. I have seen it done, on occasion."

"But what odds?" Roger demanded. The doctor looked at him with an expression compounded of admiration and pity. No doubt he admired the two of them for their devotion, Rhea thought. The idiotic old goat!

"I should say considerably against her. And one more thing. She must be kept as calm as possible. We do know that strokes are exacerbated by emotional tension and shock, and that they often occur in series. The next, if it is massive —" He shrugged. Roger and Charity looked at one another with fresh concern. The doctor fished an enormous watch from his vest pocket and consulted it, wound it a half turn and distractedly replaced it, then took it out and looked at it again, as though he had forgot to note the time. "And now, if you don't mind, I think I shall take myself home. I shall return as soon as is sensible."

After the doctor had left, Charity called in one of the servants, a girl who had been hired only weeks earlier. The two of them set about the task of undressing Rhea and putting her to bed. Then

Charity pulled a chair next to the bed and sat down. She ordered the girl to bring a damp cloth and when this had been accomplished sent the girl to her quarters. She applied the cloth to Rhea's forehead, laving off the sheen of perspiration that had gathered there. Rhea heard a knock at the door, and the girl rose.

"No," she murmured. Roger's voice squeezed through the narrow opening she had allowed, weak but intense. Roger had seen the doctor to the door. "I think not, dear," Charity said with even more authority than before. "She must rest, and I truly believe that she would prefer me here. Now go to your room and I shall have you relieve me in the morning, when you are properly rested." Without awaiting a reply she closed the door and shot the bolt. Then she returned to the side of the bed and managed a weak smile. "There now, you must rest, darling," she whispered. "One of us will be with you all the time." She sat down again, picked up the cloth and applied it to Rhea's forehead once more. Rhea strained to move and finally, at great expense in terms of energy, managed to flex her right hand. A look of concern flashed across Charity's face.

"No, darling, you mustn't," she said intently. "You must recoup your strength now. There is time for the rest later." She laid a cool hand on Rhea's forehead, then bent down impulsively and kissed her on the lips. "I shall stay the night with you," she whispered, and immediately began to peel off the dressing gown she had undoubtedly put on for the doctor's benefit. In a moment she crossed by the foot of the bed, nude, and slipped under the covers on Rhea's right. She circled the older woman's shoulders with one slender arm and drew her in close. Rhea had the impression that Charity was drawing comfort rather than bestowing it. Still, it was good to feel the girl's warmth, to hear the strong beating of her heart. Eventually she could tell that Charity had fallen asleep. Rhea felt as though she would never sleep again.

Then something in the room seemed to shift subtly, something huge and somber that filled her chambers with itself. The lamp was still alight, but as Rhea moved her gaze about quickly she could see nothing. She felt the urge to ask, to speak to the thing. It was that real. At first she thought that it might be her demon, but the feeling that emanated from this entity was unlike any she had ever known before. It frightened her, and she thought that it might have been responsible for her stroke, and that her time of restitution had come at last. But as though the thing had sensed her fear, the sensation of its propinquity altered subtly, growing warmer. Rhea felt some comfort from this, but it was slight and leavened with wariness.

Who—? What are you? she thought with all the intensity of her mind, and the answer was instantaneous.

"Do you not know me, Rhea Carter? My minions have served

you faithfully for many years."

It was not a voice, or rather it was a voice that had no sound. It seemed to fill her mind directly. It carried an enormous power, yet for all that there was an unmistakable air of melancholy about it. Rhea felt an involuntary shiver pass over her entire body. She looked about, her eyes darting over the entire room, but she could see nothing.

"You cannot look upon me, Rhea Carter. If I showed myself to you, you would be consumed. Content yourself to feel my presence, and to sense my words."

What do you want of me? Rhea asked, forming the words in her mind with great precision.

"I want everything of you. I want your service, and your devotion. I am here to claim you as my own."

No! I won't go with you, Rhea thought at the presence. Her heart accelerated, and she felt dizzy. For a moment she was frightened that she might have another stroke, and that, as the doctor had cautioned, it would kill her. By a main force of will she managed to calm herself a bit. The presence laughed, a sad and sonorous laugh that filled her brain like an echo.

"No, you will not go with me now, I am He Who Must Be Obeyed, He Who Must Be Served, He Who Cannot Be Summoned. I have come to bargain with you, Rhea Carter. To give you that which you have desired above all else for these past years."

The words made no impression on Rhea, who had glanced at the girl sleeping beside her. Charity was as deep in slumber as before. Apparently the words of this creature were for Rhea alone. Then she absorbed what had been said, and her heart accelerated afresh.

My youth? You will make me young again?

"Your youth is spent. Nothing can restore it. But if you will serve me well and loyally, I shall teach you the way to steal the youth of others." Rhea's mind, one of the finest in the world, and marvelously untouched by the stroke that had crippled her, raced.

But what of everything else? What of the blessings I've enjoyed all these years? What of my wealth, my—

"Do not concern yourself with such matters, child. For that which you have will be multiplied, and that which you expend in my service will be returned a thousandfold. Is it not mine to grant? Was it not given into my keeping, all worldly value? And that portion which you have already enjoyed, has it not come from me, lent to you to be taken away if it pleased me? How, then, can you fear to lose it in my service?" Even now, an impish sense of humor came to Rhea's assistance.

How can I serve you if I don't even know your name? she asked. *Won't you even tell where you are from, who you are?*

There was a moment when the presence didn't reply and she thought that he might be withdrawing from her.

"*Do you not know me, Rhea Carter? I have a thousand names. I stood beside the Lord God when He created the world.*"

A prickliness crept over Rhea's skin. She trembled inside, her intestines seeming to writhe with the emotion that this piece of information had incited in her.

I shall serve you, she promised reluctantly, and fought to keep from giving expression, even in her brain, to the reservation that she harbored. *Now*. Now she would serve him. Now and for so long as it seemed discreet to do so. But there had to be a way to renounce this vow, when she had learned how. *Only tell me what I must do*, she thought with intensity, deliberately drowning out the musings that rumbled through the depths of her mind.

"You must take the path which I chose long ago," the presence told her, and the voice seemed to wax infinitely sadder. Then it gained strength and authority, so that Rhea delighted in the feeling of its flowing through her. "*You must promote the suffering of your fellow beings. You must delight in their anguish and enjoy their pain.*"

Agreed — If that was all there was to it, Rhea thought wryly, it might not prove so irksome to be a servant for as long as necessary.

"*Live by my standards, Rhea Carter. Follow my commands, and you will enjoy all the pleasures of the world.*"

And then the presence was gone. It vanished instantly, so that Rhea imagined she felt a vacuum where it had hovered for an instant before. Suddenly she was filled with a great warmth, and a drowsiness that was intensely pleasurable. She let her eyes close and drifted into a deep sleep.

When she woke sunlight streamed through the window, around the draperies, making streaks on the wine red carpet. She rolled over, burying her face in the pillow to gain another moment of sleep, and then suddenly remembered the night before, the stroke, the presence, her bargain. She sat up quickly, almost frightened by the fact that she could do so. A strand of hair, thick and brown and luxurious, fell over her shoulder, and she brushed it back unthinkingly before the color and texture of it impinged on her consciousness. And then she realized that somehow, during the night, she had moved from the left side of the bed to the right. When she looked down at the form beside her she drew back, one slender, graceful hand rising to her mouth to stifle a scream of shock.

It was like looking into some horrid distorting mirror, to see that face, haggard and wrinkled with the shock of a massive stroke.

As though realizing that she was being scrutinized, the old

woman opened her eyes. The face seemed to try to smile for an instant. Then the eyes filled with confusion, panic, horror. A thin, animal scream escaped the barely parted lips, and a bubbling stream of slobber dribbled from the corner of the once opulent mouth.

Slowly, awkwardly at first, because the face was new to her, Rhea began to smile.

1976

Janet

Aside from sleeping with another woman's husband, which Janet supposed wasn't so unusual in this day and age, Rhea Carter seemed to live a very ordinary existence. Since that first day, when she had followed Phillip to the girl's apartment, Janet had kept a close vigil on her, or as close as a person could, with no help. In those two weeks Phillip had only been back once that she knew of. She had sat in her Jaguar the whole time, and had clocked the visit. He had gone at three-o-two in the afternoon, and had come out again, apparently with a fresh shave, at eight-seventeen. Janet noted all of this information in a Spiral tablet she had bought for the purpose.

There had been no other visitors with the exceptions of a teenage girl (the loveliest Janet had ever seen) and an older woman who came twice a week, apparently to clean the place. Rhea seemed to have no job. At least she didn't keep any kind of regular hours. She left her apartment, as a rule, at eleven o'clock in the morning, did some shopping, and returned early in the afternoon after a leisurely luncheon at some Los Angeles restaurant. Three times Janet had observed this routine, if it could be called that. Sometimes she skipped it altogether, and she didn't observe it punctiliously even when she did go out.

At least Janet had learned that she was a pretty good detective. For two weeks she had maintained a close surveillance on Rhea Carter and not once had she been noticed by the girl. She was careful to wear different clothes each day, and sometimes she still rented a car rather than using her Jaguar. The woman had never even glanced at her.

Then one day the weather turned surprisingly blustery for Los Angeles. It was September, and without warning the wind came through. Janet hadn't brought a coat, and she was sitting shivering in her car, trying to keep an eye on the apartment. Rhea had just come back from her shopping tour. Janet thought of giving up for the day, going home to a hot bath and a cup of coffee. Her watch told her it was nearly two in the afternoon. Her daughters would be coming home, one from school and the other from the nursery school in which Janet had enrolled her, and she should be there to greet them, she told herself. Then she heard a distant ringing sound.

For a moment she thought she was beginning to suffer from delusions brought on by her paranoid behavior of late. But the ringing sound repeated itself insistently, broken by regular intervals, and finally she noticed the phone booth just a few feet in front of the car. She had chosen this particular parking space the second or third time she had come here, precisely because there was a phone booth nearby, and had then promptly forgot it. She sat staring at the booth for a long while. *A wrong number,* she told herself. *Whoever it is will hang up in a moment.* But the ringing continued. Finally she opened the door of the Jaguar. She sat and listened to it ring again, feeling an unexplainable trepidation, as though she suspected that the phone booth was booby-trapped. The phone rang.

Getting out, she walked to the booth purposefully. If it was a wrong number, someone must be trying very hard to get hold of his party. The least she could do was inform the person that he had dialed wrong.

She picked up the receiver on what must have been the twentieth ring, tucking it beneath her long blond hair.

"Hello?"

"Well, dear, I didn't think you were going to answer," a woman's voice said. It was a young voice, with a self-assured air to it.

"Hello?" Janet repeated because she wasn't sure what she was expected to say. "What number are you trying to get?"

"The number I got," the voice said. "The telephone booth across from my apartment complex. This is Janet Stafford, isn't it, dear?" Janet felt something cold run through her like a dash of water. Her voice deserted her, along with her wits, and she just stood there, holding the receiver to her ear and staring at the phone dial like an idiot. She had neglected to close the door of the booth, and the wind whipped under her skirt, chilling her so that she shivered. "Why don't you come on inside, Janet?" the voice offered. "It's growing somewhat snappish out there, and I think you and I should meet formally at long last." *You fool,* Janet said to herself. "I've just put on a pot of tea," Rhea Carter said in that same self-assured tone. "Do come in and have a cup with me." Then she hung up.

"Well, you surely fooled her," Janet said aloud, glancing at the receiver before she hung it up.

She walked back to the Jaguar and got in, turned the key in the ignition, starting the engine. She sat for a moment listening to it purr, then turned it off. "All right, damn you," she murmured. "Maybe it is time we met."

Rhea Carter greeted her at the door in a pair of white lounging pajamas. The long black hair that she usually did up behind her head hung freely down her back, reaching her buttocks. Her face, seen at close range, was what one might call arresting. Not pretty exactly, but so fascinating that it didn't have to be. She stood regarding Janet with a touch of amusement, as though wondering whether she would have the nerve to enter. Behind her, the room was spacious, and what Janet could see of it was exquisitely furnished. She took a little breath and walked in, feeling a queasy thrill as the door closed behind her. She remembered something from Dante: *Depart from hope, all ye who enter here.*

The furniture was old and massive, well polished and undoubtedly very expensive. Some of it was authentic early American, probably two hundred years old. Mixed in with this were some Oriental pieces, including a tapestry on the far wall that showed some kind of hunting scene. The draped, heavy silk had been drawn, and a single hanging lamp turned on. A low table in front of the couch held a massive silver tea set, with a pot that swung on its own support. Across from the couch a fire crackled in a fireplace, over which hung an antique rifle or musket.

"I hope you'll forgive my casualness," Rhea said, walking past Janet toward the couch, "but I like to be comfortable at home, don't you?"

"You look lovely," Janet said without thinking, and took the end of the couch which the girl had indicated. It was she who felt a bit dowdy. She could see that Rhea Carter wasn't wearing an atom of makeup, and guessed that she never wore anything but a touch of lipstick. *She's one of those,* Janet thought with something akin to despair. Rhea sat next to her, a foot away, and poured a cup of tea.

"I'd say you're a one-spoon-of-sugar-no-cream girl, right?" she asked, reaching for the spoon in the silver sugar bowl.

"Yes, that's right." Janet shivered. She hadn't realized how cold she was until she had stepped into the warm apartment. While Rhea dropped the sugar into her cup, she noticed a black Persian cat resting in front of the fireplace. The animal looked back at her, thumped its tail once in a laconic welcome, and then went back to sleep.

"Here you are, dear." Rhea handed her the cup and then poured herself a cup without cream or sugar, sat back on the couch with one foot drawn up under the other thigh. "Don't you love my tea service?" she asked. "It's been in my family for over two hundred years."

"Oh, yes, it's beautiful." Janet glanced at the cat again, who had turned over on his back, four feet in the air, belly showing. Rhea laughed.

"That's Toby," she said. "Isn't he a character? He likes you, or he'd be in the other room by now." She took a sip of her tea, and Janet did the same. It was a bit hot, but delicious. Probably some special blend, she decided. "Now then," Rhea said in the tone of someone who was getting down to the central question, "just what do you expect to accomplish by following me around?" Doubtless the question had been intended to throw Janet off balance, but for once she was prepared.

"What do you expect to accomplish by having an affair with my husband?" she asked in return.

Rhea laughed. "Why does it have to accomplish anything? Philly is a very attractive man, and it's hardly my fault if he prefers me to you."

"Do you want to marry him?" Janet was amazed at the steadiness of her own voice.

"Not particularly, but it may end up that way. At any rate, there's not a thing you can do about it, so why don't you just retire from the lists and save everyone a lot of trouble?"

"I don't intend to give up my family that easily," Janet said, and wondered if a cup of hot tea, thrown from the distance of eighteen inches, would wash away that superior smile.

"Your family? If you mean those two little girls of yours, dear, take them with you. Philly doesn't care about them any more than I do. He just thinks he's supposed to. I'm certain you could get a very good settlement. With child support and all, you'd probably be better off than you are now. And you could probably remarry. You're still quite attractive, you know." Something about the way she said that made Janet feel clammy.

"Suppose I don't decide to 'retire'?"

"Well, then, you just don't, I guess. But you're going to lose, Janet. Don't doubt that for a moment."

"What if I decide to make trouble?" Janet asked, trying to goad the girl into saying something rash. But she just looked at Janet, her smile seeming impregnable.

"Now what kind of trouble could you possibly make for me?"

"Don't underestimate me, Miss Carter. I may be from a small town, but that doesn't make me a fool. I may get an attorney and sue you for alienation of affection or whatever."

"Oh, really?" Rhea laughed again, a merry tinkle of a laugh. "In this day and age?"

"Or I may take more direct action. I'm a gentle person by nature, but you're threatening my family, and — maybe more than that." Finally, the smile slipped a bit. Rhea Carter's delicate nostrils flared in what could have been anger.

"That idiot fortune teller said more to you than she should have, didn't she?" As soon as she had said it, she regretted it. Janet could tell, and felt a tiny glow of triumph.

"You were the woman who was seen at her door that day, weren't you?"

"That's an absurd question," Rhea said, obviously trying to hold onto her composure. "And not subject to proof. Anyway, the woman fell asleep on the couch with a lit cigarette and burned to death. That was the official finding."

"There was more to it than that. Von Baker saw something in my future. Something that had to do with you. And she was going to tell me what it was. Tell me something, Rhea. Was that fire — natural?"

"That kind of question can lead people to think you're insane, Janet," Rhea said, looking away from her and then leaning forward to place her cup on the table. "I asked you in here to give you some friendly advice, and I've given it. You can't save your marriage by these melodramatic allegations. Or by any other means." She looked at Janet again, intensely. "So why not just butt out, dear?"

"Don't try to frighten me," Janet said, preparing to stand. "Whatever Von saw, it scared her so horribly she couldn't even talk about it. That frightened me more than anything you can say. I don't think I have a thing to lose."

"Well, that's where you're wrong," Rhea hissed, leaning forward with a look of rage. "You have a good deal to lose. Your children, for instance."

Not just the words, but the intensity with which they were spoken, the obviously genuine threat implied, sent an intense cold through Janet's veins. She sat there for an instant, looking at the contorted, livid face before her, and then, without any conscious intention, she threw the remainder of her tea at Rhea Carter. The hot liquid struck her just below the breasts, wringing a cry of pained surprise from her. Rhea jumped back, half rising, striking at herself as though the tea were something flammable, but before she could move again, Janet sprang up, leaned toward the woman, and slapped her across the face more times than she could count. Toby flipped onto his feet and faced the two women, crouched as though to spring. But Janet was finished by that time. She stood upright, looking down at Rhea, who had withdrawn to the opposite end of the couch and lay there, sobbing.

"Now you listen to me, you little bitch!" Janet ordered. "You can threaten my marriage, and you can threaten me. But if you ever threaten my children again, I'll kill you. Do you understand me? I'll murder you, you goddamn little whore!" She punctuated the last word with a vicious kick that caught Rhea's shin. The cat moved forward several steps in a quick, darting motion, then stopped and observed with the alertness that cats show when they've been scared or angered. Janet's breath came in rasping, ragged gulps, and she knew her face was deep red. Rhea looked frightened, as though she expected another attack. But Janet's violence had been spent. She looked at the girl for a moment, then turned and went to the door swiftly. When she had opened it, she turned. Rhea had moved away from the corner of the couch, but she hadn't risen. "Remember what I said," Janet warned. "If anything happens to my children, anything at all, I'm going to blame you for it." Then she walked out, leaving the door open. A moment later Rhea's voice, scarcely recognizable, called her name, and Janet turned to see the woman framed in the doorway, one hand on the knob.

"Go on home," she hissed. "Go back to those two little brats you care so much about. Spend as much time with them as you can, dear. Because you just killed them!"

Janet started forward, conscious in some cold, deep part of her mind that she meant to kill this girl, to choke the life out of her just as quickly and efficiently as she could manage. Before she covered two feet of ground, Rhea jumped back and slammed the door. Janet heard a bolt thrown, the rattle of the lock, and then a chain.

She stood for a moment, breathing heavily, staring at the door with a malevolence she had never felt for anyone or anything before. Finally, because there seemed nothing else to do, she headed for her car.

When she had got in, and started the engine, it finally hit her. She laid her head on the wheel and cried, wailing like a tortured animal, her tears running down her face and her hands, and even over the wheel. She wasn't sure how long she remained there, but she knew better than to try to drive until it was past.

Finally, she sat up, threw back her head, and gripped herself with a conscious effort. She looked at the apartment complex once again. It looked malignant, somehow, like a haunted house in a horror movie. Like Dracula's castle.

She had meant it. Janet was certain of that. Rhea Carter was going to kill her children. In some weird fashion she had killed Yvonne Baker. She had known about Janet's visit, had known that Von meant to tell Janet something, and she had killed her. She had meant to kill Janet, too. That was probably what Von had seen.

"All right," she murmured. "You can kill me. But not my kids."

The trouble was that no one would believe her story. And that meant that there was nobody to stop Rhea from doing what she intended. Nobody except Janet herself. She put the Jaguar into drive, cramped the wheels to the left. A car rushed past, and then she pulled very carefully into the street.

"So be it," she murmured.

1976

Walter

After three days in San Francisco, Walter Lankershim was worn out. His eyes hurt from too much poring over microfilmed newspapers, his back was sore from sitting hunched over in front of the viewing machines, and another portion of his anatomy was particularly sore from having spent so much time with Brenda, who had proved to be just as much as Walter could handle.

She was as much as he could handle in another sense, too. The day after he found the remarkable newspaper articles in the San Francisco Public Library, he had come out of his shower at the motel and found her reading the Xerox copies. He had left them in the inside pocket of his coat, never thinking for an instant that she might be interested in any of it, and seeing her sitting there on the edge of the bed in panties and bra, perusing the things, gave him something of a start. She read on for a moment while he stood watching, then glanced up, apparently unconcerned.

"Hi," she said, and went back to her reading.

"Do you always go through a man's pockets when you're staying with him?" Walter asked, keeping his voice light. He walked to the dressing table that sat against the wall and picked up his black plastic comb. As he ran the comb through his hair he could see her in the mirror, still looking at him.

"I'm sorry. I didn't think you'd mind. I ran out of things to read, and you know how I am."

It was true that the girl was a reading freak. That, sex and food seemed to make up her entire life. Walter decided to let it go, and as he turned away from the mirror, putting down his comb, she smiled up at him in that special way, and he knew that he had just wasted a shower, and would have to take one again before they left for Los Angeles.

As he carried his bag and her knapsack out to the car, he automatically reached for the newspaper on the rack, dropping in a dime. He had read so much newspaper in the past several days that it was enervating to think of poring over another, but he hadn't gone a day without at least glancing through the major articles, since he had turned seventeen.

"I usually drive a hundred miles before I stop to eat," he told Brenda. "But if you prefer —"

"No, that's fine. I'd like to curl up and get another hour's sleep anyway." She had packed her blue jeans and was wearing a pair of blue denim shorts and a halter. Even after the rapacious half hour they had just spent in the motel room, he found the sight of her exciting. Her hair had been tied up behind her head in a tight bun. Her breasts thrust at the halter and joggled in a way that advertised her aversion to bras. In all his years of being a cockhound, Walter thought, he had never found a girl quite like this one. Even in the midst of her passion, which was awesome to behold, her control seemed uncanny. She could keep a man going for twice his normal endurance, and then wring him out like a limp rag through a wringer. He had been afraid that she might decide to remain in San Francisco, but apparently she liked either his company or the comfort of having a man around to pay for her food and lodging, because she had packed her meager belongings and made ready for the journey back to Southern California without even being asked.

Now she curled up on the far edge of the car seat, sated with sexual fulfillment, and dropped into sleep with the ease of any comfortable and well-fed animal.

The gas tank was over three-quarters full, so he decided not to bother with that until they stopped for breakfast. Once on Interstate Five he turned on his transceiver and contacted a trucker up ahead. There was a highway patrolman stashed near one of the off-ramps, the sixteen-wheeler warned him, so he should back off until he passed that spot. Walter held it to fifty-five, listening to the hum of the tires on the pavement and the crackle of the CB receiver under his dash.

He pulled into a diner and gas station a hundred and twenty-five miles south of the city and filled the tank. When he hung up the pump nozzle and walked back to the car door, Brenda was stretching like a kitten. The skin of her legs was covered with goose bumps.

"I'm ravenous," she said. "When do we eat?"

"Just as soon as you get your pretty little ass into a booth,' he told her. "I'll park the car."

When he left the car he picked up the newspaper, tucking it under his arm. Brenda was already halfway through a cup of steaming black coffee. Another stood across the table from her.

"I ordered you a pancake sandwich because that's what you had on the way up," she said. "That all right?"

"For a start." He found the waitress and ordered a side of sausages, then returned to the table. Brenda had bought a paperback book from a rack near the door and was already burying herself in it, so he picked up the paper. The President was concerned over something that had happened in the Middle East and there was a threat of a dock strike in New York. Walter turned to the funnies, read *Peanuts* and *B.C.*, and then found himself looking at the obituaries. Strange how quickly habits form, he thought wryly, and was in the process of closing the paper when something caught his eye.

"Well, for Christ's sake," he said just as the waitress arrived with their order. Brenda put down her book, thrusting a napkin inside as a mark, and looked at him questioningly. Walter shoved the paper aside so the girl could put the plates in front of him, but he didn't close it.

"What's up?" Brenda asked when they had been supplied with refills of coffee.

"That butler we interviewed. He's dead." She was pouring a sea of maple syrup over her stack of pancakes, and didn't even look up.

"That's a shame, but he was pretty old, wasn't he?" She flicked the drop of syrup off the spout of the jar, licked her fingertip, and picked up her knife and fork with obvious relish. "What did it? Heart, stroke, or cancer?" Her flippancy about the matter of a man's death irritated Walter. He looked at her with annoyance and spoke deliberately, to see if he could get through to her.

"He was murdered." She looked up at him with mild interest.

"No kidding? Who'd want to murder an old duck like that? Somebody rip him off for his junk? He had a lot of expensive-looking junk in that house." She forked an enormous morsel of pancake into her mouth and chewed laboriously.

"According to the paper, nothing is missing, unless the killer took cash. There was no sign of a struggle, either, so they think it must have been someone he knew and trusted."

"Really?" she said around the last of her mouthful of pancake. She was already cutting off another bite, just as large.

"Well, he probably couldn't have put up much of a struggle anyway."

"You don't seem overly upset about it," Walter said, putting the paper on the seat beside him and turning to his breakfast.

"Well, I didn't even know the old fart, for cripe sake," Brenda said, swallowing some coffee and forking up yet another mound of sopping pancake. Walter buttered his own cakes and cut off a chunk.

"He was stabbed, according to the paper. Between the third and fourth ribs of the left side, as though someone had stood very close in front of him and slipped the knife in, upward so it would go between the ribs into the vital organs."

"Jesus Christ, can't we talk about something else?" Brenda asked, signaling the waitress for a refill.

On the road again, she sat against the door and watched the scenery, as she had done on the way up. A silence crouched between them. Walter supposed he was being silly, and he knew he would get over it, but she had shown such crassness about the old butler's death that it had rankled him. A private detective is supposed to be casual about such things, he thought, but he had never become so, not in twenty years on the L.A.P.D. or in three years of private practice. The death of a human being was a momentous thing to him, and he had never been able to get that attitude out of his system. Still, she had been right. She hadn't known the man, so why pretend to be upset about his death?

Then he realized that there was something more to his feeling. It was something professional, an instinct he had developed in police work. She had asked the kind of questions that would relieve her of the necessity of watching her statements later. During those days he had spent at the library he had never known where she went, and the newspaper article hadn't mentioned how long the man might have lain in his home before his body was discovered.

Ridiculous. Why should a little road tramp make her way from San Francisco across the bay to Hayward just to kill someone she had never met before? Of course, it would have been easy for her to get into his house. The old man had been a lecher. He had hardly taken his eyes off her the whole time they were there. And she had mentioned that there were expensive things in his house. She might have gone over there for money, and then—

Shit! He was letting his imagination run away with him, since reading these old newspaper pieces, those pieces he had caught her reading just that morning. . . .

Mentally, he shook himself like a wet dog. This was

ludicrous. The fact that she was a young girl who seemed not to have developed much compassion and less empathy didn't make her a murdreress. He reached forward and turned off the CB, then smiled across the width of the car.

"What are you doing sitting way over there?" he asked.

"I thought you were mad about me not making a trip out of that obituary."

"Sometimes I act like an asshole," Walter said. "You have to get used to it. Come on over here. I want to put my hand between your legs." She looked at him for a moment, an impish grin at the corners of her mouth, and in the highlights of her eyes.

"All right," she consented, sliding across the seat. She snuggled against him, resting a hand lightly on his thigh. Walter dropped his right hand to her bare leg and squeezed the pliant young flesh. Christ, he thought. Two hours since I got laid, and I'm getting a hard on. Brenda moved her hand in a seemingly patternless motion, eventually finding her way to his crotch. The car swerved a bit on the road, and he looked at her with not-quite-mock severity.

"Let's not get too personal while I'm driving," he said.

"Then why don't you pull off? I see some bushes up ahead."

Walter saw the spot she meant. He hadn't done anything like that since he'd been a kid. It was ridiculous, but he found the idea exciting. Her hand had grown very convincing. Walter took his foot off the gas. He pulled the car carefully into a spot behind the foliage, where it wouldn't be visible from the road. Then he turned off the ignition and grinned at her. She turned away from him, facing toward the passenger side of the car.

"Undo me," she suggested. He pulled at the bow knot that held her halter in place, and the cloth dropped away from the thrust of her breasts. Walter slipped his arms under hers and cupped both breasts, drawing her against him. She turned her face to the side and he kissed the corner of her mouth. His right hand slipped down inside her shorts and panties, feeling the bristle of pubic hair. She was breathing quickly and in short gasps. Walter was as hard as a rock. He pulled his hand back up and yanked open the snap at the top of the shorts, then tugged at the zipper.

"Just a minute, honey," she whispered, pulling away from him. She pushed the shorts and panties down, dropping them to the floorboard of the car, then, naked, turned to face him. He was so eager for what she had to give that in that instant all his ingrained suspicion, all his laboriously developed policeman's instincts, were stilled. He caught only an instantaneous glance at the shiny thing in her hand before it slipped under his jacket. He let out a gasp and made a token effort to pull away, but she was as expert as she was quick. The thin blade of the knife slipped up between his ribs as though they had been designed to sheath it. The pain was sudden and sharp, and the shock was so intense that all the strength left his hands instantly.

His eyes widening, he fell against the back of the seat, staring at her. Brenda didn't even look into his eyes. Efficiently, she yanked the knife out of him and thrust it in again, one rib lower. Then, pulling it free, she wiped it casually on his slacks. Finally, she looked into his eyes, smiling sweetly.

"You were getting too close, dear," she said. "There's just no reason to leave loose ends like that, is there?" When she reached into his inside coat pocket he tried to stop her, but there was no strength in his arms, and she laughed amusedly at his attempt. She thrust the Xerox copies into her knapsack, closed the knife and put it in there, too, and finally pulled away from him. She pulled on her panties and then the shorts, yanking up the zipper with a hiss. After donning the halter, she opened the door and stopped, looking at him again. The pain in his side had subsided to a dull ache, throbbing slightly.

"I'd kiss you goodbye, Walter, but you might just have enough strength left to be troublesome. Don't worry, it will all be over soon. I'm really very good at my work. At every aspect of it. It's a shame, really. You were awfully good in bed, honey." A car rushed by on the other side of the bushes, the hiss of its passing dropping in pitch as it moved on. "Well, I guess I'd better be about finding a ride into L.A.," she said. *"Ciaou."* She got out and slammed the door, kissed the tip of her index finger, and blew the kiss at him through the closed window. The last he saw of Brenda was a glimpse as she rounded the bushes, moving toward the highway.

He was covered with sweat, and breathing loudly. His whole body felt incredibly weak. Another car approached, slowed, stopped. Some idiot giving Brenda a ride, he thought. The car's door opened, then slammed, and the vehicle moved on. Walter's shirt and jacket were sticky wet. He knew he had lost nearly enough blood to pass out. He was holding on by sheer force of will. That he was finished was a foregone conclusion. He had parked the car very carefully. No one would see it. The little bitch had — So why hold on so hard? What was the use? There was something — Something he could — What? His gaze fell on the dash, on the CB radio under it. Too late for help, he thought, but at least he could — He felt an incredible stab of pain as he tried to lift his arm. The sweat poured off of him, and the blood seemed to leak from his side faster with the effort.

"God help me," he murmured, and tried again. No good. *One last time*, he thought, *and I'll give up.* This time, by a supreme effort, he managed to reach the set, turn it on. He plucked the mike from its holder, keyed it up.

"Mayday." His voice was scarcely audible, even to himself. He pushed harder. "Mayday, mayday, mayday," he said, and released the mike button.

"Just a minute," someone said over the frequency. "There's somebody callin' mayday!"

"Mayday," Walter said again. "Help me, please. Behind bushes. South of diner — on Five —" He fell to the side, lying across the length of the car seat. His ears filled with a buzzing sound that wasn't coming from the CB set.

"Station calling mayday, what's happened to you, ol' buddy?" the voice from the set inquired. Walter almost laughed aloud. The mike was near to his mouth, and he managed one last time to punch the key.

"Brenda," he groaned. "Brenda. Oh, Jesus, Brenda —"

1976

Janet

The morning after Janet's visit to Rhea Carter's apartment, the kids came down with something. It didn't seem particularly serious. Janet debated with herself over the matter of letting them stay home. Cindy, the four-year-old, seemed the harder hit of the two, and nursery school wasn't all that important, so she yielded to her motherly instinct quickly. Margaret, the older, was in second grade though, and Janet couldn't see keeping the child at home over what seemed trivial. She wanted to let her stay home, but reacted to her own overprotectiveness, telling herself that she was being silly. She asked the butler to drive the girl to school, and let it go at that. Then, on second thought, she decided to take the two girls' temperatures. Cindy was running a mild temperature, just under a hundred. Margaret's was about ninety-nine, certainly not enough to justify losing a day's schooling.

So Plan A still holds, she told herself stoutly, and stood in the doorway watching as the butler drove the child away in the Jaguar.

Cindy didn't seem sick enough to have lost her interest in things. She wanted to get up and play, but Janet made her content herself with using her crayons in bed. She also brought her own Sony color set into the child's room. Then she went into the kitchen for some coffee and toast, and sat smoking and fretting. A touch of the flu, she told herself.

By noon Cindy had put down her colors and dropped into a muggy sleep. She was perspiring slightly, which was probably good, Janet thought. Sweating out the fever. Just to be certain, she got the thermometer and took her daughter's temperature again. It had gone up to a hundred and one.

"Would you like to watch television for a while?" Janet asked. Cindy shook her tiny head. "Maybe I could get the Will-O-the-Wisp set out and we could play a game or two," she suggested. It was a game she had received on her last birthday, which she loved. Once again she shook her head.

"I'm tired, mama," she said in a scratchy voice.

"Okay, lazy bones." Janet manufactured a smile. "You get some sleep then, and later I'll have some butterscotch pudding for us to share. How's that?" Cindy nodded vaguely and closed her eyes. Janet restrained an urge to touch the child, to grip her and hold her as though she might slip away. Then, to mollify her own impulses, she laid a palm on her forehead. It felt hot, and she was still sweating. Janet pulled the blankets up under Cindy's chin and sat looking at her apprehensively for a moment. Her ruminations were interrupted by a discreet rap on the door frame. It was the maid, the new one she had hired after those things had disappeared in the house. The woman was in her late thirties, rather dour but thoroughly competent. "Yes?" Janet asked.

"The telephone, ma'am. It's the school." Janet looked at the woman for a moment. It was as though she had expected this.

"All right. Thank you." She rose and walked into the hall, then went into the master bedroom and picked up the phone there.

"Mrs. Stafford?" She recognized the voice of Reverend Blake, who served as principal. "I really think we should send Margaret home. She's been complaining of headaches and tiredness since she got here this morning, and her manner seems to back it all up. The nurse just took her temperature, and she's running a hundred and two." His tone was just a bit accusatory, as though Janet should have known better than to send the child into school in the first place.

"It wasn't even a hundred this morning," Janet said, and then felt irritation with herself for having made excuses. "All right. Can someone drive her here? My other child is sick, too, and I'd rather not leave the house."

By two both girls were definitely worse. Cindy was up to a hundred and three, and damp cloths and aspirin were doing precisely no good. Margaret's reading up past a hundred and two, and she had vomited on the floor next to her bed. Janet had personally moved the child into her sister's room where she could keep an eye on both of them, asking the butler to bring one of the folding beds in from the garage. Both children had turned pale. Janet, who hated to panic over these things, decided that it was time to call the family doctor.

"I'm tied up all day," he said. "I don't see how I could possibly make it —"

"Ted, I wouldn't presume if I wasn't scared about this," Janet said. He had become the family physician because Phillip had met him at some cocktail parties. They weren't precisely friends, but she decided to proceed as though they were. In her brief acting career she had learned the technique of building up an inner emotion, holding it back and then allowing it to break through at just the right moment. This time the emotion was ready-made, and she had been holding it in for hours. She let her voice break slightly. "They're getting worse all the time."

"All right. Now don't panic, honey." There was a pause, possibly while he consulted something. "Two hours," he said. "That's the absolute best I can do. I'll have to cancel two routine examinations and a vasectomy, but maybe Les Thrall can handle everything else for me this afternoon."

"Thank you, Ted." She felt that illogical, tentative relief that comes with the knowledge that a doctor will soon be on the scene.

"In the meantime, keep them in bed —"

"Keep them in! They can't get up."

" — and try to get as much liquid down them as you can. Water, orange juice, even Kool-Aid."

"All right, Ted. And thanks again."

She managed to get a tall glass of orange juice into Cindy, and just a bit more than that into her sister. The children had become so torpid that she wanted to shake them, to try to stimulate some feeling in them, some emotion, even irritation with her. She took their temperatures again just before Ted's Continental rounded their driveway. It was up, in both cases. Alarmingly up.

"All right, now, it's possibly just the flu." She had met him at the door. He was carrying one of those little black bags, like a country doctor in an old movie. He went to the bedroom with the authority of a general taking charge, pulled two thermometers from his bag, tore off sterile wrappers, and thrust them into the girls' mouths. Janet stood staring at him, trying not to fidget. When he looked at the thermometer that had been in Cindy's mouth, he almost blanched.

"Jesus, this kid is burning up," he said, looking up at Janet in astonishment. He plucked the other thermometer out of Margaret's mouth, and his eyes widened still further. "Have you felt bad? Any symptoms? Or any of the servants?" he asked. Janet shook her head. Her eyes were spilling over, and she didn't trust her voice. "Are your kids allergic to anything?"

"Not — that I know — of," she said.

"Well, I'm going to give each of them a half million units of penicillin, and then they're going to Cedars of Lebanon Hospital."

"Are they going — to be all right?"

"Of course they're going to be all right," Ted said almost annoyedly. "But we didn't get to this any too soon. You'd better call their father."

"I tried. He's not at the studio."

"Well, have them track him down." He looked up at her as he took some vials of penicillin from his bag, and smiled. "Just because he'd never forgive me if I didn't let him play the concerned parent at a time like this," he assured her. "Now don't worry. It's just some wretched bacteria, and these days we know how to kill bacteria. Now go make that phone call."

Two hours later, at the hospital, she tried for the tenth time to reach Phillip. It finally occurred to her that he must be with Rhea. *While his children are —* She caught herself just in time to keep from articulating the terrible word in her mind. *While his children are sick he's with that little hooker.*

At five o'clock Ted came into the waiting room, looking exhausted and dazed. Janet rose from her chair and stood as though there were a wall to her back. Ted's handsome face was almost haggard looking, as though he had come up against something that had reduced his belief in an orderly universe. He had put on a white smock and pants, and he looked like one of those TV star doctors on the soaps. It almost made Janet want to laugh.

"I don't understand this," he said. "Nothing we do seems to help. It's like something supernatural." It was just an expression to him, Janet knew, but the words went through her like a flood of icy water. "Have you reached Phil?" She shook her head. "He should be here," Ted said with unconscious meaningfulness.

"How long do they have?" The words weren't her own; they just came out of her mouth, and revealed to her how much she had admitted in her unconscious. Ted looked at her for several seconds, evidently decided that it would be worse than useless to try to calm her with disingenuous assurances any longer.

"If we can't find a way to break this thing," he admitted, "until tomorrow. Maybe the next day."

"Can I talk with them?"

"They're only sporadically conscious now," he told her. "We've got them packed in ice to try to reduce their temperature." He looked at her with an expression of desperation. "It doesn't do any good." She laid a hand on his shoulder, comforting the comforter.

"Ted, I want to see them," she said gently. He nodded.

They looked incredibly tiny in their hospital beds. Some sort of rubber thing had been placed under each of them, and filled with ice. Cindy was making little mewing sounds of distress in her sleep. Margaret's eyes opened, and she looked up as Janet leaned over her bed.

"Mama, make it stop." she pleaded, and closed her eyes once again. It was funny, Janet thought. There were no tears in her now. She was intensely calm, as controlled as a champion billiard player before an intricate shot. She laid her hand on the child's burning forehead.

"All right, honey," she said. "But I'll have to go somewhere to do it." She leaned down and kissed Margaret on the forehead, then turned around and did the same to Cindy.

She drove very carefully all the way home, then went into the bedroom and started to search through the closet. The maid came in a moment later, when Janet was standing on a chair, looking through everything on the shelf over the hangers.

"How are they, ma'am?" she asked.

"The doctor isn't sure," Janet said, and continued to search.

"Can I help you, ma'am? What are you looking for?"

"Never mind. Return to your duties," Janet said stiffly. She pushed aside the last box on the shelf and climbed down from the chair.

She went through the other closets, then finally remembered, and went out to the garage, where she climbed a step ladder, finding the box on a neglected shelf, behind some packages of Christmas wrapping that had been there for years. The box was covered with a thick coating of dust, but she could make out the imprint of a rampant horse, and the words COLT WOODSMAN.

It had belonged to Phillip since he was a boy. She remembered having thrown away a half box of ammunition because she was afraid the girls might get hold of the gun. The slide functioned a bit stiffly, so she found some Three-in-One and oiled it. Then it worked perfectly. Finding one of her larger purses, she dropped the pistol inside it, then drove to a sporting goods store on Vine Street.

"A Woodsman?" the youngster behind the counter asked. "That would be .22 Long Rifle. You want regular or hollow point?"

"What's the difference?"

"The hollow points open up faster, make a bigger hole."

"I'll take the hollow points."

Janet drove to a spot a block from Rhea Carter's apartment and parked the car. Then she loaded the pistol the way Phillip had taught her before they were married. Finally, she dropped it back into her purse, along with the rest of the box of cartridges, and walked along the sidewalk until she spotted his car. *You son of a bitch*, she thought, *I should use this on you.*

She went to one of the nearby coffee shops and drank several cups of coffee, then walked back. It was growing dark. The Rolls Royce was gone. Janet walked onto the grounds of the apartment complex and sat on one of the benches. Finally, when it was close to nine o'clock, she decided to go ahead with it. The uncommon calmness that had come over her in the hospital hadn't deserted her. She knew her hand would be steady.

The door wasn't even locked. Very careless, she thought, turning the knob. The room was orderly and elegant as it had been the previous day, except that the coffee table held two used glasses and a martini pitcher. The lights were out, but she could hear the shower running upstairs. Janet walked to the couch and sat down, after closing the door. She fished the pistol out of her purse and released the safety. Then she rested it against her thigh, where it wouldn't be visible to someone coming out of the rear of the apartment.

She sat there for what seemed a very long time, and thought about going up the stairs. But finally she heard the slap of bedroom slippers, and placed her hand on the grip of the automatic. Her heart was beating wildly, but she was still certain that she would be able to hold the gun steady. Especially if she held it in both hands.

A moment later Rhea Carter came through the doorway at the head of the stairs, her body swathed in a multicolored terry bathrobe, and her head wrapped in a pink towel. She didn't notice Janet as she descended the stairs. Something moved with serpentine grace next to her feet, and Janet recognized the cat that had hissed at her the previous day. Rhea switched on a lamp, turned and looked directly at Janet for a full second, then let out a sudden, rasping cry. The cat arched its back, crouching and looking at Janet as though she were a natural enemy. Janet tightened her grasp on the gun, very careful not to press her finger against the trigger.

"Oh, it's you," Rhea said with regained composure. "I guess I should have told Philly boy to lock the door on his way out."

"I guess you should have."

"What do you want?" The cat was still hunkered down, its belly scraping the thick capret, and its wide yellow eyes were fastened to Janet. It moved forward at a glacier pace, as though stalking something patiently.

"I want my children's lives," Janet said. She injected a note of pleading into her voice. Perhaps, she thought, it would be possible to appeal to whatever decency the girl had, and then she wouldn't have to go through with this thing that was bound to change her very being.

"Do you, now?" Rhea looked at her blandly, as though considering some disclaimer. Then she smiled archly. "You should have thought of that a bit sooner."

"What have you done to them?" Janet asked calmly, almost curiously.

"Personally, nothing. I haven't been near them, as you know." The cat was still creeping closer. Janet, who had never hurt an animal in her life, decided that as soon as it came within reach she was going to stomp on it just as hard as she could.

"Whatever you're doing, why don't you do it to me? Margaret and Cindy haven't hurt you. Why don't you do it to me?" she repeated beseechingly.

"Of course, dear." Rhea thrust both hands into the pockets of her robe. "In good time. But first, the brats. I promised you. Remember? I remember."

"Then there's nothing I can do to change your mind?" Janet asked. She laid her fingertip against the trigger of the pistol, caressing the ridged metal almost sensuously. Rhea shook her head, her eyes glittering like rhinestones.

"Not a thing."

Janet raised the pistol, grasping it with both hands. She saw the sights, superimposed on Rhea's cleavage, just as the cat sprang. It made a sibilant noise that seemed to grow deeper in the instant it was airborne. The hiss became a snarl such as no house cat had ever made, and the animal's body seemed to fill the whole of Janet's vision. When it struck her it threw her back against the couch, driving the wind from her, and twisting her spine viciously. The pistol made a sharp snapping sound just before she dropped it. Janet tumbled to the floor, something lithe and powerful and incredibly heavy atop her.

"That's enough!" Rhea shouted. "Hold!" It sounded as though she were talking to a watch dog. Janet's vision cleared and she saw the animal's face hovering above her own, the huge, sleek head, covered with black hair, the alert, savage eyes that glowered down into her own, their amber pupils dilated, the two-inch fangs jutting from the powerful jaws. Saucer-sized paws bracketed her body. She felt the animal's belly against her own, pitching and contracting as the hot breath washed over her face.

She moved her head, trying to raise it, and the huge cat made another deep, snarling cough, dipping its face towards hers until the wiry whiskers of its nose scratched at her cheek. "Lie very still, Janet," Rhea advised from somewhere beyond her vision. "He gets rather excited when someone tries to harm me. He has his job, after all." She walked calmly to where the pistol had fallen and picked it up. "All right, get off her," she said. The panther didn't move. Its eyes took on a deep green glint from the lamp. "Toby! Do as I say!" Rhea commanded. With obvious reluctance, the animal backed up a step, then hopped to the side, clearing Janet's body. It stopped, looking at her with wariness. "Go in the other room," Rhea ordered in a more casual voice. "It's all right now." She held up the gun as though the animal could understand her words and gestures perfectly. The huge cat looked up at her, then back at Janet. Finally, it moved away in a low, prowling motion. Its huge paws left deep prints in the carpet. Rhea moved to a wingback chair and sat. Her robe fell open in front, revealing elegant legs. She still had the pistol in her hand.

"I have to give it to you, dear," she said. "I didn't think you had the balls to pull a stunt like this. You were almost quick enough, too. Get up, you look like an idiot lying there. Unless you'd like me to join you, that is," she purred.

Janet was barely aware of pulling herself to a sitting position, then dragging her body up to the couch. She perched on the edge like a bird ready for flight. "Quite an experience the first time you see something like that, isn't it?" Rhea said. Janet hugged herself, suddenly chilled.

"Rhea, please spare my daughters. I'll do anything, be anything you want. Take it out on me.

"I am, dear. Your children obviously mean more to you than anything else, so I'll start with them. You'll be next." Janet looked at her, and imagined for an instant that she could see the girl's skull grinning through her flesh. She seemed literally demonic. "Of course you've made things worse for them by trying this. I just can't let you get away with such antics, can I? I was going to let things go as they have been, but now I'll alter the scenario. Soon they'll regain consciousness, and they'll remain cognizant right to the end. The pains, real pains, will start in less than an hour, and increase steadily. If you try to go near them, they won't recognize you. They'll snap and bite like rabid animals. Their screams will be audible all over the hospital ward."

"Stop it!" Janet shrieked the words, but her plea only made Rhea's eyes shine the brighter.

"And then, the final symptom will be convulsions. They'll last, oh, eight or nine hours. The doctors will be very puzzled. Articles will probably be written about this one."

"You're not even human," Janet whispered, more frightened of the girl's manner than of what she was saying. There was such obvious, almost childlike relish in the way she described her atrocities. But suddenly her face contorted into a contemptuous frown.

"Stop that nonsense. There's nothing special about being human, dear. There are forces far mightier than humanity. And I mean to —" She stopped herself, as though she had been about to articulate a long held secret, and smiled again. "Let's see, now, what delightful little experiences shall I prepare for you?"

"I beg of you," Janet said, though she no longer hoped. "I'll put myself in your hands. Torture me, or humiliate me, or do anything you want."

"Of course. How would you like a case of leprosy? Or a brain disease that slowly turns you into a moron, and then an imbecile, and finally a vegetable? How would you like to wake up tomorrow to find that you have no control over your bladder or your bowels — just for a start? I haven't decided which tack to take, but I assure you, I intend to have a lot of fun with you." Janet nodded miserably.

"Anything. But give them back their lives."

Rhea placed the gun on her bare lap and then rested her elbows on the arms of her chair, making a steeple with her fingertips. She rotated them slowly, in tiny circles. There was something fascinatingly senuous about the gesture. Janet had to tear her eyes away and refocus on Rhea's face, which had taken on a marble hardness, as though her cheeks had been sculpted from stone. Her eyes were glittering gems.

"Do you really mean that, Janet? Just how far are you willing to go in order to rescue those little monsters of yours?"

It took a few seconds for the words and their implication to sink into Janet's mind. She had fallen into a comforting numbness, but now, as she looked up at the girl sitting across from her, she felt a reawakening of hope, and with it painful fright. She leaned forward, her hands clenching, the muscles gnarled and protruding.

"What do you want of me?" she asked. "Just tell me. Anything."

Rhea sat very still, even her fingertips suddenly held in

check. Janet felt certain that the girl had come to some decision, but that she was toying with her, and that if she, Janet, didn't display the requisite amount of anxiety, the right degree of supplication, Rhea would change her mind. She loosed the iron control she had maintained, just enough to set her lip to trembling, and allow a perceptible tremor to possess her hands. Rhea smiled as though staisfied by the performance.

"Come here," she said.

Janet had to push on the couch with her hand to rise. Her arms and legs were rubbery. Inside her was a tingling emotion, compounded of terror and excitement, because she knew a glimmering of a suspicion of what the girl wanted. Staggering like a drunkard, she approached the wingback chair and stood there, like a soldier ready for inspection. Languidly, Rhea placed the pistol on the floor, then took Janet's hand and tugged until the woman dropped to her lap. Janet stiffend, an abortive act of resistance, as Rhea casually flipped back her skirt, revealing slender, shapely legs. They were bare, because Janet hadn't paused to put on hose before going to the hospital, or before coming to the apartment afterward. Rhea looked at her quizzically, holding her hands clear of Janet in an open invitation to move away from her. Janet was certain that if she showed the slightest indication of doing so, there would be no second chance. The quizzical expression on Rhea's face gradually gave way to its former demonic smile. Slowly, with infinite, sensual casualness, her hand descended to rest on Janet's thigh.

The touch sent a tremor of revulsion through Janet, but despite herself she felt a tinge of excitement too, at the sheer sensuousness of Rhea's touch.

"How old are you?" Rhea asked in a slow, husky drawl.

"Twenty-nine," Janet managed to say without stammering.

"You look younger. You know, you're really a very attractive woman, Janet."

"Thank you." The words sounded stuipd in her own ears, and they deepened the smile, the glitter of Rhea's eyes.

"But you really should take better care of yourself. Your hair is a mess, and your makeup is all smudgy." Her hand slipped along Janet's thigh, then rose to the top button of her dress. Janet stiffened, but managed to withhold the protest, and the resistance, that surged through her flesh. If Rhea noticed, she ignored it. Her fingers, moving with studied slowness, opened the button, then moved to the next one. "You've been perspiring, too," Rhea whispered. "You need a shower, and some fresh perfume. Do you have any with you? No? Well, no matter. I can spare you a little. I think Shalimar would be your style." She had opened the dress to the waist, and now pushed it back over Janet's shoulders, pinning her arms. Though Janet fought it, there was a deliciousness to the helpless feeling. Rhea slipped the shoulder straps of her bra down and then pulled the bra free of her breasts, letting it rest against Janet's belly.

"My," she said in a tone that was husky and chatty at once. "You are a lovely woman. Particularly for one who's had two children." Her hand cupped one breast, and Janet's entire body convulsed in a spasm of revulsion. And excitement. Rhea's left hand slipped up her bare back, over her neck and tangled in the thick blond hair that hung loose about Janet's shoulders. Slowly, she pulled Janet's face toward her own.

"Wait, please," Janet whispered. Rhea paused, looking into her eyes with an impish and questioning expression. "How do I know you'll keep your part of the bargain?" Janet asked.

Rhea feigned puzzlement. "My attention must have wandered, darling. I didn't know we had struck any bargain. You're just being nice to me in the hope that I'll change my mind about your brats." Janet looked into the hard green eyes, so grotesquely close to her own for a moment, found them unreadable. Then, relaxing, she allowed herself to be kissed.

Later, she would wonder how many such sessions she could stand before losing her mind. Her revulsion was unabated, but Rhea Carter knew how to turn that revulsion into a weapon, to excite her with it, to bring her to a thrashing, gasping and sweaty passion such as she had never known before, even with her husband. Several times, as she lay in Rhea's bed that night, she caught herself just short of pleading for the climax she knew the girl could give her at will. Finally, when even Rhea's awesome appetites seemed slaked, she sat against the backboard of her king-size bed, taking a cigarette out of a box on the bedside table and firing it with a matching silver lighter. She took a long, delicious drag and held the smoke in her lungs for a moment. Then, letting it escape from her nostrils in two thick streams, she placed the cigarette between Janet's lips. Janet could taste the barest tang of the woman's lipstick. Rhea took back her cigarette and regarded Janet speculatively.

"Now," she said. "What shall I do with you?" Janet, sprawled next to her, rose on one elbow, suddenly tense. Her hair was a tangle, her makeup, freshly applied before their lengthy sexual interlude, smeared and patchy. She could smell the heavy musk of her own juices. "This was nice, dear," Rhea told her. "But it's just a beginning. Not that, really. The bare nub of a beginning." Reaching forward, she ran her fingers through the thick jungle of Janet's hair. There was a patronizing, proprietary air to the gesture, which ended with a brief stroking of her cheek.

"Even if I do decide to spare those two bitch pups of yours dear, I can afflict them again. Like that." She flicked her cigarette, tossing a bit of ash onto Janet's breast. It was only warm, but Janet recoiled, partly from a sense of duty. "That puts me in a very nice position, doesn't it, dear?"

"Yes. It does," Janet said in a lifeless tone.

"So if you want to keep them healthy, you're going to have to be my little slave girl. Would you object to that?" Janet shook her head. "Good." Rhea thrust her cigarette between Janet's lips again. Obediently, Janet sucked in some smoke, expelled it.

"Now," Rhea said, "you understand I'm promising nothing. You have nothing with which to bargain, after all." She paused long enough to indicate that a response was required.

"I know that," Janet acceded.

"Good." Suddenly, sharply, she looked straight into Janet's eyes. "Are you ready to serve me before all else? Answer me."

"Yes."

"Do you renounce all others?"

"I do."

"Do you, specifically," Rhea asked, exhaling another lungful of white smoke, "renounce God?" Janet shuddered. The words stuck in her throat, but she managed to nod.

"Say it, then," Rhea commanded, her voice silky.

"I renounce God."

"And reject His mercy."

"And — reject His mercy."

"And you give up, without reservations, your hope of salvation."

"I — Oh, God, please, Rhea." Her Quaker upbringing made a last, pathetic sally. But the girl's eyes were intractable. "I give up, without reservation, my hope of salvation," she recited.

"For all time."

"For all time."

"And you pledge me unquestioning obedience, in all things, good and evil."

"Yes, yes, I do, I pledge that, Rhea, I swear it," Janet sobbed.

"And you do so without hope of any compensation from me. You do so in the hope that I'll take care of my own. Swear it!"

"I swear it, Rhea." Janet felt hollow, as though everything in her that had lived had been scooped out. Rhea's smile was dazzling.

"That's fine, dear." She stretched with feline opulence.

"And now, I think I'd like to be alone."

When Janet was dressed, Rhea called her to the bedside. With languid authority, she ran a hand under Janet's skirt. "Stay by your phone, dear. I may want you to come over for another little visit. Or I may want you to run an errand for me."

"Of course. Whatever you say."

"That's right, dear. Whatever I say."

And that, Rhea thought as she drifted toward sleep, took care of Janet Stafford for all eternity. When she received word that her children had died, she would be as near to madness as a woman could come. The rest would take only a nudge. And Rhea had decided the form that nudge would take. She pulled the silk sheet, still redolent of the girl's fragrance, under her chin. For something that had begun as a near catastrophe, this night had turned out to be quite refreshing.

1976

Rhea

The next morning Rhea received a call from Brenda. It was nine o'clock.

"I thought I told you not to call this early," she said grumpily.

"I'm sorry," Brenda replied in a voice that was barely contrite enough. "I just thought you'd want to know that I got the job done."

"Fine. Any complications?"

"Of course not. It was simple. Men are so easy to manipulate, aren't they?"

"You didn't think so when I first met you, dear," Rhea reminded her. The words, and the tone in which she delivered them, conveyed a gentle threat. Brenda could easily go back to what she had been. It had been a simple matter for Rhea to arrange the alteration, and it would be just as simple to put things back as they had been. There was a pause at the other end of the wire.

"No complications," Brenda said in a voice that was considerably chastened. "I got his records. Everything he found out, and meant to send to his client. Do you want to see them?"

"No, just burn them. And then take a little vacation. Lie low. How are you fixed for money?"

"I can always use some extra, if it isn't —"

"Look in the usual place. I'll have five thousand there for you by noon."

"Thank you." She sounded cautiously brighter. "I don't see how they can possibly tie this to me. The clerk at the motel didn't see me."

"Lie low anyway. You've earned some time off. Go ruin some nice guy's life. If you keep working like this, I may decide to trust you with more of my business." Having put the girl in her place, Rhea decided that a little stroking was in order. She could almost see Brenda glow at the other end.

"Thanks. Anything I can do."

When the girl had hung up, Rhea pressed down on the cradle for a moment, then dialed Philly-boy's private office number. She let it ring six times before she hung up.

"My mind must be going," she murmured, and dialed the front desk at Cedars of Lebanon Hospital. She had him paged.

"Hello?" he said in his sexy, gravel voice.

"Hi, Philly-boy." There was a moment of silence, and she could barely hear him breathing.

"You always know where to find me, don't you?" he asked half in wonder, half in exasperation.

"I have a little bird. Tell me, are your brats still breathing?" There was a sharp intake of breath from the other end.

"I guess I'll never comprehend the depth of your depravity," he said.

Rhea laughed. "Of course you will. We're two of a kind, sweetheart."

"No. I'm not in your league."

"That's where you're mistaken, Philly-boy. Why not prove how right I am and come over here?" There was that silence again; she could feel his excitement at the suggestion.

"Jesus, you know that's impossible," he rasped.

"No, no, all you have to do is drive over. What's the matter? Are there newspaper reporters present or something? Are you afraid of the publicity?" She waited and, when he didn't answer, continued. "Don't tell me you're reluctant to leave your dear little children, because this is Rhea you're talking to, dear. I know you better than you've ever allowed yourself to know you. Now come on over. I'm going to shower and put on something nice for you."

"No." There was an ersatz finality in his voice. Rhea was sure it was meant to guard his illusions about himself. Now she would put it on a basis that wouldn't allow him to refuse, and he could continue to tell himself that it wasn't what he wanted to do.

"Now don't be perverse, darling. You know you want to. And when you get here, I'm going to make you an offer you can't refuse."

"Rhea, for Christ's sake —"

"You'll be sorry if you don't. And I promise you, you'll be very glad you did. For one thing, you might save your wife from a jail sentence. Just think of the publicity that would cause."

He was silent again. It was really quite amusing, Rhea thought, how he would lapse into silence when she surprised him, or when he didn't know what to say.

"What are you talking about?"

"A Colt Woodsman .22 automatic, dear. With your wife's fingerprints all over it. And a bullet in one of my walls that matches it perfectly. Shall I expect you in twenty minutes?"

"I'll try."

"Try very hard, dear. And, Philly-boy, aren't you glad I gave you an excuse to do what you wanted to do anyway?" She let her laughter fade away as she slowly hung up the telephone.

He made it in twenty-three minutes, unshaven and in the same clothes he had worn the previous night. Rhea had taken the time to put on a pair of gold lamé lounging pajamas with matching slippers. She had also pinned her hair up in a dramatic sweep that emphasized the graceful taper of her neck. She met him at the door and kissed him.

"You go in and shave," she said. "Then we'll get on with things."

"What's this about my wife taking a shot at you?" he demanded.

"After you've had a shave and shower. Go on, now. You know the way to the bathroom."

"How —?" He cut himself off, looking at the set of her head, the determined expression in her eyes. Ten minutes later he was back in one of the terry robes Rhea kept in her closet, shaven and showered. She gave him a cup of tea and sat next to him on the couch, pulling her knees up and sitting on her bare feet.

"All right," he said. "Now, will you tell me what this is all about?"

"You'll have to ask Janet, dear. She's the one who came over here last night with a gun in her purse."

"How did she even know about this place?"

"Oh, she's been following me about for weeks."

"And you never mentioned it to me."

"It never came up."

"It's not like her," he said, looking at Toby stretched out in front of the fireplace. "I just can't picture her doing something like that." He looked at Rhea. She looked back with a bland expression. "All right, what are you going to do about it?"

"Nothing at all. She knows better than to try something like that again. She had a rather good scare. And pretty soon she won't be around anyway." His cup rattled against his saucer, and the expression in his eyes told her a lot she already knew.

"What do you mean, not around?"

"You are priceless, Philly-boy. Don't worry, I mean every word I say. She'll be out of your way in a few days. And then you'll be free to marry me." A tic pulled at his cheek.

"This is sudden," he said.

"If you don't want to marry me, you have only to say so." She smiled at him.

"No, I won't say that."

"Fine. And we'll make a fine team, dear. We'll accomplish great things together. You can't begin to envision the plans I have for you and me."

"Then all this stuff I've been through, jumping through your hoops, has been leading up to something?"

"I've been testing you, Phill-boy. That's why I picked you up at that dull party in the first place, and why I've been getting you to do things that some men wouldn't have done, and most men would have revolted against a good deal more firmly than you did."

"To break me down, you mean."

"I haven't broken down anything but your illusions," she snorted. "Like most people you have illusions in place of principles. But you were almost honest enough to admit it. I haven't been breaking you down, Philly-boy. I've been helping you to become a more honest man."

"And now, I take it, there's some last test, and that's what I'm here for."

"Bravo! You're a very bright fellow. Yes, it's final exam time, dear." She leaned forward, closing the distance between them to scarcely a foot. She could smell the shaving lotion he had just put on, the soap from his shower. "This is where we find out what you're really made of, and whether we've been wrong about you all along."

"Who is we?"

"We is you and I, dear. No one else." There was a subtle shift to his expression. She had to hand it to him. He was a poker player. Only a hundred and eighty years of living enabled her to read him so easily. "You've developed some suspicions about me, and the source of my powers, haven't you? Well, you're right." That produced a shudder that was barely perceptible, and she laughed softly. "But don't let that scare you, dear. You'll be answerable only to me. It's time I struck out on my own. I've been preparing for a long time."

"And I'm to be your first employee?"

"One of the first, and certainly the most significant acquisition to date."

"All right," he said tiredly, but with a measure of interest in his voice. "What's the test?"

"I want you to consent to what's going to happen. To your wife and those little brats of yours." He closed his eyes, leaning his head back against the couch.

"And if I don't?" he asked.

"Then everything will be just ducky. Happy ending, just like one of those trite television shows you produce. Your children will make a miraculous recovery. Your wife will continue in good health to a ripe old age. Rhea the bitch will vanish from your life, and you can return to a routine of domestic bliss."

"If I do consent, will Janet know?" His eyes were still closed, his head resting on the couch back.

"Oh, shit, what do you care?"

"What will happen to her? I mean, I know she'll die, but will she suffer first?" His voice was flat, barely curious.

"She'll suffer deliciously. That little twat laid hands on me, dear. She called me names, and threatened me. I intend to see that she has nothing left, not even human dignity. When death comes, the only reason she won't welcome it will be that she lacks the rational faculty to recognize it," Rhea said with obvious relish.

Phillip opened his eyes and looked at her. It almost got to her, because the expression on his face was that of a man who has made peace with something he had long suspected about himself. As though he were remembering, rather than discovering. And there wasn't the fear she had expected, or even the momentary self-loathing she had come to expect in people at such moments.

She slid off the couch, kneeling before him, moving her soft, slender hands along his thighs toward his crotch, until they stopped just short of their destination.

"All right," he said, as though he had decided which morning paper to buy. "Go ahead with it."

1976

Phillip

Never had he felt such relief.

It was like discovering for the first time that all his life he had been carrying a superfluous load on his shoulders, and now someone had finally taught him that he could put it down. He remembered an old version of *Dr. Jekyll and Mr. Hyde,* in which Hyde's first words were something like, "Is this evil? I like it!"

All his life he had been playing other people's games, going by hypocritical rules he had learned from his parents, and from society. Go so far and no further. Deal sharply with competitors, and above all, win. But observe the rules outwardly, cover your tracks, pretend.

Honor they father and they mother.... Love your wife because she's your wife, love and protect your children because they're the issue of your body, and dependent on you....

It was all such bullshit, and he had never allowed himself to admit that it was, even in his own mind. He had manufactured a conscience of one-tenth imagination and nine-tenths hypocrisy.

And now he was free. His children were dead or dying, and he was relieved that his life would no longer be cluttered with them. He had only sired them because they were part of the picture of a family man, pillar of the community. They had been a bore to him, an encumbrance; he was well rid of them.

And as for Janet, her fate, whatever it might be, filled him with an awesome indifference. In a few days she would be out of the way, and then he could marry this little bitch, and that might get her out of his system, leave him free to go on with his own concerns. Why she wanted him in the first place, he didn't know. He supposed that a motion picture magnate could be of some use to her. Well, he would as well serve her as the nonsense he had been serving for most of his life.

The afternoon and evening blurred in his mind. It was always that way when he was with Rhea. All he could remember later were isolated moments and a general montage of intense pleasure. He supposed he was bewitched in some way. Well, that was all right, too. Not all right, really, but he had always been a realist. At least now she would be available to him whenever he wanted her. He wouldn't have to go through those long periods of barren waiting, wondering when and if he would see her again.

He returned to the studio. His secretary had gone home, but there was a message for him to call Cedars of Lebanon Hospital. He crumpled the note and dropped it in the empty wastebasket next to her desk, then went on into the inner office.

Two pieces of mail had arrived, both special delivery. The one on top was from Walter Lankershim. He'd have to contact that man, tell him to forget it all. The mystery was solved, or solved as much as mattered. Idly, he tore open the envelope, pulled out the sheaf of Xerox copies, and leafed through them.

At first they didn't make any logical sense to him. They had been neatly arranged in choronological order, but they were just copies of newspaper obituary pages, with certain articles boxed in red ink. Then, just as they had with Walter Lankershim, the similarities began to impinge on his consciousness. He read over them several times, then laid them face up in a stack and cleared his mind of everything extraneous, the way he had learned to do in business, thinking of only the matter that was intrinsic to the papers themselves. It was a pattern, of course. Women, fairly young women, kept dying and leaving their fortune to younger ones. It was the same pattern that Lankershim had noted before, carried back several generations. It might go back much further than that. How far? Well, that didn't matter for the moment.

Then he thought about Rhea, the things she had told him that day, the things she had hinted at. He applied those things to the pattern, and it was like a fade-in, like a big arc lamp on one of the sets being slowly activated. He chuckled to himself softly, then laughed aloud.

Rhea. Could you really be all those women?

Then, suddenly, one of the names, the last one before Susan Black, jumped out at him with such emphasis that he couldn't imagine how he had failed to notice it before.

Sally Platz.

Jesus, if he was right about this, then she had been watching him, assessing him, for twenty years! Had she been Sally when he had been screwing the girl?

No, he thought. No, that didn't seem likely. He remembered now, something he had forgot about, something he hadn't thought of since his little interlude with Sally. She had given up her chances for a career and dropped out of sight right after taking that job. That, probably, was how Rhea had learned about him.

"Christ," he said, suddenly filled with a refreshed sense of helplessness. How could he even hope to compete with a woman like that?

Then something occurred to him, something small but glimmeringly encouraging. Walter Lankershim had managed to get his information to him despite Rhea. Could it be that she didn't know about these papers? Could it be that all the time she had been manipulating him, something else had been —?

Idly, he picked up the other item, looked at it. It was a large manila envelope, with a flap at one end, tied in place with a little string, and sealed as well. It was addressed to him, and marked with the little code symbol that forbade even his private secretary to open it. No more than a dozen people in the world knew of that code. He hadn't even told Walter Lankershim about it, but, to avoid the proliferation that could render the gimmick worthless, had instructed his private secretary to convey all items from Lankershim without opening them.

He looked at the envelope for a moment, then tore it open, feeling a dull excitement deep in his belly. Inside was another envelope, only slightly smaller. Where the address should have been, there was only his name. And where the return address would normally have been written, there was, in thick red letters, large and blocked, a single name: BRENDA.

He sat looking at it for a moment, his heart mildly accelerated. He didn't know why, but he had the feeling that this strange-looking envelope had something to do with the smaller one he had just opened. He laid it on his desk and walked to the bar, mixing himself a bourbon and water. Walking to the door, he locked it, just in case the night watchman might come by. He shot the bolt, too.

Finally, like a kid putting off opening a birthday present until the last moment, he walked back, sat down and set his drink on the green blotter, precisely over the circular mark where another had been set before. Then he picked up the manila envelope and held it in his hands for a moment. It was thick, obviously stuffed with several layers of paper. At last he tore it open and pulled out the contents.

The first thing he saw was a Xerox of one of the newspaper clippings, exactly like the copies Lankershim had sent him. Under it were several others, all those he had found in the first envelope. Had he been a less methodical man, he might have missed, at least for the moment, the salient materials, which were on the bottom.

The bottom two sheets were genuine newspaper clippings, not Xerox copies. They were fresh, torn out carefully and folded to fit into the envelope. The first thing he saw was a picture of Walter Lankershim. It was an old photo, of a much younger man, without the moustache, but instantly recognizable. He was dressed in a police uniform. The legend at the top of the clipping told him it was from the Los Angeles *Times*. Under the picture was a headline, medium-size.

L.A. PRIVATE DET. MURDERED IN CAR

Beneath that was a story relating how the body of one Walter Lankershim had been found in a 1971 Ford sedan beside Interstate Five. He had been stabbed at least twice. There was no sign of a struggle, it said, so apparently the murderer had been someone he had trusted. The story went on to say that the body might not have been found until routine maintenance had led someone to the spot, which was secluded behind a large mass of foliage, except that just before dying Lankershim had made a call over his Citizen's Band radio. A Union Oil trucker had picked up the call, but all he had got from Lankershim was the name "Brenda," which the private detective had called several times. It wasn't much of a lead, the Highway Patrol admitted, but it was all they had at the moment, and they were following it up. It was possible that the party, Brenda, had been a hitchhiker. This passage had been circled in red ink.

The second clipping was a repeat of the first, but from a northern newspaper. It was headlined in much larger type, doubtless because it was the biggest piece of news in the area. There was no picture of Lankershim this time, but there was in its place a photo of his car being towed out from behind a clump of bushes. Nearby was a sign, one of those that lined the freeways, announcing that the road was Interstate Five. The photo had been circled in red, like the mention of the hitchhiker theory in the *Times* piece.

Phillip sat looking at the photo for several minutes, sipping at his drink until it was exhausted. Then he took the glass back to the bar for a refill. He sat down again, read both the pieces over several more times, and looked at the photo some more. Obviously Brenda, whoever she might be, had sent him this material for a reason. She was trying to tell him something. Or to suck him into something. If she had killed Lankershim, then she was no one to mess with. But if she hadn't killed him, and expected Phillip to clear her somehow, then it was really no concern of his. Unless she had something to trade.

He looked at the clock on his desk. Four-twenty-two. He had been tired when he had come into the office, but now he was hyped up. His eyes didn't even feel gritty. He picked up the materials from the two envelopes and the envelopes themselves, tucked it all under his arm, then walked to the door. In the outer office, he locked the door behind him and then entered the hallway, locking the outer door, too.

Under the seat of the Rolls Royce was the Woodsman. Rhea had given it to him as a present, she had said, to celebrate his coming of age. There were eight rounds in the magazine and one still locked in the chamber. He made certain the safety was on before placing the gun under the seat once more. The car purred into life with a flick of the ignition and he slipped in into reverse, backing out of his parking space and turning onto the street, heading toward Interstate Five.

The sun had come up and was well over the hills by the time he neared the spot mentioned in the paper. The name of the town had been a help. He had bought a map at one of the local service stations, then had driven at fifty-five until he was near to where the town was located. He slowed and drove along the road, looking to the left until he spotted what looked like the same clump of bushes. Pulling over, he looked at the photo again, then at the foliage. There was the shield announcing CALIFORNIA INTERSTATE FIVE SOUTH in bold letters. He looked both ways, making certain there were no Highway Patrol cars nearby, then pulled the gun from under the seat. Placing it next to him, using the pressure of his butt to hold it in place, he set the car in motion.

He drove to the next offramp, found an underpass that placed him on the opposite side of the freeway. He drove along until he saw the foliage again, and the sign just beyond it.

Several sets of tracks headed into or out of the spot, some of them very deep. A heavy truck had been pulling Lankershim's car back onto the road.

His heart was trying to beat its way through his ribcage. He looked down to check the position of the gun, as though he couldn't feel it under his buttock. Then, slowing down, he glanced into both mirrors and up ahead. No one was around. It was almost eery, the way the freeway was deserted. As though it had been cleared for a shot in a film. Cramping the wheel to the right, Phillip pulled around behind the foliage and braked to a stop.

For a while nothing happened. He was beginning to feel the hours now. He hadn't been to sleep in over twenty-four hours. This entire trek seemed silly, and he wished he had had sense enough to stay in Los Angeles. It was cool under all those shrubs and trees, and comfortable, even with all the windows rolled up. The last thing he thought about before dozing off was that he was in for a bit of hell if Rhea found out about his journey.

The first thing he became aware of was something tapping against the passenger side window. He jerked upright, feeling foolish because he had fallen asleep, and afraid for a moment that some cop had decided to check behind the bushes. But it was no cop.

A girl peered in the window. She looked to be about nineteen, very pretty, with light brown hair that hung partly down her back and partly over her left shoulder. She was wearing one of those halters that looked like a red bandana, and Phillip could see her belly. It was a very tight, flat belly. If this was Brenda, he could see how she managed to catch Lankershim off guard. He remembered something Lankershim had said about wishing to take Phillip's place and be destroyed by Rhea. Perhaps he had made it.

"Hey! Aren't you going to let me in?" Her voice was muffled by the thick glass window. She was grinning at him.

Reaching over with his left hand, Phillip flicked the switch for the passenger side front window. It whirred down quietly. The girl reached for the locking button.

"Are you Brenda?" he asked, interrupting her motion. She stared at him for a moment, that grin still playing at the corners of her mouth.

"Sure. Who else?" She unlocked the door and opened it. She was wearing Levis cut off as short as they could be and still leave the crotch in place, and she carried some kind of bag, a military-looking thing with flaps and pockets all over it. She hefted it and started to slide into the car. Phillip picked up the automatic and aimed it at her clearly visible navel. The girl froze. "Hey, take it easy, Mr. Stafford," she said, giving him an innocent-little-girl expression.

"You can toss that in back," he said. "On the floor."

"You're the boss." She lifted the bag by one strap and dropped it over the back of the seat. "May I get in now?"

"I'll tell you when" He looked her over carefully. She

wasn't wearing much, but he supposed it was possible to hide a knife in a hip pocket, under the shorts, or even in the halter. "Turn around," he ordered. "Slowly." she grinned again, stepped back.

"Sure. Look me over," she said in a voice that tinkled with amusement. When she was finished he nodded.

"All right. Get in, but keep your hands up high."

"You want to pat me down?" she asked when she had slid onto the beige leather seat. Her tiny hands were poking dents in the headliner. Phillip looked her over for a moment before answering.

"Yes," he said.

"Primo! Be my guest." She hitched her fanny toward him a couple of notches, then sat waiting. Phillip leaned toward her, pressing the cold muzzle of the gun into her side. It made a little indentation in her skin, and caused her to shudder a bit. "Jesus, that's cold," she said. Ignoring her chatter, Phillip patted the front of the halter. There was nothing under it but soft jouncy breasts. He was starting to get an erection, but he chose to ignore that too, for the time being. Next he patted the front of the shorts. She gave a little jerk when he touched her there, then laughed. "I only carry one kind of weapon there," she said.

"Lean forward."

"Yes, sir." She bent at the waist, placing her hands atop the dash and tossing her head so that her long brown hair spilled forward, baring her back. Phillip ran his hand under the back of the halter, clear across her back. "If you pull the short end, it comes undone," she said helpfully. Phillip ran his fingers down inside her Levi shorts, feeling her buttocks and the crack between. Her body trembled again. "You want me to strip so you can run a skin search?"

"I guess not."

"Oh. Rats."

"Hoist your ass." She hesitated a moment, as though not quite certain he had meant it, then, with a little grunt, lifted herself clear. The leather seat made a creaking sound that seemed very loud in the car's interior. Phillip ran his hand down farther inside the shorts. There was nothing there but fanny. Finally, he relaxed a bit.

"All right, you can pull your hands down now." He slid back to the far side of the car, keeping the gun leveled at her, as she arranged herself. She closed the door and leaned against it, laying her left leg across the seat to show him the inside of her thigh.

"All right, now we can talk," he said.

"Talk? After that I don't feel much like talking."

"Did you kill Walter Lankershim?" If he had expected to jar her with that one, he was disappointed. She just looked at him for a moment, then nodded. "Why?"

"I was told to."

"By Rhea Carter?"

"You're pretty sharp, aren't you?"

"Never mind the bullshit. How did Rhea know about Lankershim?"

"How does Rhea know about all the things Rhea knows about?" she shot back with a note of impatience. "Look, if you don't mind, I don't think it makes much sense to hang around here too long, you know?"

Phillip looked at her for a moment, then placed the gun on the floor, between the seat and the door. He backed out carefully, looked around to make certain there were no cars coming, then put the transmission in drive and accelerated to fifty, holding the righthand lane.

"You want to tell me what's been going on?" he asked without taking his eyes off the road.

"How much do you know already?"

"I know there's something unnatural about it all. And I suspect Rhea's a bit older than she looks." Brenda laughed. "Also, I have the feeling that she's recruiting me for something. But I'd like to know exactly what it is."

"She's recruiting you for herself, love. Rhea is supposed to be serving a power above herself, but she's started to get a bit pushy lately. She's been around so long, and gained so much power, that she thinks she's the whole show. She has the authority to impress people into the service of our master, but she's forgotten why that power was given to her in the first place. It was really her idea to go after you. She knows you're a very sharp guy, and you'd be in a position to recruit a lot of very attractive people, as head of a major film studio. Getting you under her power is a big step ahead. It makes her even more important than she was, or so she thinks."

"I still don't know what the hell you're talking about. What kind of importance are you referring to? And who is this master you're talking about?"

"Oh, stop. I know this is the twentieth century, and you're an enlightened man and all that, but you must have figured that part out by now. His name doesn't strike fear into many people's hearts anymore. And that's just the way he wants it."

"You're talking about the devil?" There. He had said it, and he didn't feel quite the fool he had expected.

"Rhea's been serving him for well over a hundred years. I don't know much more about her. She likes to know all about people, but she doesn't do much advertising herself."

"Christ, this is like something out of *Dark Shadows*."

"Well, I'd advise you to take it seriously. Haven't some strange things been happening to you lately?"

"To say the least."

"Then believe what I'm telling you. Sure it sounds fantastic at first. But if you believe that one impossible thing, then the rest of it makes sense, doesn't it?"

"All but one thing." He saw her from the corner of his eye as she looked at him questioningly. "You. You don't make a damn bit of sense. If you killed for Rhea, why are you telling me all this now? Aren't you taking a chance?" She produced a smile that made him shiver.

"The master lets people get away with things just as long as he wishes. Then he cracks down. Rhea thinks she knows everything, but actually she only knows as much as he wants her to. She's a very bright lady, but in some ways she's incredibly stupid. She knows she can cancel the powers of those who are subordinate to her, but it never occurs to her that her own powers can be extinguished just as easily and just as effectively by the big boss. One obvious example of that is you, right now. Did you get a hard on when you were feeling me up back there?"

"Of course. So—" He stopped, aware of her answer before she spoke it.

"How long has it been since you could get it up for any woman but Rhea?"

"Since I met her." He felt an intense exhilaration, similar to that of a prisoner who has been released after a long term.

"Don't get the idea that her power over you has been cancelled," Brenda cautioned. "It's only been suspended. Whether it will be cancelled is up to you."

"What do I have to do?"

"Why don't you pull in up here, honey?" she suggested. Ahead was an offramp, and beside the freeway a small gathering of businesses, including a motel. "You look awfully tired, and I could use some sack time myself." The suggestion made his heart race. He felt like a kid about to score for the first time, "I'm damn near as good in the sack as Rhea is," she assured him, reaching across the width of the car and laying a hand on his genitals. "We've got all day. And after that I'll tell you where you have to go and what you have to do, and who you have to deal with."

1976

Phillip

When they left the motel room at dusk, Phillip was in a better frame of mind than he could remember at any time in his life. Certainly better than he had known since meeting Rhea. If Brenda's statement was true, and Rhea's power over him had only been suspended, then it would be worth whatever it might cost him to make the arrangement permanent.

He had had precious little sleep in the motel room. Brenda's bedroom demeanor left nothing to be desired even by comparison with Rhea, whose expertise, until now, had seemed without equal.

"That's because we're both gifted," she told him when, between sexual encounters, he mentioned it to her. She lay on the bare sheet, with the covers folded back, her superb young body naked and tanned. "Once an ordinary person has fucked someone with the gift, that person can never be satisfied with anyone else again," Brenda explained as though talking to an interested undergraduate. Phillip hoisted himself on one elbow and looked down at her. She was smiling.

"You mean I'm stuck with you and Rhea for the rest of my life? No one else —?"

"Only if you remain an ordinary person," she said. She sat up, adjusted the pillow on her side of the double bed, and scooted up to lean against it. "If you're initiated, then it's a whole new ball game. You'll be able to get it up with anyone you want, just like I can get it on with you."

"And it will be as good as it used to be?" Phillip asked almost plaintively. Brenda laughed, her face crinkling attractively.

"Shit, it'll be a thousand times better. For one thing, there's the satisfaction of being in complete control every second. And knowing that when you fuck somebody, that person becomes an addict. I've had a lot of fun with that one. Men have come back to me, begging for more, because they just can't make it with another woman, no matter who she is. One guy drew a thousand dollars out of his bank account so he could try it with a top-flight call girl."

"And it was wasted money," Phillip said grimly.

"He couldn't even get it up for her." Brenda's eyes took on an expression of relish. "He came back to me crawling, begging. I laughed in his face. And what made it even sweeter was that he'd always been a big stud. That was all he lived for. You know what he finally did?" She cocked her head to one side, clearly enjoying her nostalgia trip.

"Blew his brains out."

"You've got it." She shivered a bit with excitement, and a tiny pulse ticked in her left cheek. Her eyes were like coals, burning in their sockets. "He came to me first, showed me the gun, told me he was going to do it. I told him to go ahead and stop boring me with his plans, because I had a date that night. He said I thought he was bluffing, and I said, 'No, I believe you mean it, sweetie. It's just a matter of complete indifference to me, that's all.' And I could tell he believed me, that he was sure then that I really didn't care what he did. Actually, I did care in a way. I thought it would be neat to have a guy blow his brains out for me." She chuckled.

"You enjoy telling these little stories, don't you?"

"You just bet I do!" She picked up his hand, placed it on her vagina, "I wasn't always the girl you just fucked, honey. When Rhea found me, I was thirty years old, and the proverbial old maid school teacher. I'd been screwed exactly twice by two different men who were drunk when they did it, and who never even phoned me later. Why shouldn't I enjoy myself now?"

"What the hell are you talking about? Thirty years old?"

"Oh, come on, haven't you even figured that out yet? Do you think Rhea's as young as she looks?" It made his head spin to think about it.

"She changes bodies."

"And what she can do for herself, she can do for someone else. I picked this body out. It used to belong to a student of mine. Cheerleader, junior prom queen, all that bullshit. All the things I'd never been able to be. She didn't have brain one. She was flunking my class, and I invited her to my house for some tutoring and Rhea made it happen. The little bitch fell asleep and I laid out a suicide note I'd written, and then took a slow-acting poison. Then it happened. I was in her body and she was in mine. It was a disconcerting experience, watching myself die in agony. But it was gratifying, too. That stupid little girl didn't deserve a body like this." During this speech Brenda's whole manner changed. She seemed to become older. Phillip had noticed discrepancies in her vocabulary, as though she tried, sluggishly and sporadically, to sound as young as she looked. Now she grinned. "Creepy, huh?" She reached out languidly and took his penis in her hand, caressing it into a fresh rigidity. "Come on," she breathed, moving toward him. "Less talk, more work."

Later, she scooted against the headboard again, drawing her knees up against her breasts and hugging them.

"How would you like to be my boss?" she asked, dimpling a grin at him.

"I can't say I'd mind," Phillip answered cautiously. "How do I land the job?" She looked at him for a moment as though considering her next words with care. Then she shrugged, barely preceptibly.

"I was told to offer you the position. Right now Rhea's my boss. I answer directly to her. She answers only to the Master."

"I thought you said you had 'the gift'." The word tasted strange in his mouth.

"There are all levels of gift. Mine's pretty low, and Rhea's is as high as you can get."

"Then her powers must be immense."

"Her power is whatever the Master chooses to give her, just like mine. Right now, sure, if I weren't on a special mission, under the Master's protection, she could wish me right into the deepest pit. But that could change tomorrow. Or tonight. She's been a naughty girl, and the Master wants to replace her." Phillip felt a thrill of excitement that was almost painful, and he knew she could tell. He was afraid to ask.

"Replace her with me?" For the first time since he could recall, except when he had spoken to Rhea, his voice trembled. Brenda nodded.

When they left the motel, the foothills in the west had begun to chip away the bottom of the sun's disk. Brenda, dressed again in her cut-off blue jeans, stood in the doorway of the office as Phillip dropped off the key. The clerk, a kid in his early twenties, fought the urge to gape at her and satisfied himself with an envious and resentful look at Phillip. Suddenly Phillip realized the nature of what he was being offered. In that moment he got a glimpse of the way things could be, and he grinned directly at the boy.

"You don't know the tenth part of it, son," he said, and broke into his rich, baritone laugh for the first time in months. When he turned to Brenda, she was laughing too, and they walked to his car arm in arm, leaving the clerk scowling angrily after them. They drove thirty miles north on Interstate Five and then, at Brenda's direction, Phillip turned off onto a side road, crossed over the freeway, and drove for a half hour. There were farms on both sides of them, open fields with houses and barns that looked tiny with distance. Phillip lost count of the farms, but finally she nudged his thigh with her left index finger and nodded toward a lopsided-looking barn and a dirty white farmhouse. Phillip let up on the gas, applied a little brake, and turned right down a dirt road that was badly in need of filling in. He took it easy because it would be very possible to break an axle or blow out a tire.

When they were halfway down the driveway, a brace of huge German shepherds ran out and took up their places, one on each side of the car, barking their fool heads off, snarling with rage, occasionally nipping at the tires. Phillip had never seen such big dogs. They could have been timber wolves. He eased the car up beside the house and looked at Brenda. She laughed, opening the door on her side. One of the dogs made a lunge for her slender brown leg and, with exquisite accuracy, she kicked it directly on the nose. Dazed and surprised, the animal drew back, emitting something between a squeal and a snarl.

"Get out of here, you asshole!" Brenda stooped over and scooped up a large rock, hurling it at the dog's flanks. The shepherd gave a face-saving growl, but backed off a step and then turned and walked away, looking back belligerently from time to time. His partner seemed to have taken his cue. Brenda leaned in the Rolls Royce and smiled at Phillip. "Don't worry, they won't hurt you. They're all show and no go."

"I hope you're right."

"Sure. They only act mean because they're frustrated and confused." She leaned toward him conspiratorially and whispered, "They weren't always dogs."

Phillip opened the car door and alighted cautiously. The dog looked him over, apparently seeking some sign of fear. When Phillip slammed the door and gave the dog a confident look, it slunk away.

There was a small service porch on the near corner of the house, with a screen from waist height. Phillip saw a girl looking at him through the fine mesh. She seemed young, possibly in her middle teens, and she was wearing some kind of halter that nearly revealed a pair of precociously developed breasts. When she saw Brenda the girl brightened, waving at her through the screen. She walked to a screen door and pushed it open against the pull of a back coil spring that creaked.

"Well, come the hell on in!" she called in a cordial voice. The tenor of it convinced Phillip that he had guessed right about her age. There was an artifical punch to the profanity, as though she were still growing accustomed to the luxury of using it.

Reddish-brown hair hung down her back, reaching her fanny, and when Brenda took hold of the door, the girl began to twist the hair into braids. She was a mass of freckles, and one of the most attractive girls he had ever seen. Despite her extreme youth, or perhaps because of it, there was an intense sensuousness to her. Below the halter she was dressed in faded cotton shorts that were as tight as the bark on a tree. Her legs, as freckled as her face and shoulders, were luscious. She backed away from the doorway to allow them to enter, and as the screen door creaked and slammed she raked Phillip with a frankly speculative glance.

"I'm Cynthia," she said with a touch of dare in her tone. "People who know me call me Cyn." Something told Phillip that it would be better to keep this little squirt at a distance, at least for the moment.

"I'm Phillip Stafford. People who know me call me Mr. Stafford." The bold look faded from Cyn's eyes and she backed off a step, suddenly a little girl again. She indicated a door with a jerk of the head.

"Oh. Well, won't you come in, Mr. Stafford? I was just about to put on a pot of coffee." She was still braiding her hair, and he noticed that her feet were naked. He didn't believe she had been about to put on any coffee, but he followed Brenda into a spacious kitchen with cracked linoleum and a 1950's refrigerator in one corner. He half expected to see a pump, but the sink sported ancient-looking taps. A rusty dish drainer rested on one sinkboard, piled high with thick dinnerware. Opposite, looking out of place in the homey surroundings, stood a sparkling Amana range with an overhead oven. Like the dinnerware, it was white.

"Bobby'll be out in just a minute," Cyn said, and offered them each a seat at an old wooden table at the far end of the room. Her braiding job finished, she set about preparing a pot of coffee, true to her word.

"Well, hi, Brenda." Phillip looked up to see a young boy enter from a hallway that led out of the kitchen at right angles to the door through which they had entered. The boy was tall and gangly and good-looking, with squared bones and a thick mass of red hair. He wore a pair of bib overalls, into which he was stuffing the tail of a cotton shirt. His feet padded on the linoleum, as bare as Cyn's. "Want to introduce me to your friend?" he said, smiling at Phillip. The smile was open and youthful, with wide eyes trained ingenuously on Phillip's own. Something about it set Phillip on edge. He couldn't isolate the element, but responded to it as instinctively as would one of the dogs outside.

"This is Mr. Stafford, Bobby. He's the gentleman I told you about." Bobby's eyes registered fresh interest as he thrust forth a large, horny hand. His shake was firm and strong and honest feeling, but it made Phillip's skin creep a bit, just as that boyish smile did. A glint appeared deep in Bobby's eyes, as though he had let his guard down for an instant, and Phillip realized what it was about the boyish grin that bothered him: it was as though Bobby weren't well enough practiced in it, and had to concentrate to keep it up.

"How do, Mr. Stafford. I hope Cyn hasn't been talkin' the leg off ya."

"She's thoroughly charming," Phillip said. Cyn looked around, her smile revived, and then, like a dog that has heard its name spoken in a cordial tone, walked up beside Bobby, who had snaked a lanky leg over the nearest chair to sit. She stood next to him and placed a tiny, freckled hand on his neck. Bobby's arm circled her hips, a hand resting lightly on her abdomen.

"I kinda think so, too," he said.

"Mr. Stafford is interested in joining us, Bobby," Brenda said. "He hasn't made up his mind yet, but I think he's willing to hear the proposal." She looked at Phillip with a slightly questioning expression, and he nodded slightly. Bobby turned back to him just in time to catch the gesture, smiling. Boyishly.

"Well, I'll tell you all I can now, Mr. Stafford. I understand you've been sort of took over by Rhea Carter?" Phillip neither agreed with the assumption nor denied it. "That's a pretty rough experience. Only one way to get out of it without killin' yourself, and you got to be made the offer. You're one of the lucky ones, sir."

"All right, I'm one of the lucky ones. What do I have to do to be rid of Rhea's — obsession?"

"Well, now, the Master wants to make a deal with you. And it'll be bindin' on both sides. What I'm gonna tell you right now is just preliminary. If you decide to go ahead, then I'll take you into the parlor and show you the whole story. After that, the deal is made, better or worse. Okay?"

"That sounds fair enough." Cyn disentangled herself from Bobby and walked to the range, where the coffee had been perking. She turned down the heat and plucked two thick mugs off the drainer. Bobby, apparently unaware that she had moved, leaned his elbows on the table.

"Okay, sir, here it is. You want to be rid of Rhea Carter's influence. And maybe you'd like to get even with her a little bit for the way she's made you jump through her hoop. That's very understandable. The Master's willin' to put you in her position. That's a right high position, Mr. Stafford. Nobody higher in his followin', and maybe six people as high in the whole world. None in this country."

"What are the advantages?" Cyn came to the table with two cups of coffee. Her hip brushed Phillip's arm slightly. He didn't look up, but positioned the cup in front of him. It was a thick white mug with a slight waist, like a shaving cup.

"Advantages? Listen, Mr. Stafford, you're in the movie business, right? Well, how'd you like to own that studio of yours? How'd you like the kind of judgment and luck that makes it impossible to do the wrong thing? How'd you like to back the competition right off the map? How'd you like to corner the whole friggin' world movie market?"

"Sounds interesting."

"Then there's the standard benefits, of course. Little things, like bein' able to eat and drink all the time, and never have to face the consequences like other people. And there's sex. You'd be able to go all the time, you know. Twenty-four hours a day if you like. And with any woman you chose, because they won't be able to say no."

"And once I've screwed a woman, she won't want any other man, right?" Phillip asked with a glance across the table at Brenda. She smiled. Cyn had brought two more cups of coffee for herself and Brenda, and once more took her place beside Bobby.

"Well, I wouldn't say any other man. Just those who're in on things."

"You make it sound pretty good.

"Well, Jesus, Mr. Stafford, it is pretty good. I mean, what could be sweeter? Then there's the matter of Rhea. I can't go into any particulars about that, but you'll be able to even the score with her and come out ahead, too." Bobby picked up his cup and took a sip of the hot black coffee. "Well, what do you think?"

"What's my end of the bargain?"

"Okay. Just that you agree to serve the Master, that's all."

"How do I know I won't end up just like Rhea?"

"That's entirely up to you, sir. Rhea's been a bad girl. She hasn't kept her end of the bargain. She did at first, but lately she's been gettin' a little too smart for her own good. She's been gatherin' disciples, but for herself, not the Master. That's what she tried to do with Brenda, but Brenda was too smart for her. She made her own separate covenant. Rhea thinks she's puttin' somethin' over on Satan!" Bobby grinned at the sheer hubris of the idea, and Cyn laughed outright.

"How do I serve him?"

"Simple. You use the powers he gives you to influence others in his service. That won't cut into your enjoyment at all. You make the kind of movies he wants people to see, which won't be too hard in this day and age. You give young actors breaks, providin' they're willing to join the team. That kind of thing. The Master don't give this kind of position to just anybody. You're in a good position to do him a lot of favors. And he's willin' to be a lot more generous than most, in return." Phillip looked at the boy for a long time. He turned his gaze on Cyn, and then Brenda. All of them were watching him expectantly.

"What's my alternative?"

"Very simple. You just go out and get in that fancy car and you drive back to L.A. and Rhea. You go right back to where you were before you came up here. Only one thing: you don't tell Rhea nor nobody else about us, or the offer I just made you. 'Cause if you start to, well, sir, the words just won't even get out of your mouth."

"And I spend the rest of my life obsessed with Rhea Carter?"

" 'Lessen somebody else takes her place, yeah."

"I seem to have been maneuvered into a position of having only one sensible choice."

"I guess," Bobby grinned broadly. "But it's a real nice choice, don't you think? A lot of men would be happy to trade places with you, me included."

"All right," Phillip said. He felt like he was pulling a tigger without being entirely certain of the direction in which the gun was pointing.

"Well, good, then. Yes, sir," Bobby said, the grin growing even wider and more boyish.

"Do I have to sign in blood or something?" The other three people laughed brightly.

"Nothing like that, Mr. Stafford," Cyn assured him. "Just your consent is enough."

"Right." Bobby pushed back his chair, took another sip of

coffee, then rose. "Now if you'll excuse us, me and my sister have to make some preparations."

"Brother and sister," Phillip mused to Brenda when they were alone. "I had the impression they were lovers."

"Why shouldn't they be? They've always had a yen for each other, but they wouldn't admit it until about a year ago, when their father died and left them orphaned." Phillip looked at her for a moment.

"Was it really the father who died?" The question came as a sudden inspiration. Brenda's smile suggested amusement and admiration.

"You're going to do all right," she said with a kind of excitement in her voice. "You catch on quickly. But don't mention it in front of Cyn, will you? She isn't aware of the switch."

A few minutes later Bobby and Cyn were back. Bobby looked down at Phillip expectantly, and Phillip rose with a scrape of his chair on the linoleum. The two girls sat looking at the men.

"This way, Mr. Stafford."

Phillip followed the boy into the hallway from which he had emerged originally. There were four doors leading off it, two on the right, apparently leading into bedrooms, and two on the left. They passed the first door on the left and walked to the end of the hall. They stopped in front of the last door, which was closed.

"This is as far as I go, sir," Bobby said. "I want to remind you that you can still back out. But if you go through that door, the deal is made."

"Why would I want to back out?" Phillip's voice shook just a bit bringing an amused grin to the boy's face.

"Good. Now don't be scared, Mr. Stafford. All you're gonna do in there is watch a little show. Kind of like a documentary. Like on TV, but without the TV." He shook hands with Phillip and turned back toward the kitchen. Phillip watched him until he closed the door behind him, then turned to the door reserved for him. He thought the knob felt unnaturally warm under his hand as he turned it.

The room was neat in a worn and shabby way. Opposite the door was a huge window, heavily draped. An ancient upright piano stood next to the door, on his left. In front of the window rested a swayback couch that was bright red, and very much out of place in the surrounding drabness. The carpet was worn to the nap in places.

Phillip advanced to the couch, where he sat. Then he realized that he had left the door open, so he went back and closed it, then returned to the couch. He was beginning to feel like a fool, sitting in this old parlor waiting for a supernatural sign. Sounds, seemingly without source, reached his ears.

Old houses creak at night, he told himself.

Specks of something, glinting in the dimness of the room's one dim lamp, seemed to appear in the air at random, with no pattern at all. They swirled and spun and gathered, forming a loose spiral that grew tighter, closer with each second. Phillip's heart pounded like a prisoner against his ribcage.

He fought an impulse to cry out, gripping the arm of the couch with his left hand, and the cushion with his right. What the hell am I doing here? he asked himself. The spiral grew more compact. Then, in the center of it, a light began to glow. It had a blue cast, like a television tube, and Phillip remembered Bobby's description: like a TV, but without the TV. In the center of the flow, colors began to swirl, to take shape.

Then he saw a woman, tall and beautiful, dressed like a character in a period movie. He had never seen the woman before, yet there was something about her, her gait and carriage, that seemed familiar. Phillip's thighs hurt from muscular tension, and his stomach was filled with a tight nausea that threatened to erupt at any moment. The woman stood on a cobbled street. A man came out of a building, spoke to her. Phillip didn't hear the words. It was like watching a color film with the sound track omitted. Man and woman walked down the street together, speaking casually. There seemed a tension about the woman which gradually transferred itself to the man in the form of an excited caution. The sene changed instantly. The same man and woman alone in a room. Both were taking off their clothes. Phillip saw them get into bed together, saw them couple.

After that it was like watching a carefully, even brilliantly edited film. He saw Rhea Carter's birth, saw her first encounter with a demon, and the results. Bits of sound reached him when they were necessary, but he soon grasped the plot, and then it was easy to follow.

If he had been maneuvered, Rhea had certainly been manipulated all the while she thought she was controlling her own fate, and that of others. He saw her brief affair with Raymond Wakeling, the result of it, Wakeling a crippled and bitter old man and Rhea a cruel, sadistic, middle-aged woman. He saw her peering through a hole in the wall at Charity Mead, growing intensely excited and embarking on her first homosexual affair. He was there when she made her pact and took over Charity Mead's body.

He saw the rest of her career, too, all of it, right through her taking over of Susan Black's body, the body in which he had seen her, the desecration and murder of Yvonne Baker, Janet's attempt to kill Rhea, and the panther's defense of its mistress. He saw himself doing all the things Rhea told him to do, yielding to the need she had planted in him, and, seeing it all laid out before him like that, grew to hate her even more ravenously. Rhea's sexual interlude with his wife left him curiously unmoved, except for a mild erotic thrill.

Then the picture took on a smybolic quality, and he knew he was seeing not what had happened, or even, literally, what was to happen, but rather a depiction in symbolic images of the way things could be in the future if he willed it.

There were flames, white at the edges and tips, blue at the center, a vast pit of fire that hissed with supernatural intensity, and stretching up from it a spool of thread. Climbing laboriously up the thread, a naked Rhea, sweating, exhausted, yet driven by the terror of those flames. From below, in the center of the fire, came the shrieks of the eternally damned, as they writhed in their blistering agony. As Rhea pulled herself along the taut thread, it slipped downward at a rate nearly equal to her progress, so that she barely moved away from the fire.

From time to time a stray flame leaped upward, licking at her skin and sending her scrambling upward with renewed vigor. Huge blisters erupted on the soles of her feet, on her calves. Her hair smoked threateningly. Finally, her strength gone, she wound the thread about her hands and hung limply, resting for a moment.

The thread inched downward more quickly. And then, from the depths of the flame leaped forms, horribly misshapen but recognizable. The souls of the damned. Phillip recognized some of them. Rhea's mother was there. So were Yvonne Baker, Janet, and his children. Charity Mead and her brother, Theresa Dalrymple and Raymond Wakeling. Warped and charred, they leapt and clutched at Rhea, snapping with horrid yellow fangs and hideous claws that left bloody trails along her skin. Rhea shrieked and began to climb again. The thread slowed to its former pace, and she made some progress, finally dragging herself out of their reach. The swaying of the thread seemed to grow less wild as she neared the top.

Phillip saw the thread hung from something, but it took him a moment to recognize the object as a giant hand. From a comparison with Rhea's body, the palm and fingers must combine to stretch a hundred feet in length. Hanging by one hand, Rhea clawed futilely at the knuckles, seeking some means to pull herself through to safety. The thread continued to slide downward, and her one hand grasp slipped, letting her drop more quickly. She clutched at the thread with both hands once again, pulling herself up those scant inches, as the souls below, encouraged, began to leap at her again like fish jumping from some infernal lake.

Then it was like a slow, reverse zoom shot, like the camera backing away. He saw the hand, and below it the thread, and Rhea clutching and scrambling alternately, and he realized that she was pleading with someone, the owner of the hand, and just before the scene opened enough to reveal the fact, Phillip realized that the hand was his own.

1976

Janet

There was certainly something in the room.
Janet lay very still in the bed and waited to see what was going to happen next. She didn't cry out, or attempt to call the servants, because she had done too much of that already, and they were starting to look at one another knowingly. There was never anything there when they arrived. She was certain there wouldn't be anything here this time either. But it was here now, here with her, just for her. It was a gift from Rhea Carter.

She could turn on the light. That was what she had done the last several times it had come to her. But it was never visible in the light. She had caught a glimpse of it occasionally in the darkness, a massive form against the draped windows. She had always panicked and switched on the light, and the thing vanished with a rustling chuckle, and a vague rushing sound as though the air were closing the space it had vacated. She wanted to face it this time. If it was her imagination, something dredged up from her own primitive fear, then it was best to confront it. The trouble was that she still had that mindless terror, something too acute to have come from the simple knowledge that she was not alone when she should have been. She felt as though there were a fear center somewhere in her brain and this thing stimulated it directly by some means of its own.

And her resistance to the fear had been eroded by

exhaustion. She hadn't slept for more than a few seconds at a time in the past thirty-six hours. She hadn't been able to make herself eat either, but had subsisted on liquids. Now she was aware of her bladder, full and beginning to ache. She made that her excuse, justifying a postponement of the confrontation with her denizen, whatever it might be. Reaching to the lamp on the bedside table, she turned it on, blinked in the sudden diffused light. She was sure she had heard that chuckle again, as though the thing knew she had turned on the light to keep from facing it.

There was nothing in the room except herself, and the objects so familiar to her, the things that had once spelled a measure of security, but that now seemed to squat like giant spiders, mocking her. Janet threw back the bedding and stood up. Her nightgown had hiked above her waist, and just before it fell into place she thought she heard that sighing chuckle again. Ignoring it, she bit her lip and moved toward the bathroom.

The door was ajar. She pushed it open and walked into the darkened room. Just as she passed through the doorway, something touched her bare shoulder. It was a light whisper of a touch, a suggestion of cold, scaly wetness. Janet spun around, stumbling backward to careen off the basin, bruising her left hip, and then lurched into the bathtub. The scream that tried to force its way from her was stifled, coming out as a vocalized gasp. Her legs buckled and she fell back over the edge of the tub, flailing wildly for some grip. There was nothing but air and, behind her, slick enameled wall. She sat down hard in the tub, slamming her spine against the edge. She started to cry, the sobs lasting only a moment before she realized that the thing was still with her, still in the bathroom, somewhere between herself and the door. She could hear it moving, not footsteps, but a slithering sound. And for the first time she could smell it, a sharp tang in the air, as though something had forgotten to die.

"Get away from me!" she cried. "Leave me alone, whatever you are!"

There was nothing there. She had caught a glimpse of the form, like a massive shoulder silhouetted against the open door, and then she knew she was alone.

"I've given up," she sobbed aloud to nothing. "I've surrendered to her. I even gave her my soul. What more does she want?"

Slowly, she regained control of herself, stifling the sobs and the tremors that wracked her body. It took all the strength she had left. Her nightgown was soaked. In that moment of total fear she had lost control of her bladder.

"Goddamn you," she wept. "Goddamn you!" The odor of

urine assaulted her nostrils. Was that what she had smelled before? "No," she said to herself. "It smelled different. It did —" But talking was unwise. She was beginning to lose control again as her voice cracked. It was better to shut up.

Rising from the tub gingerly, she took off her nightgown and dropped it in a corner. She snapped on the light and looked about the empty bathroom. It was frustratingly uninhabited. Even the scent of the thing had vanished. Lowering herself to the toilet seat, Janet hugged herself and let the tears and the sobs have their way. She sat there for a long time, rocking slightly, feeling the warm wetness run down her face to drop to her thighs.

"Stop this," she said finally. She was on the edge of hysteria. She rose and walked to the shower stall, turning on the hot tap and adjusting the temperature with the cold until it was just bearable. When she was under the shower head, she gripped the handle of the soap niche with both hands. Her skin turned lobster pink under the scalding stream. When the feeling began to leave her, she twisted the center control, nearly in a state of shock. But the hot water treatment had done its job. Besides cleaning her skin, it had shocked her into a nearly normal state of calm.

A perfunctory toweling and she went back into the bedroom. It was too much trouble to put on a fresh nightgown, so she lay down, still damp, atop the folded covers, then turned off the bedside lamp and waited.

In a moment she thought she detected the presence again. She could smell it, more weakly, as though the creature were farther from her and the larger room diluted the effect. Staring at the ceiling, Janet gripped the sheet under her with both hands and waited. The sounds were soft, like a mouse running across the carpet, and separated by inconsistent lapses of time. Once, from sheer exhaustion, she drifted into sleep for an instant. She jerked back into awareness, raising her head with a snap to see the form against the diffused light from the window. It was giant, vaguely humanlike, with thick shoulders and a round, apparently hairless head that seemed to bear some kind of protruding ridge at the sides and back. The body was only a silhouette, but there was a feeling of solidity about it, a definite reality that told Janet that none of it had been imagination. It moved toward her in fitful motions, with the patience of a stalking serpent. The smell was stronger, almost overwhelming. She wanted to vomit. A whimpering sound rose in her throat, but she swallowed it. She needed to see this thing. A clear look might dispel her terror, she thought. Nothing could be as terrible as she imagined. But she was shaking so badly, and she couldn't stop.

Letting go of the sheet with her right hand, she moved her arm toward the bedside table with the same slowness that the creature displayed. She didn't turn her head, or even roll her eyes in that direction, but relied on the instinctive knowledge acquired by years of living and sleeping in this room. Her knuckles brushed the base of the lamp, allowing her a perspective on which to base her subsequent movements. Slowly, she raised her hand and groped for the socket, then the switch. She held it between her thumb and forefinger, watching the thing move toward her slowly, as inexorable as death itself. The stink was almost solid now, as palpable as a filthy rag. Finally, the form lost its distinctness, blotting out the entire window. Janet turned on the lamp.

The bulb flared brilliantly and died. That incandescent blink showed her the domed and ridged head, the watery yellow eyes under protruding, scaly lids, the thick manlike chest also scaled, each scale exuding its own slickness, the taut, trunklike waist that trailed into a heavy snakelike tail. The eyes blinked and sparked in the momentary light and then, in the darkness, she felt the thing move toward her.

For a moment she was paralyzed. She couldn't move or make a sound. Then a choked screech clogged her throat and she tried to roll away from it, but a hand grasped her arm. It was cold and rough and slimy, the same hand she had felt on her shoulder in the bathroom. Janet tried to scream, tried to beg, tried to pull away, but none of it was any good. The monster's grip was incredibly potent. For just a moment it was painful. Then her arm went numb, the nerves and bloodstream pinched off. She could only feel the roughness of its skin on hers, the pressure as he pulled her, struggling, toward him.

The fear welled up until it seemed it would burst her body. A dizziness came over her, making her head spin, filling her with a nausea that had already begun to grow from the stink of the thing.

If it keeps on touching me, I'll lose my mind, Janet thought. Then she was on the edge of the bed, her right leg kicking against the side of the mattress. The bulk of the creature moved forward until it pressed against the mattress and frame. Gradually, horribly, she became aware that its other hand was fumbling with something, an appendage in front of its body. It turned slightly, as though deliberately lining up with the window so she could see what was being done.

The penis was massive, thick and heavy as a sapling's trunk. It stood out from the front of the monster's body, stiff and pulsing with obscene virlity. Then, as the creature's hand turned it slightly, she perceived with fresh awe that it was forked like a serpent's tongue, ending in two thickly ridged heads, each the diameter of a silver dollar. The organ glistened in the dim light, as did the rest of the thing's body.

The hand dropped the penis but it stood, barely drooping, as the monster turned toward her. Janet felt the hand scoop her head from the pillow and draw it closer, heard the low, hissing chuckle. Her brain was roiling, ready to burst with fear and revulsion.

This can't happen, she told herself. If it does, I'll go insane.

She tried to clamp her jaws together, but the creature's hands parted them with the ease of a grown man opening a book. Her mouth hung open, vulnerable, accepting, as the twin heads of the penis came together like the blades of some hideous scissors. Janet felt the scales tear at her lips, felt the slickness of the organ pass between them and her teeth and across her tongue until she gagged on its hugeness.

There was no warmth in it. It throbbed with life, but was as cold as a toad. Janet lay still, realizing finally the futility of resistance. She prayed for unconsicsouness, but her brain was perversely alert. The penis moved, sliding back and forth in a parody of sexual activity, even as the monster forced her head to rock in converse and reinforcing motions. Janet's mouth grew unbearably sore as the scaly organ scraped against it. Then, all at once, the penis seemed to expand, to throb more strenuously than before, and a cold, bitter substance spewed into her throat, burning her with an alkaline sting.

The creature withdrew from her slightly, maintaining its grip on her arm. Janet turned her head to the side and vomited. The bitter fluid gushed onto the sheet and onto her lips, making her sick all over again. Blood mixed with it, exuded by her torn lips and tongue. Her body contracted in hard, twisting convulsions, but there was nothing left in her to heave.

She felt herself being turned over. Her face rolled onto the slick dampness of the sheet where she had vomited, and she seemed ready to break, but finally she was on her belly. There was nothing left in her to resist, nothing but a shuddering, submissive horror.

The hand left her arm, and then both of the creature's hands closed on her thighs, yanking them apart so hard she thought he would split her in two. He lifted her clear of the bed as easily as though she had been an inflated doll. She was pulled to the very edge of the mattress, her knees hanging over and almost reaching the floor until the creature picked her up again.

When it entered her, the pain was almost enough to make her pass out. Her face was flat against the mattress, and finally the emitted a muffled scream. It was like having two jagged icicles shoved into her orifices at once.

And now she knew the purpose of the forked penis.

1976

Rhea

She woke with the kind of foreboding she had forgotten long ago. Part of the feeling came from a dream she had endured. In the dream she was chasing something that seemed small and helpless, and she was exhilarated because she knew that very soon she would catch it. And then she had sensed a change, and the thing she had been pursuing turned on her, suddenly huge and powerful, and moving faster than she could.

Rhea knew she had cried out in her sleep, and when she woke the sheets were damp. She shook her head and stared at the ceiling for a moment, then rose and walked to the window, naked. Parting the draperies slightly, she looked out at a day that was uncommonly brilliant for Los Angeles. It hurt her eyes, and the base of her brain. She hadn't had a headache since — since that night in 1847, just before she had taken what's-her-name's body. There was no aspirin in the apartment, because she had never had a need for such things.

She was being ridiculous. So she had a little headache. That didn't justify this unshakable feeling of alarm. All she needed was a cup of coffee. She was sorry now that she had let Philly-boy leave. He always made the coffee.

Rhea put on her terry robe and a pair of pink fuzzy mules, then plodded into the kitchen, where she started the coffee. It was perking when she heard the door open. At first she thought she was imagining things, because she was certain she had locked it, and there was no one else who had a key. Then she remembered that Philly-boy had left. If he had forgot to lock up behind him again, she was going to give him a very bad time about it, she thought. But who was this barging into her home?

With some apprehension, and wishing Toby were in sight, she walked to the door and leaned forward at the waist, looking into the living room.

Philly-boy stood there, freshly shaven and dressed in clean, pressed clothes. He was just standing there in the middle of the room, looking as casual as though he owned the place. The knot in Rhea's stomach got bigger and harder. Where the hell was Toby? Why wasn't he here when someone came walking into the apartment? She thrust her hands into the pockets of her robe and entered the living room.

"After this, call before you come over here," she said. Then she jumped visibly, startled. Sitting in the wingback chair near the wall was Brenda. She was dressed in that same ragged pair of shorts in which Rhea had seen her when she was about to go on the road, with her red halter. One foot was drawn up under her opposite thigh, and sitting in her lap, purring so loudly it was audible clear across the room, was that damned cat. "What is this?" Rhea demanded a bit shrilly. "A goddamn convention? Toby, get over here!" The cat looked at her balefully, then curled up on Brenda's lap and closed its eyes.

"Hi, Rhea!" Brenda chirped, petting Toby luxuriously. This was all wrong. It had never been like this, not in — not in a very long time. Rhea looked at Philly-boy, who was smiling at her with an assured grin that disconcerted her even more. It did something else to her, too. She felt a surge of sexual excitement deep in her bowels. It was so powerful it almost drove the breath from her. She felt perspiration form on her upper lip and in the creases of her knees. Philly-boy walked over to her with a slow, deliberate pace and then, just as deliberately, raised his right hand and slapped her across the face. The blow left a burning sensation on her cheek.

She fell to the floor, landing on her rump in a very ungraceful way. The robe parted, revealing her thighs and a dark triangle of pubic hair. She tugged it closed, staring up at him blankly.

"How are you, Rhea?" he asked.

"What the hell do you think you're —?" She stopped, choked off, as he reached under his coat and produced a gun, the same one his wife had tried to use on her. He leveled it at the middle of her face. She could see the narrow black tunnel of the bore. "Take that thing out of my face," she commanded with a show of courage she didn't feel. "Or I'll make you eat it." He laughed. She heard a click as he switched off the safety. It was too confusing, and her headache, which was worsening, didn't help her to figure any of it out. It seemed as though her nightmare were still going on. She looked at Brenda, the cat curled on her lap contentedly. "Toby!" she shrieked. He looked up at her for a moment, not a flicker of interest in his eyes.

"Come on over here, Toby," Phillip ordered, and the cat jumped off of Brenda's lap and darted to his side. Rhea shrank back from it instinctively. "Toby, why don't you show Rhea who's running things?" Phillip ordered. Toby looked at her belligerently for a moment. With a whining snarl he leaped at her, swiping with his paw. Tiny claws left a track of red lines down Rhea's thigh.

She screamed, jumping back, trying to get away from the animal. But the attack was already spent. His point made, Toby looked up questioningly at his new master. Phillip nodded and the cat lay down by his foot, paws lined up before him, looking at Rhea with mild and insolent interest. Gradually, the sense of the situation began to filter into Rhea's consciousness, bringing with it a needle sharp fear that manifested itself as rage. Rhea's head swiveled to the wingback chair where Brenda still sat, smiling at Rhea with saucy impertinence. That look in her eyes, an amalgamation of hatred and triumph and sadistic satisfaction, bit more deeply than any of it. Rhea gathered herself to rise.

"You," she breathed, her voice coming out in its accustomed serpentine hiss. "You're in on this!" She pushed herself to her feet, wavering for a moment because the pain in her head was reaching the unbearable stage. She determined to ignore the pain and her rage sustained her. "You dared," she whispered. "You really dared!" There was an instant when Brenda threw back her head and Rhea heard the first syllable of an arch laugh, and then she flung herself at the girl. The pain in her head exploded in a giant, throbbing blast, and she lost her balance and momentum, but then gathered herself for another rush. Only a momentary, reflexive look of apprehension appeared in the girl's eyes as Rhea hurtled toward her, hands raised, fingers arched into claws.

With a soft, amused chuckle, Phillip thrust out his foot, catching Rhea's ankle deftly. Her mule tangled over her toes when she tried to clear herself, and she felt a jolt of pain as her leg was yanked almost out of its hip socket. In the instant of her fall, she tried to protect herself, tried to brace her arms against the impact, but her muscles wouldn't respond. Helplessly, she tumbled to the carpet, jarring every bone, every joint and ligament in her body. Tears were running down her face in a wild cascade, tears of pain and rage and sudden, hopeless fear, but somewhere she found a grain of determination and rose to her knees, turning on Phillip now, raising her clawed hands.

Toby raised a screeching howl, instantly on his feet, his back arched, every hair on his body bristling. The lines of his form wavered a moment, as though he were about to charge, and the thought gave Rhea such a sick turn that she hesitated in her attack. Her pause was long enough. Phillip dropped the gun to the floor and reached down to grasp her wrists. The iron strength of that grasp numbed Rhea's wrists and forearms, and the sexual desire she had noted before surged up again, so powerful it left her gasping, her nipples tingling, her breathing ragged. As though he could read her thoughts, Phillip smiled down at her and slowly pulled her up, off her knees, drawing her face closer to his own. Rhea could feel the heat of his body, smell his skin and the cologne he wore, and she went totally weak inside. Involuntarily, her lips parted, her warm, wet tongue extended itself slightly from her mouth.

And then he spat on her. Rhea gasped, her head jerking back so hard she felt it in her spine. All the fight was gone from her, the resistance extinguished as she belatedly recognized the futility of her position. The snapping rage in her eyes melted, displaced by an imploring expression that brought a giggle of delight from Brenda. Phillip dropped her, letting her strike the floor with a force that jarred her knees. His form towered over her own, erect and dominant, suggesting a strength and control that warmed her even as it cowed and incensed her. Unconsciously, she raised a hand to wipe away the globule of spit he had deposited on her face. Phillip, in a perfunctory move, parried the gesture. The spit rested on her cheek, unmolested by anything but her tears.

"Now," Phillip said in a complacent tone, "I think you're in a proper frame of mind to discuss your future."

1977

Rhea

The guests began clearing out at three a.m., but there were the inveitable hangers-on who would be there until sunrise, and who might finally consent to stay the night. In the past two hours Rhea's migraine had reached the intolerable stage, and her feet and legs hurt too, because as hostess she was expected to keep circulating, to see those to the door who were determined to leave, and to replenish the glasses of the others. She was also expected to remain cheerful to the end, to smile and simulate the best of moods, as though she hadn't the slightest worry or discomfort.

Jennifer Bradley finished some mindless joke, and Rhea laughed along with those guests, mostly men, who were gathered about her. Jennifer flashed Rhea a little smile that made Rhea want to rip the girl's heart out. Instead, she plucked a bottle of champagne out of a nearby bucket and freshened Jennifer's glass, wondering if Jennifer really thought that she, Rhea, was the only person in the room who didn't know about her and Phillip. They hadn't been very subtle about things, and she probably would have figured it out even if not for the fact that Phillip took such plain and obvious delight in rubbing her nose in his extramarital affairs. Half the members of the movie colony were amused at her, and the other half pitied her, and Rhea wasn't certain which was more galling. Poor little Rhea Stafford. How can she blind herself to that tomcat husband and his ways?

What made it even worse was that she knew a lot more than they did. She knew, for instance, that Jennifer Bradley wasn't going to get that series role she thought she had sewn up. She knew how many of the men who were here, or had been here, this night, had wives who had fallen into bed with Phillip. And she knew something far more fundamental than that.

She knew why those women found Phillip literally irresistible.

She didn't want to think, not about this, not about anything. The headache had reached such a fine pitch that she was getting dizzy. The room rocked and swayed around her, and voices grew faded and indistinct. She heard laughter and joined in it like Pavlov's dog. Laughing made it hurt worse, and she knew there were tears in her eyes. She had to get out of this room, away from these people for a while. She hated them, every last one, almost as much as she hated Phillip. Not really, she thought as she made her excuses and headed for the stairs. Not nearly as much as she hated Phillip. If only she didn't love him so much.

She had reached the head of the stairs, and she leaned against the wall with one hand, laughing softly at herself, and beginning to sob because the pain in her head had begun to throb now, and it was more than human flesh could tolerate. Dimly, she heard a door open farther down the hall, and she pushed herself upright, opening her eyes to see Brenda coming toward her. She was wearing one of Rhea's dresses, a green off-the-shoulder number she had bought because Phillip had mentioned casually one day that he thought she looked good in green. Brenda's hair was freshly brushed, and her makeup newly applied. The effect was more suggestive than if she had been tousled and unkempt. She gave Rhea that saucy and maddening little smile.

"Headache, darling? What a shame." She brushed past without breaking stride. "If you're looking for your husband, he's in my room."

Rhea forced herself to move forward, past the children's room, from which she heard the muffled sounds of laughter and horseplay. It was known to all, now, that since their miraculous recovery the children did much as they pleased. Acquaintances assumed that after their ordeal Phillip lacked the heart to deny them anything. They openly defied Rhea's desultory efforts to discipline them, sensing as they did her helplessness. At times they were emboldened to the point of punching or kicking her, and if Phillip happened to be present he would laugh with such open amusement that the brats knew her place in the pecking order. Once, when they had tried it while alone with her, Rhea had attempted a physical reprisal. She had been stopped by an orgasm of pain so savage it had made her sick. That particular headache had lasted three days, teaching her a lesson she had never forgot since.

Rhea had been ironically correct about one thing: when she had told Janet Stafford that her children's case would be written up in the medical journals, she hadn't realized the sense in which her prophesy would come true. The medics were still baffled by their sudden affliction, and even more puzzled by their inexplicable and total recovery. It was no enigma to Rhea: they had been given a reprieve, that was all. A bit more time on earth to reach the age of consent, and to develop the tastes and habits that would damn them.

Rhea almost passed Brenda's door, because she had to concentrate so hard just to keep going that she wasn't fully aware of where she was. She paused, one slim hand on the knob, and then stood upright and opened the door.

He was in his undershirt and trousers, smelling of shaving cream and talc. Rhea felt the same overwhelming sexual desire that always struck her in his presence. It cut right through the agony of her mirgaine, leaving her with the familiar, watery weakness. He glanced at her and shrugged into a fresh shirt that had been laid out on the bed. Rhea moved to the wingback chair in the corner and fell into it, leaning her head on one hand.

"Who's looking after our guests?" Phillip asked. He was buttoning the shirt, looking in the mirror over Brenda's vanity.

"I excused myself," she said softly, and began to cry in earnest. "Phillip, I can't stand this pain any longer. You've got to make it go away." Phillip tucked the shirt into his waistband and picked up his black tie.

"That's an irrational statement, dear. What do I have to do with your headache?"

"Darling, please don't do this to me," she whined. Then, because she knew that whining annoyed him, she took control of her voice. "It's going to kill me, or drive me insane."

"You mean the way my first wife went insane before she died?" he asked, knotting the tie and inspecting it with satisfaction.

"That — I'm sorry about that. I've told you, I'm very, very sorry." It would be useless to point out to him that his wife's fate couldn't have occurred if he hadn't willed it. She had laid the curse, but he had maintained it once her power had been given to him.

"Well, I'm very, very sorry about your headache,

sweetums," he said, picking up his coat from where it lay across a chair. "Why don't you take something for it?" Rhea laid her head back against the chair and closed her eyes. Even so, the light from the lamp on the vanity seemed to penetrate them, making her head hurt all the more.

"Phillip, please don't do this. At least talk sense to me."

"All right." He walked to where she sat, towering over her, staring down with that implacable expression. "I'll talk sense. Get off your ass." She stared at him for a moment, unable to believe he meant it. Then, shakily, she rose. She could feel the heat of his body, smell the soap from Brenda's bathroom. "Now fix your face," he ordered. "You look like a piece of shit."

"Yes. All right." It was useless. She had known that anyway. Somehow, she would have to get through this night and maybe he would let the pain stop in the morning. "And then I want you to go back down to our guests," he said in a firm voice, as though he were talking to a slightly retarded child. "And try to act like a lady. And make my excuses." She raised her eyes to his, reaching forward impulsively to touch the sleeve of his coat.

"Are you going somewhere?"

"I offered to drive Jennifer home." He went to the door, opened it, and paused. "Don't wait up for me, honey."

Alone, she stood for a moment, dizzy and sick with pain. Then she went across the hall to her own room. Sitting down in front of the dressing table, she inspected herself in the mirror. Her face was still unlined, and there were no gray hairs yet. For the first time since 1847, she was aware of age, and afraid of it. There would be no more stealing of others' bodies. Not unless Phillip allowed it. He could let her stay young, or he could make her get old and — She didn't want to think about that possibility. She opened a jar of cleansing cream and began to wipe away her makeup.

How long? she thought. How long would it amuse him to keep her around, to go on punishing her? When would he grow tired of it? That was something else she lived with, the fear of boring him. It was just as nagging as the headaches that popped up at the worst times. And the desire for him that never seemed to lessen. She tried to remember how long it had been since he had touched her. Months. It might be more months before he did so again. Or it might be never. Once she had tried to slake her desire with another man, but the indifference she had felt for him had turned to repugnance when she had found herself alone with him in his car, and then outright revulsion when he had tried to put his hands on her. She had run from his room barely dressed, choking on the bitterness of her vomit. And she had known better than to try that sort of thing again. As though Phillip had sensed her abortive indiscretion, she had had the worst headache so far right after that night. It had endured more than a week, growing steadily in intensity until, at the end, she had fallen recurringly into fainting spells. Similar episodes had followed her few halfhearted attempts to resist his will, or to speak up for herself. Or when she had dared to be less than ingratiating around one of his current mistresses.

Picking up a Kleenex, she wiped away the cream and started to apply fresh eye makeup.

The worst thing of all was the realization that had slowly dawned on her that it had been leading to this all along. From the very first time when, as a child, she had summoned up a demon. Just as she had manipulated Phillip before the switch, so she had been manipulated by the demons, and by Him Who Must Be Served.

She refreshed her lipstick, then placed her fists on the dressing table and lifted herself to her feet. The room, the table, her image in the mirror, swam before her. Her head felt as though something inside it were swelling, crumbling her skull, squashing her brain. She forced herself to concentrate, to clear her vision.

It was time to see to the guests.